# RIO CLARO

*A Brazilian Plantation System, 1820-1920*

# RIO CLARO

*A Brazilian Plantation System, 1820-1920*

## WARREN DEAN

STANFORD UNIVERSITY PRESS, STANFORD, CALIFORNIA

1976

Stanford University Press
Stanford, California
© 1976 by the Board of Trustees of the
Leland Stanford Junior University
Printed in the United States of America
ISBN 0-8047-0902-5    LC 75-25149

Published with the assistance of
The Andrew W. Mellon Foundation

For Russell Bach, Sidney Dean,
and William Thomas

# Contents

Preface  xi      Abbreviations  xvii

1. Expropriation of the Land      1

2. The Organization of Plantations      24

3. Slave Labor      50

4. An Experiment in Free Labor      88

5. The End of Slavery      124

6. The Wage Labor Regime      156

   Conclusions      194

   Notes  201      Index  229

*Maps are given on pp. 5, 28, and 29.*

# Tables

1.1 Agricultural Production of Free Households, 1822 and
    1835    8

1.2 Labor Inputs and Productivity in Agriculture, 1856    9

1.3 Cash Income of Free Agricultural Households, 1822    10

1.4 Structure of the Agricultural Sector, 1822–57    18

1.5 Production and Apparent Consumption of Corn,
    1822 and 1835    19

2.1 Sugar Production, 1822–62    26

2.2 Capital Investment in a Sugar Plantation, 1851    27

2.3 Capital Investment in a Coffee Plantation, 1861    34

2.4 Sources of Credit on Plantations, 1850–59    34

2.5 Coffee Production, 1835–1929    39

2.6 Concentration of Coffee Production, 1860    46

3.1 Slave Population, 1822–88    51

3.2 Slave Occupations, 1872    52

3.3 Yearly Cost of Maintaining an Adult Slave, 1857    53

3.4 Prices of Male Slaves, Aged 15–29, 1843–87    55

3.5 Provenance of Slaves    57

3.6 Aging of Adult Slave Population    59

3.7 Sex Ratio of Slaves    59

3.8 Ratio of African to Creole Slaves    59

3.9 Apparent Racial Composition, Slave Population and
    Free Population of Color    61

3.10 Surviving Females of Childbearing Age Compared to
    Surviving Children, by Apparent Racial Group    62

3.11 Comparison Log of Slave Survivals, 1822–35    77

3.12  Slave Marriages, 1822–72                                      78
3.13  Absent Population, 1872                                       83
4.1  Accounts of Indentured Workers, Ibicaba Plantation,
       1851                                                         93
4.2  Indenture Colonies in Rio Claro and Limeira, 1847–57          94
4.3  Estimated Initial Indebtedness of Indentured Family,
       1856                                                        105
4.4  Shares of the Coffee Harvest, Ibicaba Plantation, 1856        107
4.5  Wages in Contracts por Ajuste, 1856–80                        119
4.6  Accounts of Indentured Workers, Ibicaba Plantation,
       1862–72                                                     120
5.1  Slaves Freed, 1857–87                                         133
5.2  Slaves Classified for the Emancipation Fund, 1882            134
5.3  Slave Population, 1875–76                                     135
5.4  Ingênuo Population, 1875–76                                   136
6.1  Immigrant Arrivals, 1883–1921                                 160
6.2  Population, 1822–1920                                         160
6.3  Condition of Coffee Trees, 1909                               161
6.4  Concentration of Coffee Production, 1892 and 1905            163
6.5  Coffee and Corn Output per Worker, by Size of
       Producer, 1905                                              164
6.6  Coffee Production, Santa Gertrudes Plantation,
       1857–1916                                                   166
6.7  Wages in Coffee Culture, Santa Gertrudes Plantation,
       1886–1915                                                   169
6.8  Payrolls, Santa Gertrudes Plantation, 1896–99               171
6.9  Employment of Nationals on Plantations, 1905                 172
6.10  Productivity of Nationals on Plantations, 1905             173
6.11  Colonos' Balances, Santa Gertrudes Plantation,
       1885–89                                                     174
6.12  Estimated Yearly Income of Colonos, 1885–1911              175
6.13  Nationality of Landowners, 1905                              188
6.14  Number of Rural Properties, 1822–1964                       190

# Preface

THIS IS a study of plantation labor in the county of Rio Claro, in the state of São Paulo, Brazil. It begins with expropriation of the thinly populated frontier land in the second decade of the nineteenth century, and ends a hundred years later, when relative soil exhaustion led to partial fractioning of the plantations and transfer of capital and labor force to newer regions farther inland. The hundred-year cycle of the plantation system, mainly coffee plantations, straddles in this region of São Paulo the transition from slave to free labor. In Rio Claro attempts were made to engage European immigrants for plantation work beginning in the 1840's, and mass Italian immigration finally began in 1888, the year of abolition. There were many plantations on which, for many years, free workers and slaves labored in adjoining groves, and after emancipation the freedmen continued to participate in large numbers in the plantation regime.

The transition to wage labor was unquestionably the crucial social issue in nineteenth-century Brazil. The region of the Paulista West, a fan spreading from Campinas northwestward to include Rio Claro, and extending to Bauru and Ribeirão Preto, was from the 1850's the most rapidly growing in population and wealth. The breakdown of forced labor and the experimentation with free workers in that area therefore influenced national debate enormously, for its planters were clearly the future prop of government finances and the major beneficiaries of the traditional social system that supported the empire. If slavery failed to function

there, or if free labor proved more profitable there, then the rest
of Brazil would bend to the inevitable.

The study of a single county has its rationale. The county
(*município*) is the basic political unit in Brazil, and in the nineteenth century it was usually quite large. Its boundaries often
followed a certain geographical and economic logic, although
they were continually revised by planters who, finding themselves
in local political opposition, persuaded the provincial legislatures
to redistrict their estates to neighboring counties. Agents of county
government generated most of the historical record regarding the
labor regime of the plantations. The notarial offices—two in Rio
Claro—endorsed contracts of all kinds and copied probated wills,
the land registry recorded sales and kept trial records, and the
county council kept minutes of its sessions and copies of correspondence, tax rolls, and contracts. There were county newspapers, but
only one is preserved in a long run, beginning in 1901. Others are
available in scattered issues in archives in the city of São Paulo. In
the state archive considerable correspondence is filed by county,
and in the Museu Paulista dispersed material on Rio Claro is
indexed by county.

For practical considerations, therefore, Brazilian historians have
sometimes chosen to base their studies upon one county. Undoubtedly they gained thereby a sense of interrelationships, of details, of perceptions and motives, that fade and disappear at a
longer distance. In this study great quantities of other materials,
mainly political and social, have been uncovered. They may be
employed sometime in other tangential studies, but they were
valuable to this monograph in establishing a context that has
provided inferential validity to much that is discussed here. The
historical experience of Rio Claro is in some senses generalizable.
Counties were dependencies of the provincial legislature, and the
president of the province, who debated its budget, appointed most
of its officials and determined policies, province-wide, that were
critical to the fortunes of the plantations of Rio Claro. Planters,
especially the most wealthy, were not residents of a single county,
but had wider interests, and increasingly became absentee land-

lords. The mass of the population was highly mobile, so that Rio Claro was a perch for transients crisscrossing a wide frontier.*

Rio Claro was not selected out of any criteria of uniqueness or typicality. No doubt amendments might have to be made to some of the statements in this study before they would apply to other counties in the Paulista West. Rio Claro was convenient in that its archives were preserved and even partially catalogued, and its faculty of arts and sciences gave kind welcome to an outside researcher. The county was challenging because it was in several respects the site of significant transitions: between the colonial and national land grant regimes, between monarchy and republic (its seat was one of the first to found a chapter of the Republican Party), and between slavery and free labor. Its planters were among the most influential in deciding provincial and even national policy. Furthermore the county seat of Rio Claro, on account of geographical circumstances, became an urban center of some importance, as railhead and as manufacturing and service center, so that its economy exemplified the eventual diversification that is remarkably characteristic of the state of São Paulo.

The historiography of slave and immigrant labor for the most part accepts the self-appraisals and the world view of the planters. The requisite separation between the historian and the clerks who produced the documents, in this case directly or indirectly employees of the planters, has seldom been consistent or self-conscious. This study attempts to maintain a critical guard, and in so doing doubtless will grate upon some sensibilities, which may feel in the attitude, paradoxically, a lack of objectivity, on the assumption that in more "traditional" societies the ideologies of the elite were paradigms of the social order, or at least outwardly uncontested.

The author's concern, it must be admitted, has its own ideological basis. The people have a right to their own history. That land, labor, and profit were expropriated is of less consequence than that the expropriation should have been justified, and justi-

---

* A monograph dealing with a single county which has considerably influenced this study is Stanley Stein, *Vassouras* (Cambridge, Mass.: Harvard University Press, 1957).

fied in such a way that those who suffered expropriation are demeaned. At a congress held in Rio de Janeiro in 1950 to consider the status of the black in Brazilian society, one of the participants rejected entirely the study of the slave past: "We need to forget this brutal treatment, to keep from feeling hatred. Why should the Congress recall that my father was beaten, my mother was beaten? Why?" For scientific purposes, said the chairman; to show the whites the error of their ways, said other participants; to show that blacks nevertheless had always cooperated; to show that things have got better. The speaker's anguish was unconfrontable. The panel was hurriedly adjourned. The reply ought to have been: Your father and mother deserve remembrance because they suffered, and even more because they resisted and overcame. The record shows not submission and resignation, but survival and retribution. The study of plantation labor has egalitarian implications, but the effort, it must be protested in advance, is to restore perspectives distorted through special pleading, not to introduce a distortion where none was before.*

The author was very well treated by Rioclarenses. They made available documents, sometimes at considerable personal inconvenience. In particular, the author wishes to express his gratitude to Mssrs. Tomaz Macha, Sérgio Pereira, and Osório Morato Filho, notaries; to Mr. José Machado, secretary of the county council; and to Mssrs. Oscar Arruda Penteado and José Constante Barreto, local historians. At the Faculdade de Filosofia, Ciências e Letras de Rio Claro, members of the departments of history, geography, and political science were of great assistance, but special thanks are owed to Professor Jeanne Berrance de Castro, whose vast efforts in organizing the local historical museum were fundamental to this study. In São Paulo the staffs of the Arquivo Público do Estado de São Paulo and the Biblioteca Municipal provided constant help in locating and microfilming materials. The intervention of Pro-

* A. de Nascimento, ed., *O negro revoltado* (São Paulo: Edições GRD, 1968), pp. 201–3. I am indebted to Alison Rafael for this quote. A powerful appeal for populist historiography has been made by José Honorio Rodrigues; among his other works, see *Conciliação e reforma no Brasil* (Rio de Janeiro: Editôra Civilização Brasileira, 1965).

fessor Sérgio Buarque de Holanda and Professor Emília Viotti and her students Professors Alice Canabrava and Eddie Stols opened doors to valuable public collections and to private estates. Fellow researchers Professors Samuel Baily, Robert Mattoon, Norris Lyle, Joseph Love, Thomas Holloway, Thomas Flory, and Rae Flory located documents essential to this study. Professors Gabriel and Clélia Bolaffi, good friends, were always ready with introductions to the intellectual life of São Paulo. Ms. Judith Dean accepted dislocation, a commuting schedule, and an interruption of her own studies to accompany the author, whose gratitude and admiration are herewith offered. Parts of two chapters of this book were presented before the Columbia University seminar on Brazil, whose members and chairman, Professor Douglas Chalmers, made useful suggestions. Funds for research were provided by the Social Science Research Council of New York and the University of Texas. A second trip to São Paulo, sponsored by the Faculty of Arts and Sciences at Assis, enabled me to add material in the final stages of editing.

This study was carried out in Brazil during a year of great political ferment, when it appeared that the military dictatorship might abandon its authoritarian rule in the face of opposition that included the universities. The author was uncomfortably aware of his relative immunity, and lamented the damage that was being done to the progress of historical studies in Brazil. Many colleagues lost their positions, and were jailed because they had exercised rights of citizenship and responsibilities of their craft honestly and honorably. A special debt of inspiration is owed to Caio Prado Junior, who suffered imprisonment at an age when he should have been awarded an endowed chair. To him and other brave scholars this book is dedicated.

                                                                      W.D.

# Abbreviations

AMI-P    Arquivo do Museu Imperial, Petrópolis

APESP    Arquivo Público do Estado de São Paulo

LN    Livros de Notas

MHP-ABV    Museu Histórico Paulista "Amador Bueno da Veiga"

MP-AA    Museu Paulista, Arquivo Aguirra

NCC    Núcleo Colonial de Cascalho

OD/RC    Ofícios Diversos, Rio Claro

RC/C-1    Rio Claro, Cartório do Primeiro Ofício

RC/C-2    Rio Claro, Cartório do Segundo Ofício

RGTP    Repartição Geral das Terras Públicas

SG    Santa Gertrudes Plantation

SP(P)    São Paulo (Province)

SP(S)    São Paulo (State)

# RIO CLARO

*A Brazilian Plantation System, 1820-1920*

# CHAPTER 1

# Expropriation of the Land

S TANDING ON the bluff north of town one looks down on a land-
scape several times transformed: pasturage, mostly unimproved,
second growth and stands of eucalyptus on the hilltops, and, on
the outcroppings of red granitic soils where the land is still fertile
after 200 years of cultivation, cane fields and orange groves or
smaller patches of corn, rice, and beans. At the beginning of the
eighteenth century some of this was *campo cerrado**—open fields
where the soil is sandy and thin, dotted with scattered brush
and trees—but most was wooded. Nearby in Araras a few hectares
of virgin forest have been preserved on the plantation that once
belonged to Martinico Prado. It is an awesome sight. From a canopy of trees 150 feet tall—cabreúvas, perobas, jequitibás, smooth-
trunked and dainty-leafed—the morning light filters down through
the tangled strands of runners and lianas. The bulging trunks of
the figueiras look like ruined battlements, hardly resisting the
broaching waves of ferns and vines. One feels gratitude to the
first owner of this land for sparing a corner of it, even though he
may have been expressing less a reverence for this that remains
than hubris for his despoilment of the rest.

These luxuriant forests were inviting in their mildness and
temperateness, for here the climate is not tropical: at 600 meters
above sea level the temperature varies little from a yearly average
of 20 degrees centigrade. Throughout most of the year first one, and
then another, species of flowering tree spreads a canopy of purple,

* The spelling of Portuguese words in the text conforms to modern orthography. Authors' names in notes have also been modernized.

pink, and yellow overhead. This sight is still to be seen in the town square, where a marvelous grove of ipês and paineiras has survived. Other trees provided edible fruits and berries—goiaba, maracaju, jaboticaba, jaca, jatobá—and beneath their branches roamed tapirs, pacas, and capivaras, timid and slow-witted game.

What became the county of Rio Claro was for thousands of years the dwelling place of nomadic hunters whose chipping and cutting stones litter the banks of its streams. Their bones and whatever else they may have produced have been dissolved in acid soil and the heavy summer rains. About 1,000 years ago they were succeeded by other tribes, ceramicists and semi-sedentary. These were Tupi-Guarani, a group that the Portuguese found spread along the entire Brazilian coast when they arrived early in the sixteenth century. Everywhere the Europeans acted rapaciously in their first contacts with the primitive inhabitants of the new world. In Brazil they were hunted for slaves to work on the coastal plantations. Raid after raid decimated them and shattered their culture. Most of the survivors withdrew far into the backlands. A few tribes sued for peace and were placed on reservations near settled areas where they were catechized and gradually assimilated. This experience of aboriginal culture, as violent and exploitive as it was, yet influenced the Portuguese profoundly. As servants and auxiliaries the Tupi taught them how to dominate the wilderness; as concubines they bestowed upon them a mestizo population.[1]

By the beginning of the eighteenth century the primeval inhabitants had retreated a little beyond the region of Rio Claro. By that time the Europeanized population of the captaincy of São Paulo was no more than 50,000. Only nine settlements on the edge of the plateau, including the capital, had been granted town charters. This vast region of fertile soil and temperate climate had become accessible to pioneer occupation. It was a frontier. The word is marvelously evocative, because on frontiers men not only can taste a temporary freedom from the restraints of their society; they can, if they will, recast it to a permanently different mold. Only in revolution is there any parallel, but even revolution lacks the sense of the unknown, of telluric strangeness that makes the frontier a powerfully attractive place and time to be alive. One might expect to see on the frontier, at least on a frontier invaded by Europeans, the opportunity grasped to make each man a smallholder, and to see as a consequence the withering of social distinctions and privilege that crabbed and stifled them at home. In São Paulo the environment was adequate to accommodate this kind of settlement, and in its beginnings the pioneer fringe was indeed an area of smallholdings.

In between the decamping aborigines and the nodes of town life on the edge of the plateau stretched a broad territory, still insecure and unclaimed, where only scattered army posts intruded. Into this were drawn people who sought a refuge from the oppressiveness of colonial rule. The landless could find land. The young and able were free of the draft, a terrible scourge because of intermittent war with Spain in the River Plate. Criminals were beyond the reach of the law. In fact the law often exiled them to the frontier. As late as the middle of the eighteenth century a judge at Itu was imposing banishment: the convicted man was ordered to proceed by boat to the falls at Piracicaba and then to march northward. The escaped slave headed for the frontier often—the hired slave hunter was called for good reason the "captain of the forest."[2]

The discovery of gold in Mato Grosso in 1718 increased slightly the tempo of settlement in the region of Rio Claro. To reach that extraordinarily remote and inaccessible place the inhabitants of São Paulo usually followed the Tietê River into the Paraná basin, sailing in great yearly convoys. Some, however, in order to avoid the fevers of the lowlands, struck out overland from the Piracicaba falls, across gently rolling countryside. At a point 30 kilometers to the north the travelers encountered a series of bluffs, 200 meters higher than the valley floor, marking the beginning of another plateau level. On the north and west these basalt palisades are unbroken and difficult to traverse, but in between there is a corridor of more eroded and subsided terrain where only isolated outcroppings remain, bearing names like Watchtower Hill and Bald Hill. The trail through this pass was opened between 1719 and 1727, then abandoned and reopened between 1765 and 1775. It was to be expected that the mule drivers would stage a resting place before starting the tiring climb. The way station at Ribeirão Claro —Clear Creek—was probably nothing more than a thatched roof suspended on poles. It was located along a flowing brook across a broad holm that is now a square in the part of town called Santa Cruz. Above it a chapel was erected, the first in the area.[3]

The mule trains needed supplies. A few of the muleteers turned merchants. Thus a desultory trade in staples grew slowly and supported a scattered population for a century. Rio Claro came to be thought of as the *boca do sertão*—the mouth of the backlands— for beyond it on the plateau stretched what the inhabitants considered the true wilderness, the Sertão de Araraquara. Meanwhile settled town life gradually edged forward. Piracicaba, to which village Rio Claro was attached, was elevated to a parish in 1770. Mogi-Mirim, 65 kilometers to the east, and Campinas, 75 kilometers southeast, were granted town charters in 1751 and 1797. The towns were only slightly less rustic than the frontier. "Most of them are towns only in name, . . . composed of a few Indian families, some few whites, all of them extremely poor," reported one traveler in the mid-eighteenth century. The French naturalists d'Alincourt and Saint-Hilaire found little more than mule drivers' sheds at Mogi-Mirim in 1818, while Campinas, more prosperous, had only houses made of *taipa*—packed earth. Jundiaí, a minor ruin, was in decline from better days it had known in the seventeenth century. All of these towns were still separated from one another by virgin forest.[4]

By the beginning of the nineteenth century there were several hundred families in the area of Rio Claro. The census of 1822 lists 1,033 free persons, living in 231 households. Nearly all of the heads of households, according to the census, had been born elsewhere, mainly nearby places that were somewhat removed from the frontier. Most were from Mogi-Mirim, Bragança, and Nazaré, counties to the southeast with a high proportion of smallholdings in decline. Some were from Campinas and Itu, to the south, a few were from counties farther off (Sorocaba, Santo Amaro, Jundiaí), and a few were from the province of Minas Gerais. Only four

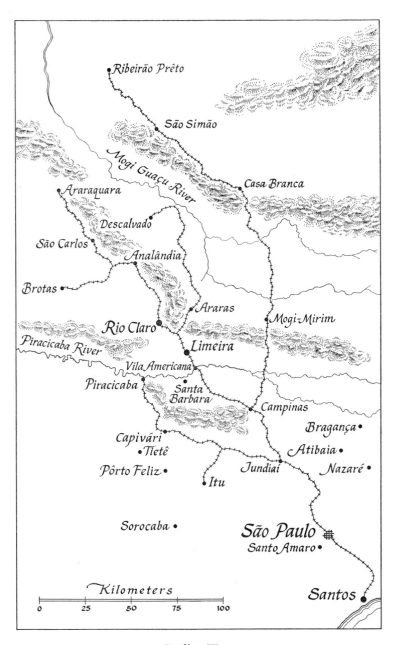

Ribeirão Prêto

São Simão

*Mogi Guaçu River*

Casa Branca

Araraquara

Descalvado

São Carlos

Analândia

Brotas

Araras

Rio Claro

Mogi-Mirim

*Piracicaba River*

Limeira

Vila Americana

Piracicaba

Santa Barbara

Campinas

Bragança

Atibaia

Capivári

Tietê

Nazaré

Pôrto Feliz

Jundiaí

Itu

Sorocaba

São Paulo

Santo Amaro

Kilometers

0    25    50    75    100

Santos

Paulista West

came from Portugal, and only seven reported that they had been born in "this" county, which may have meant Piracicaba. Within this limited ambit the population flowed ceaselessly. Of the 112 farm families working their own claims, 21 reported they had arrived that year. Less than 10 percent of the free households present in 1822 were to be found in the next census thirteen years later. In the latter, one of the census takers conscientiously copied the birthplace of each member of the family. In his wards 16 out of 35 heads of families had taken a wife from a different town; 30 of the families had children who were born in at least one other town besides Rio Claro, 13 families' children were born in at least two other towns. The average number of years resident, for 83 families with children, was 5.2.[5]

The households were invariably nuclear, husband and wife—or a surviving partner—and children. This structure was dominant in São Paulo at least since the time of the first census in the mid-eighteenth century. Of the sixteen families with female heads, mostly widows, half begged for a living. Some marriages were unacknowledged by the male partner. The census taker copied down the word *agregada*—"dependent" instead of "wife"—to refer to his companion, even though there were children. A few of the families had *agregados* of other kinds, either very young or elderly. In these cases the dependents were probably related. The nuclear families were not social isolates. There was, apparently, a strong tendency among the settlers to move to areas where relatives were already located. This is easily observed in the reappearance of family names among settlers resident in the same ward or declaring the same place of origin. Of the 21 householders from Mogi-Mirim in 1822, only four had unique family names.[6]

The free population was recorded as mainly white—85 percent in 1822, but only 66 percent in 1835. All but a few of the nonwhites were listed as *pardos*, that is, mulattos. These distinctions reflect, undoubtedly, a considerable uncertainty of criteria and delicacy of social usage. There were probably many pardos categorized as whites in the earlier census, and perhaps in the latter census as well. Saint-Hilaire, the French botanist, noted in his travels in São Paulo that the white population was, in fact, mestizo, a category not employed at all in the census. Some of the pardos were probably as well classified as black, but this was a term thought demeaning to apply to a free man. The single free black listed in 1822 and the seven in 1835 were possibly known locally to be manumitted Africans. The census takers of 1822 did not record any marriages between whites and mulattos, again a social imprecision, or perhaps it was less effort to assign the same racial designation to everyone in the same household. In 1835, however, in about half the wards the census takers went to the trouble of making distinctions. There they found, out of 255 couples, 22 with partners differently classified: twelve white males with pardo females, eight pardo males with white females, and two black males with pardo females. Since there were 91 other households in these wards in which both partners were classified as mulatto, nearly 20 percent of that racial group participated in marriages with whites. The children in two of the pardo-white households were listed not as pardo but as white. Perhaps they were the offspring of earlier marriages, or possibly they were sufficiently light to be recategorized. In the eyes of their social superiors in the towns, these free householders, regardless of their race, were merely *caboclos,* a faintly mocking term, implying both rustic and half-breed, with none of the favorable connotations of words like pioneer or frontiersman.[7]

One of the reasons for the extraordinary transiency of settlers in Rio Claro was their employment of swidden farming. The settlers made temporary clearings in the forest by burning it down. Near the end of the dry winter season underbrush and lianas were hacked away with machetes and two-handled sickles. The farmer then waited a few weeks for the brush to dry, and on a day when the wind was right, he set it all on fire. The blaze would burn violently and the smoke could be seen for miles. The clearing that resulted, two or three hectares in size, would not resemble an open field. It was full of blackened tree hulks, of fallen trunks and upended roots—but it was extremely fertile. The farmer planted with a digging stick, a few seeds to a mound, and took little care thereafter except to hoe a time or two and thin the plantings. Each

TABLE 1.1

*Agricultural Production of Free Households, 1822 and 1835*

| Category | 1822 | 1835 |
|---|---|---|
| Total number of households without slaves | 102 | 196 |
| Number of households reporting: | | |
| Corn | 96 | 166 |
| Beans | 66 | 137 |
| Rice | 16 | 88 |
| Production per household (liters): | | |
| Corn | 3,010 | 5,476 |
| Beans | 326 | 254 |
| Rice | 435 | 326 |

SOURCE. APESP, População Piracicaba, 1822, 1835–36.

NOTE. Production has been converted from alqueires (dry measure, equal to 36.27 liters). New households, not yet in production, have been omitted.

year the clearing was burned before planting until, after five or six years, it was abandoned and allowed to return to forest. The swidden farmer had few fixed investments to lose: a hut, flimsily constructed of wattle and daub, dirt-floored and roofed with palm fronds, and usually a corn crib and a *monjolo*—a lever-action corn mill worked by hand.[8]

The principal crop was corn, which Luis Lisanti has calculated as 80 to 90 percent of the settlers' calories. The censuses show most households growing some. In 1822 an average 83 *alqueires**（3,000 liters) was produced per household. The corn was ground into meal or grits, for cooking in cakes or mush. The other staples were beans, grown by two-thirds of the households, and rice, grown by one out of six (Table 1.1). Both required well-cleared land and some extra attention; therefore on the average only 12 alqueires of rice were grown per household, and only nine of beans (Table 1.2). There were lesser crops. Manioc, which was valuable because it could be harvested almost all the year through and was less demanding of the soil, was not listed in the census, but was probably grown by some of the households, along with other tubers—gourds,

* An alqueire was equal to 36.27 liters before 1874 and to 40 or 50 liters after 1874.

TABLE 1.2
*Labor Inputs and Productivity in Agriculture, 1856*

| Activity | Days of labor to plant one alqueire | Output in liters |
|---|---|---|
| Clearing, felling, burning | 30 | — |
| Cultivation of: | | |
| Corn | 8 | 1,740 |
| Beans | 30 | 1,450 |
| Rice | 20 | 3,630 |
| Manioc | 30 | ? |

SOURCE. APESP, OD/RC 396, Subdelegate to President of Province, Jan. 1856 (day illegible).
NOTE. The same report showed that the current wage in hoe work, no food provided, was .80 milreis per day.

pumpkins, sweet potatoes, and yams. Much of the animal protein came from fish and game, but many families also kept pigs, which could be left to root, semi-wild, in the forest. There were never any chickens, because they were defenseless against snakes. Some families grew cotton and wove homespun. There was some exchange of soap, candles, and tobacco. The wilderness provided fruits and medicinal and cooking herbs, as well as the materials for house-building.[9]

According to the census only a few of the free householders of Rio Claro were tied into the larger economy of the province. Sixteen families sold hogs, a total of 95 locally and 97 in Itu, São Paulo (the provincial capital), Campinas, and Pôrto Feliz. In the latter town, three Rio Claro farmers sold a total of 140 *arrobas**
(2,050 kilograms) of tobacco, possibly for shipment on the Tietê River to places farther inland. The trade in hogs was especially suitable for the frontier because the settler could drive them to market on the hoof. Of those who sold in the market in 1822, only one earned more than 100 milreis,† while the average was only 32 milreis (at the time one milreis exchanged for 1.25 dollars, and

* An arroba was equal to 14.69 kilograms before 1874 and to 15.00 kilograms after 1874.
† Throughout the text, only the milreis has been referred to, and references to other values have been avoided to eliminate confusion. When necessary to refer to fractions, hundredths of milreis were used, in conformity with the modern centavo. The milreis became the cruzeiro in 1942.

TABLE 1.3
*Cash Income of Free Agricultural Households, 1822*

| Product | Number of households | Quantity | Value in milreis |
|---|---|---|---|
| Pigs | 16 | 192 | 503.12 |
| Corn | 2 | 870 liters | 3.84 |
| Beans | 3 | 870 liters | 15.36 |
| Tobacco | 3 | 2,050 kgs. | 257.60 |
| TOTAL | 24 | | 779.92 |
| Average per household | | | 32.40 |

SOURCE. APESP, População Piracicaba, 1822.

a day's farm labor was worth .64 milreis; see Table 1.3). By 1835 the extent of involvement in the market was considerably greater. The later census unfortunately does not record sales or prices, but cash-cropping can be inferred from the increase in corn production and households raising pigs—23 households, 594 head—and the appearance of cows—11 households, 115 head. There were also goats, castor beans, and peanuts. In part this greater variety was made possible by larger forest clearings, but it was also related to the appearance of a town nucleus in Rio Claro itself.[10]

Although the free settlers were becoming more numerous, and their clearings more permanent and increasingly tied to a market economy, they were unable to maintain their holdings. Outsiders from regions more distant from the frontier acquired legal title to most of it, evicted many of the smallholders, and subordinated the rest to tenancy of a sort. Even the earliest census of 1822 does not capture the way of life of the fully independent frontier; by that date there were already 40 farm households that employed workers—slave workers. By 1835 smallholders were reduced to a third of the population. The reason for this displacement was that the cash surplus generated by the colonial economy, accumulated mainly by plantation owners of the coast and by merchants, bureaucrats, and professionals of the towns, was reinvested by them in new lands.

The acquisition of land, even though beyond the limits of potential exploitation for export crops, was nevertheless founded upon economic considerations. As sheer speculation, improvements in transportation or increases in world market prices might extend the perimeter of profitable cultivation. The acquisition of virgin land was as necessary to the export cultivators as to the swidden farmers, since both depended on the higher fertility of newly deforested land to maintain output. In the meantime reserve lands might be subdivided for profit or used as guarantees for loans. Landownership, furthermore, within the colonial polity represented a more secure investment than any other. It was not taxed, it was not affected by inflation, it was not as ostentatious or liquid as trade goods, animals, or cash; therefore the governor could not confiscate it when he became desperate for revenue or envious. On the other hand, he considered landowners especially deserving of government contracts and concessions and high offices through which further wealth might be amassed.

Unquestionably, title to vast tracts of land represented status, and the owner of them considered himself thereby peculiarly worthy to command and to exact deference. These feelings may be characterized as seignorial, but they were engendered by actions intended to increase access to resources, and thereby to achieve monopoly gains in an active, capitalistic market.

It was to the advantage of the merchants and others who sought to make large investments in land that the system of *sesmarias*, or grants of crown land, be continued. Sesmarias, which were conceded by the viceroy or the governor, were the only titles to land recognized in court, until the land law of 1850. Typically they were a square league (44 square kilometers) in size, and they cost, in bureaucratic fees, 300 to 400 milreis to establish. Such a sum was not utterly beyond the capability of a free settler, if he was engaged already in some form of cash-cropping. Credit would be nearly impossible, but he might pool the resources of kinsmen, if he was lucky enough to be part of a large family all of whose members were prosperous. In fact one of the sesmarias of Rio Claro seems to have been established by such an association, that of the Pereiras, who were engaged in raising cattle and horses. It was far more likely, however, that the governor or the viceroy would bestow the immense favor of free land upon persons rich and politically influential in the towns.[11]

The first of the grants in the area, in fact, was fraudulently acquired. José Ignácio Ribeiro Ferreira, legally restrained from acquiring his own sesmaria because he was secretary to the governor, used front men to obtain five of them—one in Rio Claro—totaling 566 square kilometers. Two other grants were made before 1800, apparently to speculators who never made the beginnings of cultivation called for in the grants, so that they eventually lapsed. The rest of the ten grants in the area of Rio Claro were made in the last few years before independence put an end to the sesmaria system in 1822. Except for the grant made to the Pereira clan, all were bestowed upon persons of considerable wealth, with positions in the militia or civil service, all of whom already owned plantations elsewhere. Five of these sesmarias were made to associations of several related partners, another to a retired Portuguese-born officer, Francisco da Costa Alves, who already had a plantation in Jundiaí. The other three were granted to associations of persons already resident at the time of legalization, but none of these were ordinary squatters, since they all had introduced retinues of slaves and tenants. The original settlers were relegated to an extremely marginal position. Validated holdings of no more than 170 hectares in size by 1818 amounted to a mere 2 percent of all registered property, although they were held by half of the proprietors of the Rio Claro area.[12]

It seems strange that the frontier of São Paulo, so temperate and so amenable to European agricultural technique, could have been so abruptly closed to the development of smallholding. The latifundia-sized sesmaria had been, perhaps, a necessary incentive to effect the transfer of Portuguese settlers during the first two centuries of the colony, but this was no longer the case by the late eighteenth century. It might have been expected that the royal bureaucracy, interested in the fullest development of the region, albeit within the strictures of the mercantilist system, might have insisted on the predominance of smallholding and free labor. The concept was available intellectually. In 1810 the solicitor-general of São Paulo strongly recommended to the king not only the gradual abolition of slavery, but also the granting of free homesteads to immigrants and freedmen alike, and the establishment of a fund to provide credit so that smallholders might compete with plantations. His motive was to augment the resources of the state, which "would always increase progressively along with the farming, the settlement, and the industry of the people. It would be therefore a very wise law."[13]

The crown, furthermore, was not wholly without resources to bend the colonials to whatever policies seemed in the best interests of the metropolis. It had enforced in the past a considerable number of draconian social reforms in order to increase production or to improve its military position. Furthermore, São Paulo was beginning to receive the attention of the viceregal government after a long period of neglect and of depopulation by army recruiting officers. As revenues from the mines declined, the potential of agriculture came to appear more promising. The government therefore constructed between 1785 and 1795 a greatly improved road up the coastal escarpment from the port of Santos, thereby reducing significantly the cost of transport.

Unfortunately, the royal administrators could never entertain seriously a reform that would bring about not only the desired increase in revenues but also what would appear to them to be a social revolution. The only organization they could conceive for the immense colony had to be a society precisely as aristocratic as that of the metropolis. Throughout the colonial period, therefore, land grants represented the most essential privilege in the power of the king to bestow. "The social condition of the concessionaire," Passos Guimarães has written, "was, in the final instance, the decisive factor in the system of donations."[14]

This is not to deny the crown's desire for profit. The administrators could not be expected to grant property rights to a social class that they considered irresponsible and unproductive. The twin vices of the settlers, according to the governor in 1766, were "presumption and sloth." It was the calculation of the bureaucrats that the smallholder, if he were left in undisturbed possession of his land, would never engage in cash-cropping. Standing on its head the image of society that served as ideology for the smallholders in English North America, the makers of policy in Brazil believed that only the rich and the well-born could be expected to display entrepreneurial qualities, for the others "have no idea of property, nor the desire for distinctions and social vanities, that are the powerful springs which put in action the civilized man." The caboclos, complained another, "have become of a new nature, bereft of that well-regulated ambition that causes States to flourish and impells men to work and crafts."[15]

Frontiersmen, they lamented, were neither courageous nor energetic. Nature was too openhanded in São Paulo; there was no goad of hunger. Although they were "strong enough for any kind of work," they "labored only to feed themselves and their families." Royal governors, desperately squeezing the settlers for their surplus to feed the troops, agreed with the civil officials and the landowners. "There is no production in this captaincy because of the indolent liberty in which the greater part of its inhabitants live, engaged in vagrancy and reduced to a total impoverishment, disdaining any work," wrote one in 1788. The contempt and rage of the aristocrat for the unmanageable lower class are evident in another official's description of a *mutirão*, or cooperative effort, for land clearing: "After dining well and drinking better, they pick up their machetes and sickles, more animated by the spirit of rum than the love of work. . . . So shiftless are they that in order to get them to work for two or three months of the year, they must be led forth as if to an entertainment." It was essential, therefore, in order to recreate the repressive and authoritarian society of the metropolis, and to extract the maximum possible revenue for the crown, that these "adventurers, exiles, murderers, misanthropes, enemies of social contact," as a latter-day apologist for the great landowners has described the caboclos, be swept aside, so that the "real settlement could begin."[16]

The new grantees began immediately to speculate in their land. Excluding the Pereira grant, no more than half of the grantees ever took up residence in Rio Claro. All of them began to sell off parts of their shares, always in fairly large pieces, to other parties who founded plantations or sold their interests to still other persons.

By 1835 seven of the twelve sugar mills in operation were built by persons who had purchased parts of the sesmarias. Five of these planters are identifiable as members of families already growing sugar in the region of Campinas and Itu, including one, Joaquim José de Andrade, who married into the family of one of the grant- ees. The other two were a priest and an army officer. The latter, Estevão Cardoso de Negreiros, had possibly used his advantageous post of commander of the fort at the port of Santos to accumulate his initial capital.[17]

Although records relating to land transfers are very scattered for the earliest period—some of the contracts of sale were verbal in any case—references to earlier sales in later contracts give the impression of an extraordinary turnover in ownership. In 1855, at the time of the first general land registry, many of the declarations show three or more owners succeeding the original grantee of 30- odd years before. Many of the intervening owners were never resi- dent in Rio Claro. They were speculators, counting on further subdivision for a profit. Nearly half of the landowners in the parish of Rio Claro who declared the date their properties were acquired had gotten them less than six months before. The velocity of trans- fers through purchase exceeded inheritances. In the same registry of 1855 only 20 percent of those declaring the basis of their titles indicate inheritance or donation. Although some of the entries that show purchase or exchange were, in fact, arrangements among co-heirs, it appears that land was more commonly sold than be- queathed. The declarations of the largest property owners display numerous transactions between neighbors—fencing-in and fencing- out. Nicolau Vergueiro's plantation, as an extreme, was made up of about two dozen separate tracts totaling more than 100 square kilometers. Land in Rio Claro was evidently wholly within a market economy that was active and fluid.[18]

The concession of the sesmarias did not wholly eliminate squat- ters' claims. The titles to about a third of the land area of Rio Claro derive merely from *posse*, that is, original occupation. This was because some of the sesmaria-sized claims were occupied too late to be legitimized by a subsequent grant. The independent

Brazilian government found itself incapable of formulating a land law to substitute for the system of royal grants. The embarrassed claimants of Rio Claro had to employ makeshift forms of recognition. They mingled their interests with others by selling off tracts to third parties, who could then be counted on to uphold the original alienation. The tax paid on these transfers could be represented as official acquiescence. In Rio Claro one of the more important squatters, Manuel Paes de Arruda, improved his position by donating part of his *posse* to serve as the county seat. By 1835 the county council of Piracicaba reported blandly to the provincial president that there were no public lands left in the region. Indeed, they had all been usurped.[19]

Some of the original settlers' claims also survived, in spite of the concession of the sesmarias. Certain tracts with poor soils were never coveted by outsiders, and therefore never underwent any kind of legal alienation. Thus the parish of Itaqueri, later named Itirapina, remained an isolated region of subsistence farms, where titles were based on squatting. Some of the original settlers' clearings that lay along the borders of the sesmarias were left undisturbed so as not to provoke a dispute between the grantees. The last of the sesmarias conceded in Rio Claro provided a kind of recognition of squatters' rights: the grantee was enjoined from impinging on the claims of persons already occupying land within the sesmaria's boundaries. At least one of the grantees did desist from a claim in the Rio Claro area because he encountered "too many squatters," not on account of any legal right they might insist on but because in this instance an excessive amount of force might have been called for.

Even though the original settlers had come to possess an incipient legal claim to the land they were farming, most of them were evicted by the grantees as a matter of policy. To allow them to remain, even when the new owner had no immediate intention of farming it, put in question the legality of his own title and offered a bad example to the tenants whom the grantee may have installed on the property. The rich usually did not employ the courts against these settlers. It was inconvenient and implied a distasteful equality of rights. It was quicker to arm a foreman and a few tenants and send them after the squatters, who were referred to after the fact as "intruders." Threats and calculated damage to the squatters' plantings preceded any greater violence, so that the removal was usually effected without bloodshed. Although simple eviction was not very difficult, there were many purchases of small tracts by the grantees and their successors. These may have been inspired by the hope of adding tangibility to the uncertain bounds of the sesmaria. The sales may, however, have been coerced, and thus may represent only a variation on the customary pattern of eviction.[20]

It is likely that the extremely casual method of farming along the frontier was partly a result of the near impossibility of establishing title to a squatter's claim. It is also possible that swidden agriculture limited the extent of the conflict generated by removal of the caboclos. All that was at stake was a clearing that would have to be abandoned in a few seasons in any case. Very rarely did the settlers choose the alternative of requesting a tenancy on the sesmaria. There was always the forest ahead, free of any rent at all. The direction of population flow, as rapid as it was, was ever in the direction of the wilderness. In the 1835 census only one family in all of Rio Claro came from the Sertão de Araraquara. Meanwhile the new tenants established on the plantations tended increasingly to be natives of counties with poor soils and not much opportunity for cash-cropping. Jundiaí, Bragança, Atibaia, Mogi-Mirim, and eastern Minas Gerais provided 57 percent of the family heads in 1822, and 74 percent in 1835. The modest rents in kind collected by the new plantation owners left them with a better subsistence than they could have provided themselves in those counties, even when they had been smallholders.[21]

The grantees, then, managed to take over most of the best soils in Rio Claro with less need for violence than might seem to have been necessary. Even in retreat the caboclos were useful to the plantation system. By allowing themselves to be pushed constantly forward into the unoccupied land between the aborigines and the plantations, the squatters performed the supremely valuable, although unacknowledged, function of keeping the primitives at bay. The plantations of Rio Claro were not attacked by them, though they were exposed and undefended by the army. The squatters alone suffered aboriginal reprisals for the loss of their lands. Since the squatters' existence was not recognized by the state, there was no need to spend public funds to assist them. The landowners were safeguarded from the hostility of the caboclos as well, since the latter vented their frustrations against the more accessible of their enemies, and despised the aborigines as much as the landowners despised them.

The alienation of crown lands and the introduction of slave labor did not completely eliminate smallholding. The censuses of 1822 and 1835, and the land registry of 1855–57, show a decline in the proportion of rural households farming their own claims (Table 1.4), but not much. Some 54 percent of rural households in 1822 were free, working their own claims; the proportion had fallen to 48 percent 35 years later. The area covered by these holdings relative to the total, on the other hand, had decreased. Among the families with land were 149 who, according to the parish priest, were "miserable farmers" too poor to pay the two or three milreis needed to enter their claims in the register. These were minifundia, "little remnants of land," inadequate to provide an income or even

TABLE 1.4
*Structure of the Agricultural Sector, 1822–57*

| Category | Number | | | Percent | | |
|---|---|---|---|---|---|---|
| | 1822 | 1835 | 1857 | 1822 | 1835 | 1857 |
| Total number of rural households | 224 | 401 | 820[a] | 100.0% | 100.0% | 100.0% |
| Farming own claims | 151 | 258 | 448 | 67.4 | 64.3 | 54.6 |
| *With slaves* | *31* | *62* | *55* | *13.8* | *15.4* | *6.7* |
| *Without slaves* | *120* | *196* | *393* | *53.6* | *48.8* | *47.9* |
| Tenants, agregados, and colonos | 10 | 28 | 372 | 27.7 | 35.2 | 45.4 |
| *With slaves* | *9* | *3* | | | | |
| *Without slaves* | *1* | *25* | | | | |
| Laborers without tenure | 52 | 113 | | | | |
| Beggars, no occupation | 11 | 2 | — | 4.9 | 0.5 | |

SOURCES. APESP, População Piracicaba, 1822, 1835; Registro de Terras, 1855–57; OD/RC 397, Vicar to President of Province, Aug. 18, 1858. The 1857 total estimate from SP(P), President of Province, *Relatorio*, May 1, 1854.
  NOTE. Tenants include administrators, foremen, and *foreiros*. Laborers include *jornaleiros, camaradas*, and those living *de suas agências*.
  [a] Estimated.

TABLE 1.5
*Production and Apparent Consumption of Corn,
1822 and 1835*

| Category | 1822 | 1835 |
|---|---|---|
| Per capita production in liters: | | |
| Slave farm households | 430 | 319 |
| Free farm households | 635 | 1,095 |
| Per capita apparent consumption: | | |
| All households, including nonfarm | 446 | 473 |

SOURCE. APESP, População Piracicaba, 1822, 1835.

subsistence. At the other end of the income scale, the slave-owning households, whose number had not doubled during the period, possessed among them more than three times as many slaves.

At the beginning of the plantation regime at least, smallholders in Rio Claro seem to have experienced a growing market for their surplus. Production of corn by free farm households grew from 274,000 to 909,000 liters from 1822 to 1835, a per capita output more than 70 percent greater than before (Table 1.5). It is likely that the surplus went to fatten hogs, to feed the growing town population and to make up the deficit on the plantations, and perhaps also to feed the increasing transient population of mule drivers, not listed as residents but nevertheless dependent on the county for part of their supplies.

The appearance of minifundia by 1857 implies strongly that many of the smallholders were being marginalized—from suppliers of commodities to part-time suppliers of labor. They were in another significant way dependents within the plantation system. The planters occupied all political posts, including those of justice of the peace, police delegate, school inspector, and commander of the militia. It was not possible for the smallholders to survive without favors from the plantation owners. The plantation owners, in turn, required of them just one favor: their vote. According to the 1824 Constitution, only persons with property or a business could vote, and employees were excluded. The smallholder, therefore, formed the only electoral following in the empire, and mobilizing him constituted the chief fraud of the regime. This relationship entitled the smallholder to formal, respectful treatment from the planters—they called him neighbor, sat at his table, and restrained themselves from taking advantage of his women. On the other hand, the smallholder was enrolled in the militia, which obliged him to guard the polls on election day, chase after runaway slaves sometimes and perhaps his fellows on other occasions. Thus the quarrels of the great became his, and his personal and party loyalties were irrevocably publicly displayed, as though he had been branded.[22]

Simultaneously the plantation owners admitted to their estates a certain number of farm laborers who were completely landless. Those who achieved a certain degree of tenure were called *agregados*, like the dependent relatives in the smallholders' households, but quite distinctly in this case in the sense of "retainer." Sixteen of the slave-owning households kept agregados in 1835, a total of 45 persons. There were, besides, a floating population of laborers—*camaradas*—whose position was precarious, since they were hired to perform a given task or to assist in the harvest. Neither of these groups was fully mobilizable for the steady work of the plantation. Their labor was casual and restricted to certain specialties, such as clearing forest, road-building, and carting. The planters could not demand more of them, not only because they could abandon the plantation fairly easily, but also because the planters had more need of their loyalty. The camaradas were clearly a volatile element among the free population. Most obviously dispossessed, subject to arrest for vagabondage when they departed the plantation, denied the protection bestowed upon the smallholder and the agregado, they were also free to exercise their own wills. They perceived the intention of the plantation owners to adapt them to unremitting toil in the groves as exploitation, as indeed it was. The planters, on the other hand, reviled them for laziness and improvidence. Yet the landowners had need of them, because they were intrepid, hardy, and resigned to remaining landless. The contradiction was insoluble within the embryonic market economy of the Paulista West, however. A wage sufficiently high to tempt the camaradas to steady labor would have enabled them to buy a homestead within a reasonable period of time. Rather than countenance such an outcome, the planters frequently mused upon the application of force to them as well as to the slaves. It was sometimes suggested that the landless rural population be dragooned into an "agricultural militia," along with the freedmen. Although coercive labor systems were imposed elsewhere in the New World after chattel slavery ceased to be viable, operating such a system parallel to slavery would surely have proved impractical, and would have interfered further with the transition to free wage labor based on European immigration.[23]

The social system of the great estates was intensely violent. The forcible eviction of squatters, the defense of vague estate boundaries, the control of the slave labor force, and the social domination of the landless all required the application of considerable force. Agregados were recruited as private police—*capangas* who guarded boundaries and carried out any violent act the owner might order, including murder. Sometimes men were found who relished the life of the bully, but more often the tenants dreaded capanga duties, since these exposed them to the dangers of private vengeance. Camaradas, rootless and insecure, engaged frequently in random violence, mostly directed against their fellows. The murder rate in the interior of São Paulo in 1835 was 32 per thousand, and in the district that included Rio Claro it was in that year a staggering 176 per thousand. Undoubtedly the leading edge of the frontier suffered the highest rate of violence. It appears that Rio Claro was the scene of political crimes in 1842 and 1846, during province-wide crises, and at a time when the local oligarchy was not yet firmly organized.[24]

By 1830 about 2,000 resided in Rio Claro. A church was built, and the place was designated a parish, a term with civil administrative as well as clerical significance. The plantation owners formed a "Society of the Commonweal," whose purpose was to act as a local government while petitioning the province to incorporate the area formally. The society decided where the town center would be located, a significant political act, since it determined thenceforth every landowner's cost of transport. Since the center was a *patri-mônio*, donated land, the society empowered itself to lay it out and sell lots. The funds were used for purposes of local administration and to build a church. From the beginning, then, the politics of Rio Claro were arranged by the plantation owners.

The county by 1835 contained some 60 households that pursued nonagricultural occupations in the town center. Twenty-three were in trade, nineteen in construction—mostly carpentry—fifteen in crafts, including, surprisingly, a jeweler. There were another 35 households that reported earning their living from day labor, which was probably farming. A secretary to the justice of the peace, who acted as notary, and the vicar were members of a sort of middle class ex officio. Besides them, only six of the town households reported income of more than 200 milreis, the wealthiest being one of the storekeepers, a cloth merchant who earned 600 milreis.

In 1842 Rio Claro was detached from the county of Piracicaba. Administratively, in Brazil the local unit of government is the *município*, which tended to be the size of a county in the United States. Its seat is not separate politically; instead the whole area of the *município*, including the seat and whatever other villages may lie within the county line, are governed by a single *câmara*, or council. The county of Rio Claro had outlying parishes of its own. Brotas and Descalvado soon became separate counties, in 1859 and 1865, respectively. Itaqueri remained administratively a part of Rio Claro. In 1845 the county was raised from the rank of *vila* to that of *cidade*, which brought a slight additional autonomy from the provincial legislature. Together Rio Claro and the parish of Itaqueri enclosed about 1,600 square kilometers.

In this part of the Paulista West the extinction of the aboriginal population and its replacement by Europeanized *caboclo* settlers took place gradually through the eighteenth century. Even in its beginnings the inruption of the mestizo-mulatto squatters was tied to the economy of the coast, since these marginal, cast-off people gathered at way stations along the road to the mines in Mato Grosso. The original settlers had to hew small and temporary clearings from a dense and luxuriant primeval forest, but they managed quite easily to maintain a subsistence regime, and even a certain amount of trade with towns nearer the coast.

Around 1820 many of the settlers of Rio Claro were suddenly expropriated by a few persons with enough cash and political influence to secure titles in the form of sesmarias. The expropriation of value added to the land through clearing and prior cultivation represented an initial act of capital accumulation. Soon even more wealthy and influential persons began to put together holdings that would be suitable for large-scale agricultural exploitation. Rio Claro had become, in local usage, a *frente pioneira,* that is, it had entered the perimeter of the capitalistic, export-oriented coastal economy.[25]

Land appropriation did not wholly eliminate the smallholders. Those who remained, however, were mobilized for subordinate and dependent roles within the export economy. By the time of its separation from Piracicaba, then, Rio Claro's landholding pattern and social structure conformed with those of the coastal towns. Nevertheless, the transformation was not complete. The propertied class had to make a profit from its lands, preferably from a crop that could be sold abroad.

# CHAPTER 2

# The Organization of Plantations

THE APPEARANCE of some sort of export crop was essential to the maintenance of a social system based upon great estates. Had there been no cash crop profitable enough to attract capital, the sesmarias would undoubtedly have fragmented within a few generations, and slaves would never have been introduced. That was the outcome in other areas where no cash-cropping was possible. On the other hand, in the western end of the Paraíba Valley, where the sesmarias of a century before had already been dismembered, landholding became concentrated once more when sugar and slaves were brought in during the 1770's. Inevitably, the planters sought out overseas markets for their products. The Brazilian population was rural and self-sufficient and the few towns offered only a weak demand for farm goods. The domestic economy lacked capital except at very high interest rates. Slaves—the most costly element in the organization of a plantation—often required foreign exchange. Therefore the frontier region of São Paulo continued into the nineteenth century the plantation regime that the Portuguese had installed on Brazil's coast nearly 300 years before.

For the first 30 years the plantations of Rio Claro cultivated sugar. The owners of the original grants and most of the persons to whom they sold parts of their sesmarias were members of sugar-planting families from the region of Itu and Campinas. They were, in fact, transferring their operations to another area. Sugar was not a crop with very favorable prospects, however. The moribund trade had been supplied for centuries by planters in the northeast, and more lately from the eastern lowlands of the province of Rio de Janeiro and from the coast of São Paulo east of Santos. The planters of the plateau, lacking capital, could not match even the retrograde techniques of the coastal mills and had to pay much higher costs of transport. Nevertheless, the frontier possessed some advantages for raising cane: the soil was extremely fertile, and there was limitless wood for stoking boilers and ample pasturage for the animals employed in carting and turning the grinding wheels. Sugar cultivation was more demanding of the soil than the caboclos' swidden farming. Sugar land required fallow periods every three to ten years and was usually abandoned permanently after twenty. Therefore the planters were nearly as itinerant as the squatter settlers, clearing and burning wider and wider swathes of the grants until at last new forest land had to be acquired. This predatory regime was nonetheless "economical" since the extreme scarcity of labor and credit made it unprofitable to expend any effort on the preservation of soil fertility.[1]

Sugar cultivation, encouraged by crown authorities in the 1750's, began on the black soils of Itu. In the 1770's it was extended to the red soils of Campinas. By 1818, there were 60 *engenhos*, sugar mills, located there, and its population of 6,000 was half-slave. Campinas was succeeded by Piracicaba as a sugar frontier a generation later. In 1816 there were eighteen engenhos in Piracicaba, and twelve more were under construction. By 1822 there were eight in Rio Claro and three others were being built.[2]

The engenhos were fairly expensive. An animal-powered mill with the necessary vats cost more than the validation of the sesmaria itself, and a water-powered mill might cost ten times as much. The engenho ran efficiently only if a large amount of cane —more than a single family could grow—was fed steadily into it. The colonial government, after 1802, sought to ensure the viability of the existing mills by restricting the building of new ones. For all these reasons sugarcane was an enterprise attempted only by those with a lot of capital, a supply of slaves, and title to a large stand of virgin forest. In Rio Claro there never developed any subsidiary layer of cane suppliers dependent on mill owners. Unlike the sugar areas of the northeast, where there were numerous tenants and

TABLE 2.1
Sugar Production, 1822–62

| Category | 1822 | 1835 | 1853 | 1862 |
|---|---|---|---|---|
| Number of cane growers | 18 | 13 | — | 8 |
| Number of mills in operation | 8 | 12 | 13 | 6 |
| Slaves employed | 262 | 299 | — | — |
| Sugar production, metric tons | 158 | 177 | 522 | 264 |
| Cane brandy production, kiloliters | — | 202 | — | 145 |
| Price of sugar per arroba, milreis | — | 1.00 | 1.44 | 2.50 |

SOURCES. 1822, 1835: APESP, População Piracicaba. 1853: APESP, OD/RC 396, Report to President of Province from Câmara, Jan. 26, 1854. 1862: MHP-ABV, Report, Oct. 14, 1862. Sugar production in 1822 and 1835 is estimated.

planters without mills, in São Paulo nearly all the sugar was raised by the mill owner on his domain with his own gang of slaves. Undoubtedly this exclusiveness related to the small capacities of the mills in Rio Claro—only three of them in 1835 ground more than 1,000 arrobas (14.7 metric tons).[3]

The cane fields continued to expand in the region of Itu, Parnaíba, and Piracicaba while in Campinas the planters were shifting to coffee. The apogee of the sugar cycle was reached in Campinas around 1836, when 93 mills ground 2,320 metric tons of sugar. By 1854 only 44 mills remained, producing 910 tons. Rio Claro followed the example of Campinas. The high point of its output probably came before 1853, when 522 tons were ground (Table 2.1). After 1862 sugar steadily lost ground to coffee until, according to a report of 1873, the county was not even producing enough for its own consumption. The cane cycle in Rio Claro was clearly undercapitalized and speculative. The planters of Rio Claro financed local production from their earnings on estates in Campinas and Itu. The exhaustion of the forests and the soil in the older regions would eventually have turned the county into a major cane-growing area, but by then coffee had replaced cane.[4]

The inventory of the owners of one of the more important sugar plantations suggests a modest rate of profit, indeed a negative one if depreciation and interest are considered (Table 2.2). The plantation of Palmeiras included 254 *alqueires* (615 hectares).* The

* The land measure of one alqueire was equal to 2.42 hectares.

TABLE 2.2

*Capital Investment in a Sugar Plantation, 1851*

| Investment | Milreis |
|---|---|
| Slaves (25, of whom 14 males) | 10,400 |
| Land, including residences, storage, and quadrado | 7,100 |
| Engenho, including shed and still | 2,600 |
| Other equipment and tools | 1,000 |
| Animals | 500 |
| TOTAL | 21,600 |

SOURCE. RC/C-1, Inventories, Maço 3, May 19, 1851: inventory of the property of Manuel José de Carvalho and his deceased wife, Matilda, Palmeiras plantation.

family possessed 1,670 milreis in personal property and a store in town worth another 1,000. The inventory listed 1,324 milreis in sugar on hand. Probably that was all that year's crop, though some may already have been sold; a report of 1854 shows this plantation producing a thousand arrobas of sugar, at the time worth 1,440 milreis. Since the mill was also equipped to distill cane brandy, perhaps another 200 milreis should be added to that income.

The output per slave on Palmeiras was only 40 arrobas, as it was on the average of all plantations in Rio Claro in 1822 and 1835. According to Saint-Hilaire, the French botanist who visited the region in 1818, the average should have been about 100 arrobas. Possibly the plantations of Rio Claro were much less efficient than those of Campinas, but it may be that Saint-Hilaire was only considering the efforts of slaves directly involved in sugar production, and that in Rio Claro more than half the slave force was engaged in raising subsistence and other cash crops.[5]

Palmeiras, then, yielded less than 7 percent on fixed investment. Slaves and equipment should have been written off in twenty years, an average decline of 685 milreis per year. Several local planters owed the family 3,400 milreis, but they in turn owed other planters, mostly relatives, an astonishing 18,600 milreis. Interest on the net indebtedness must have amounted to more than 2,000 milreis. Surprisingly, Carvalho was still the owner of Palmeiras in 1862, according to another report that showed he had shifted to coffee growing. By then all eight of the plantations still raising

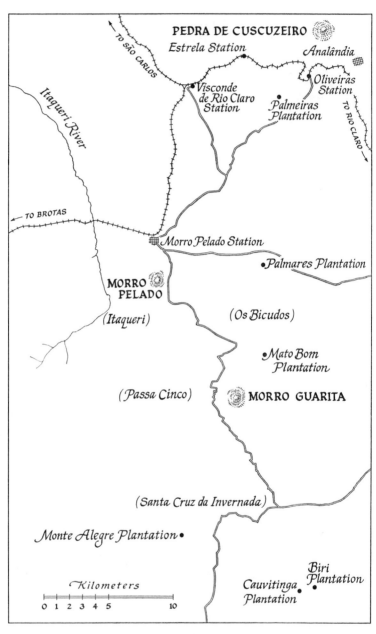

*Region of Rio Claro—West, ca. 1905*

Region of Rio Claro—East, ca. 1905

sugar were also growing coffee; for each of them it had become a relatively unimportant sideline.[6]

*Coffea arabica* had been brought to Brazil early in the eighteenth century. In the 1790's commercial exploitation of the plant was successful in the hills behind Rio de Janeiro. By 1830 it covered large areas of the Paraíba Valley, across the provincial boundary into São Paulo as far as Jacareí. It is not hard to understand why the cultivation of coffee substituted for sugarcane on the great estates. First of all, world demand for coffee was a good deal stronger than that for sugar through most of the early nineteenth century. Furthermore, costs of production were somewhat lower. Coffee was more economical of labor. Although harvesting and processing the two crops required about the same amount of effort, sugar had to be replanted usually every three years. The coffee groves, on the other hand, might last 30 or 40. Although the coffee trees could have been managed more carefully, they flourished in the same soils suitable for sugar with relatively small managerial input on the part of the planters. Finally, coffee allowed a better margin of profit above the cost of transport to the port of Santos. It had a higher value by weight, and it was less subject to spoilage on the way.[7]

Seeds from Rio de Janeiro were planted in Campinas as early as 1817, and in Limeira, on Vergueiro's Ibicaba plantation, in 1828. Other planters, it seems, acquired seedlings after a few years from those early plantings. Antônio Paes de Barros and Joaquim José de Andrade had producing trees by 1835. But these first groves were for a long time regarded as experiments, or mere curiosities. Not until the mid-1840's were large-scale plantings of coffee carried out in the Paulista West, from Campinas to Rio Claro. The planters became convinced of the feasibility of coffee growing in 1841, when a hard freeze in the region proved that the tree was at least as resistant as sugar at altitudes much higher than the Paraíba Valley. Then, in the mid-1840's, the general decline in export prices led planters far removed from the coast to favor coffee over sugar. Although there were at least six treatises on coffee growing published in Rio de Janeiro before 1850, the first in 1813, it appears that the planters of Rio Claro obtained their knowledge of the plant by visiting plantations in the Paraíba Valley, and then passing the information to relatives and friends.[8]

The example of the province of Rio de Janeiro was not sufficient, however, because the climate and soils of the Paulista West presented many dissimilarities. The best soils for growing coffee spread north and westward from Campinas. The decomposed gneissic and granitic earth of the region contains nutritive elements in low concentration, but it is deep and very porous. In the summer rains the humus on the surface quickly decomposes and seeps into the thick upper layer. Coffee trees send their roots ten or twenty meters into this material before reaching bedrock. The hilliness of the region is an advantage, because drainage is more rapid. These soils are quite variable in fertility, but the planter had only a few rough tests to help him decide where to plant. He relied greatly on color. "Red" soils, the color of terra cotta, were the most common and signified moderate fertility. The more yellow the soil, the greater the intrusion of clay and sand, and therefore the less valuable. The soils of deepest red are called *terra roxa*, "purple earth." These, richer in iron oxides, are the most fertile and the most sought out. Color was not a certain test, however. There are red soils called *catanduva* that are low in quality, and there is a yellow soil called *massapé*, of basaltic and granitic origin, that is nearly as fertile as *terra roxa*.[9]

Only forested land, it was assumed, could support coffee trees, and within the forest certain species of trees were hunted out as *padrões*, or models—sure signs that the coffee tree would flourish in the same place. Pau d'alho, jangada brava, and white fig were especially highly prized. Sometimes one of these trees would be left standing in the midst of a grove to prove to neighbors or prospective buyers that the coffee trees were vigorous. It was essential to avoid planting on land subject to frost. One or two hours of cold below zero centigrade withered branches and reduced yields for several years. A night of such cold would destroy the trees. The planters, therefore, did not set out groves in creek bottoms, where the cold was caught in pockets at night and where the higher humidity increased the danger. Hillsides above 600 meters were thought safer. The *padrões* were as sensitive to cold as the coffee tree, and therefore were doubly proof of a favorable location. Certain other more resistant trees were signs of cold ground that was to be avoided.

In order to begin cultivating coffee, it was not necessary immediately to cut down more of the forest. There was already much open field and second growth after nearly a century of subsistence farming and a generation of sugarcane cultivation, on account of the enormous appetite of the engenho's wood-burning boilers. Besides, the planters were reluctant to set out groves on land still too exuberantly fertile because they would be overrun with weeds. Instead, land that had just been cleared would first be planted in corn, which demanded little attention, even among the burned-out, fallen trunks. After a few seasons the clearing was allowed to return to second growth. Then, after a second burning, the groves were finally set out. In spite of these rule-of-thumb standards, a large proportion of Rio Claro's trees were planted on inappropriate lands, so that their productive life was short. Possibly this was the result of haste and speculation; more likely it was because Rio Claro was of the first generation of coffee growing and possessed too great a variety of soil conditions. Planting was necessarily experimental and hazardous, therefore. At any rate, a number of plantations laid out in the shadows of the bluffs on the western and northern edge of the county never flourished and finally were abandoned.[10]

Planting was done from seeds when prices were rising and the planter was short-handed, but in the long run better results were achieved by transplanting from a nursery in a shady forest clearing. Sometimes the nurseries were planted with seeds thickly sown, but it was more common for seedlings already germinated in the groves to be brought there and allowed to grow for another year or two. At the beginning of the rainy season the seedlings of various ages were either dug up in clumps or yanked out of the loosened soil one by one for replanting in the grove. There holes would be dug aligned on the square or diamond pattern, 15 or 16 *palmos* (3.3 or 3.5 meters) apart. In each of them three or four seedlings were inserted and the hole was partly refilled with earth. The coffee tree, therefore, was really a cluster, called a *pé*, or "foot" of bushes. Each cluster was then partly shielded from the sun with a lean-to shelter of cornstalks or scraps of wood and bark. In three or four years the trees would grow to a height of about four meters and would begin to bear. During this time the grove would have to be hoed clear of weeds, but the effort was compensated by planting corn between the rows.[11]

The cost of "forming" a coffee grove in the early 1850's can be estimated from two reports sent the provincial government. Cleared land cost 40 milreis per hectare, half of that representing the cost of clearing. Since a hectare accommodated 920 trees, land for a 100,000-tree plantation cost 4,350 milreis. Planting the trees and tending them to maturity was much more expensive. The four years of labor would add 35,450 milreis. Drying terraces and processing equipment for a plantation of such a size would cost about 10,000 more. To these expenses must be added yearly interest charges of 15 percent on the cost of land and improvements. The total cost of shifting a cane plantation to coffee, with some allowances for minor expenses, would amount to about 50,000 milreis ($32,500) per 100,000 trees. Compare the inventory of Boa Vista de Passa Cinco plantation (Table 2.3), whose grove was valued at that rate. By the year 1859 there were about 2.6 million trees in Rio Claro; consequently, in the first ten years of commercial exploitation about 1,300,000 milreis ($845,000) had been transferred into coffee.[12]

Part of this sum had been reinvested from sugar profits. From 1845 to 1854 the planters of Rio Claro sold about 6,000 tons of sugar for about 400,000 milreis, excluding transport and commissions. Not much of this would have been available for the expenses of conversion, since normal operating expenses and the servicing of

TABLE 2.3

*Capital Investment in a Coffee Plantation, 1861*

| Investment | Milreis |
|---|---|
| Slaves (71, of whom 46 males) | 106,244 |
| Land, including residences, 200,000-tree grove | 122,790 |
| Processing equipment | 14,890 |
| Other equipment and tools, draft animals | 20,370 |
| Other animals | 3,576 |
| TOTAL | 267,870 |

SOURCE. RC/C-1, Inventories, Maço 6, Feb. 9, 1861: inventory of the property of Benedito Antônio de Camargo, Boa Vista de Passa Cinco plantation.

mortgages were quite onerous, especially in view of the necessity of abandoning existing mills and cutting back on the cane plantings. Thirty-nine mortgages and probated wills registered from 1850 to 1859 provide some evidence of the source of the rest of the capital (Table 2.4). It should be emphasized that the security for mortgages was almost never land, but slaves. Lenders preferred slaves as mortgage security, probably because they were a far more liquid form of capital. It cannot be assumed that the total of 886,900 milreis represented over half the hypothetical 1,300,000 mentioned above, because a portion of it went to pay for another kind of "equipment"—the slave gang. In fact, since many mortgage contracts would have been registered in São Paulo, Santos, and even Rio de Janeiro, the total indebtedness cannot be calculated. Contracts registered in Rio Claro are certain to overstate the significance of local lenders.

Nevertheless, it is clear that the indirect infusion of capital from

TABLE 2.4

*Sources of Credit on Plantations, 1850–59*

| Lenders ($N = 39$) | Milreis | Percent |
|---|---|---|
| Planters and merchants, Rio Claro | 54,670 | 6% |
| Planters and merchants, rest of São Paulo | 127,630 | 14 |
| Exporters and merchants, Santos and Rio | 704,600 | 80 |
| TOTAL | 886,900 | 100% |

SOURCE. RC/C-1, LN and Inventories, 1850–59.

abroad, represented by exporters' loans, was essential to the organization of the coffee plantations in the Paulista West. The significance of foreign capital to the adoption of coffee cultivation in the area may also be inferred circumstantially. Before 1828 Santos shipped nearly all its goods to Rio de Janeiro, where Portuguese merchants resold them to exporters. Not until 1848 was Rio de Janeiro finally eliminated as entrepôt, when English and German exporters established themselves in Santos. Undoubtedly, their presence stimulated the demand for coffee and encouraged the abandonment of sugar, a product their home offices preferred to buy elsewhere.[18]

The work of clearing land, planting the trees, and tending them to maturity might be carried out with the planter's own slaves or agregados, but it was usually contracted to "entrepreneurs" who were owners of slave gangs. The planter thereby avoided the considerable risk of having his investment wiped out by frost or insects. Dead trees had to be replaced by the contractor, and the planter paid only for mature trees turned over to him, not for labor expended. Sometimes the entrepreneurs were free laborers contracting individually or with relatives. Probably they were, like the slave-owning entrepreneurs, from less favored regions like central Minas Gerais, agregados cast out of declining estates. The slave-owning entrepreneurs appear to have been in some cases failed landowners, in others inheritors of slaves without land. Contracts were located for the planting of more than a million trees by entrepreneurs, who together introduced 332 slaves into the county.[14]

If they came to Rio Claro with the hope of acquiring their own plantations, they were mistaken. Typically the contract they signed relieved them of a former debt contracted elsewhere and presented them with a sizable advance, often half the value of their slaves. In turn they mortgaged their slave gang as security for fulfillment of the contract. The landowner provided shelter, seeds, and direction in aligning the rows. The planting of subsistence crops was permitted between the trees, and some extra land was made available for pasture. At the end of the term, usually four years, the entrepreneur was paid a certain sum for each tree surviving, and proportionately less for replants. The entrepreneur was also allowed to keep any berries he may have harvested in the final year, when some of the trees might have reached maturity.

The contracts of the 1860's seem not to have permitted the entrepreneur to accumulate enough in four years to pay off the principal, much less make a profit. For example, when João Baptista do Prado took on 40,000 trees on the estate of Antônio José Vieira Barbosa in 1864, with an advance of 8,000 milreis guaranteed by his twelve slaves, a schedule of payments was specified that could not have exceeded 16,000 milreis, and would have been only 14,000 if he suffered a yearly loss of no more than 5 percent of the trees. On the other hand, his slaves had to be clothed and a few might have to be replaced. It is not surprising that none of the 22 entrepreneurs who signed local contracts ever bought property in the county.[15]

The planter took over the mature groves with his own slaves, who tended them in gangs, under the direction of drivers, called *feitores*. During the rainy season, from spring to early fall, the ground had to be hoed several times to uproot the weeds that compete with the trees for moisture, and to keep the surface loose so that as much rain as possible might be absorbed. When there were enough hands, three or four hoeings would be carried out. Otherwise there might only be two, or a hoeing might be replaced by a mere scything of the weeds. The last hoeing was called the "crowning." In this operation the debris from the hoeing was raked away from each tree, forming smooth circular clearings at the bases. This was in preparation for the harvest, which began in April or May, as the weather turned dry and cool. The picking was done with as little care as the hoeing. The picker stripped a whole branch at once, allowing the berries, withered, ripe, and green indiscriminately, to fall to the ground, where other members of the gang had spread out sheets to collect them. Leaves and branches were plucked from the sheets or cast out by winnowing on large flat sieves. A worker was able to pick about 250 liters a day in this fashion.

Little else was done to maintain the productivity of the trees. A lack of hoeing and carelessness in harvesting manifestly reduced the yield, but the planter, chronically short of working capital, had no choice. The only skilled labor was that of the *feitores*, carters, and sometimes pruners, who were employed after frosts to remove blackened branches before they killed the rest of the tree. Some laborers were skilled in exterminating saúva ants, whose underground networks attacked the roots. No attempt was made to fertilize the grove, except for the return, after the harvest, of the debris to the base of the trees to serve as mulch.[16]

The preparation of the coffee for market was complex and time-consuming. It was the only stage of production that was both labor- and capital-intensive. The first step was to remove dirt, leaves, and overripe berries by washing the coffee in vats of water. Then the berries were conveyed through gutters to the *terreiro*, a large, flat terrace surfaced with bricks, where the coffee was spread out to dry. The coffee bean is enclosed in a berry consisting of an outer shell, a pulpy layer, and a soft inner husk. The drying had to be prolonged until the pulp and the shell were desiccated enough to be easily cracked. For several days or even several weeks the berries on the terrace were turned two or three times a day and heaped up at night to protect them from the dew. The lack of rain in the winter months is at this point a great advantage. When an unseasonable storm threatened, the workers frantically rushed to rake up the half-dried beans and cover them with oilcloth or bundles of straw. The planters were satisfied to protract the drying; they sought thereby to induce a slight amount of fermentation inside the shell that improved the color and quality of the bean. When the berries were quite dry, they were hulled by machine. A variety of mechanical hulling devices were employed. Probably the most common were the *pilão*, a multiple wooden trip-hammer activated by water power, and the *ripa*, or *carretão*, a pair of wheels that revolved on a flat wooden basin, usually turned by animal power. After the broken shells were blown away with mechanical ventilators, the beans were spread out on tables or on the floor of the warehouse and hand-sorted.[17]

This method was not only wasteful of labor; it also yielded uncertain results. Therefore the planters were willing to invest much capital in further mechanization. Machines were patented early in the 1850's that were able to crack the hull of the berry before it was dried. This was a great advantage because fermentation was more easily controlled and drying time was reduced when the shelling was done first. At the same time these machines made possible a much more even quality, since they rejected green berries that had been picked along with the mature fruit. After the pulp was washed off the beans and they were dried on the terrace, a second huller was employed to remove the inner husk. This huller was run in tandem with mechanical ventilators and sorters, all moved by water or steam power, that eliminated most of the rest of the hand labor and greatly improved the marketability of the product. The cost of installing the new processing equipment was considerable; a report of 1875 said 20,000 milreis and inventories confirm that estimate. By that date three of the town's coffee agents had set up hulling machinery to which the smaller planters of the county were obliged to resort.[18]

Coffee remained the dominant plantation crop from the 1850's to the 1930's. In 1854 more than 1,000 tons was harvested; the high point was reached in 1901, when nearly 15,000 tons was produced (Table 2.5). Coffee was challenged only briefly by cotton in the late 1860's, during the temporary prostration of the U.S. South. More than 30 local planters were growing cotton by 1873, but no record remains of the techniques, output, or commercialization of the crop. Apparently large-scale planting was not yet profitable when the brief speculation subsided.[19]

The plantations of Rio Claro were largely self-sufficient in foodstuffs, construction materials, draft animals, and some handcrafts. Although the chronic shortage of slaves tempted the planters to specialize wholly in coffee, the market was too small to supply the needs of the plantations without sharply increasing prices. In Rio Claro the price of corn and beans doubled between 1850 and 1856, partly because of the decreased self-sufficiency of the planters as they converted suddenly to coffee. Nevertheless the plantations

TABLE 2.5

*Coffee Production, 1835–1929*

| Year | Number of growers | Metric tons | Year | Number of growers | Metric tons |
|---|---|---|---|---|---|
| 1835 | 2 | 0.5 | 1897 | — | 9,300 |
| 1851 | — | 294 | 1898 | — | 9,815 |
| 1852 | — | 470 | 1899 | — | 11,378 |
| 1853 | — | 756 | 1900 | — | 10,503 |
| 1854 | 25 | 1,671 | 1901 | — | 14,824 |
| 1855 | — | 1,466 | 1903 | — | 9,071 |
| 1857–59 ave. | 44 | 1,764 | 1905 | 394 | 13,172 |
| 1862 | — | 2,557 | 1907 | — | 14,642 |
| 1874 | — | 4,410 | 1909 | — | 12,356 |
| 1876 | 91 | 6,000 | 1911 | — | 8,940 |
| 1884 | — | 6,000 | 1913 | — | 9,135 |
| 1886 | — | 9,000 | 1915 | — | 10,785 |
| 1892 | 152 | 7,895 | 1917 | — | 10,980 |
| 1894 | — | 6,269 | 1919 | 287 | 8,070 |
| 1895 | 213 | 8,024 | 1929 | 507 | 4,050 |

SOURCES. 1835: APESP, População Piracicaba. 1851, 1853, 1854, 1857–59, 1876, 1884: APESP, OD/RC 396, 397, 398. 1852: SP(P), President of Province, *Relatorio*, 1853. 1855: Paulo Pestana, *O café em São Paulo* (Sao Paulo: Typographia Levi, 1927). 1862: MHP-ABV, Report to President of Province from Câmara, Oct. 14, 1862. 1874: *Correio Paulistano*, Feb. 11, 1874. 1886: SP(P), Conselho Central de Estatística, *Relatorio*, 1888. 1892: MHP-ABV, "Relatorio dos agricultores de café . . . 1892." 1897: SP(S), Repartição de Estatística e Arquivo, *Relatorio*, 1897. 1894, 1895, 1898–1903, 1907–17: Companhia Paulista de Estradas de Ferro, *Relatorio*, 1894–1918. 1905: SP(S), Secretaria de Agricultura, Comércio e Obras Públicas, *Estatistica agricola e zootechnica, 1904–1905.* 1919: Census. 1929: SP(S), Secretaria de Agricultura, Indústria e Comércio, *O café, estatistica de producção e commercio*, 1929.

were not very diversified. Besides the staple corn, beans, and rice, generally some cows were kept along with the horses and mules, and sometimes goats and sheep. Sugarcane was grown in small amounts, at least for its juice and to make cane brandy. Cotton was grown and given to the slaves to be spun and weaved into homespun, but it was more common by the early 1870's to buy English yard goods. The larger estates were frequently equipped with a sawmill and grist mill activated by the same steam or hydraulic power that ran the coffee hullers. In Rio Claro there are scattered deposits of lime and clay. A few planters had limeworks and brickyards, usually leased, that supplied the town and the rest of the county.[20]

The town supplied the plantations with a few manufactured goods, wagons and other kinds of carpentry, wrought iron, and saddlery. Most of the rest of the plantations' supplies were imports —construction hardware, barbed wire, hoes and machetes, kitchenware, medicines, and kerosene. The local smallholders probably sold some corn to the plantations, but not steadily. They appear to have been the chief suppliers of the salt pork consumed on the plantations but rarely produced there.[21]

Rio Claro in the 1850's and 1860's was at the farthest limit of profitable coffee cultivation. Beyond it the cost of transportation to Santos absorbed too much of the sale price. The routes to Santos were mere trails, only two meters wide at best. They could not be traversed by wheeled vehicles. Numerous streams had to be forded or crossed on unsteady ferries; therefore the coffee of the Paulista West had to be brought to market on muleback. Each of the mules carried about 120 to 150 kilograms. Driven in pack trains of about ten animals, they took ten days to reach Santos. The journey was arduous; observers saw mules mired up to their bellies and carcasses and spoiled cargos littering the roadsides. Since a pack mule could manage no more than six trips at a harvest, Rio Claro's coffee must have employed about 3,000 mules by the 1860's, when the county's output was 2,600 tons.[22]

Not that many were available. A planter complained to the county council in 1857 that he had two years' harvest in his storerooms because he couldn't get any mules, which "greatly distressed him." A few of the planters owned their own pack trains; more commonly they advanced money to independent mule drivers, in return for the exclusive use of their animals. The practice was easier for the larger planters to engage in, another factor that favored concentration in the exporting sector. A few contracts registered in 1859 show that this primitive form of transport cost about 1.60 milreis per arroba from Rio Claro to Santos, which is to say .43 milreis per ton kilometer. Since coffee sold in the port for an average 5.00 milreis per arroba (1858 to 1860), the mule trains represented nearly a third of the planter's sale price.[23]

Clearly, if the roads could be improved, the margin would be much enlarged. But the provincial government was hard-pressed even to maintain the inadequate system of trails. Those connecting

Rio Claro with other towns—Limeira and Piracicaba to the south, Descalvado to the north, and São Carlos and Brotas to the north-west by way of Itaqueri—cost about 10,000 milreis to keep up. Their repair was the immediate responsibility of the local property owners, who had to detail slaves and tenants for corvée labor, but materials and engineering were paid for by the province. All of this was so poorly executed that the county council complained continually: "Few repairs have been made, which produce only ephemeral improvements."[24]

The planters of the Paulista West strongly pressed the provincial government for a wagon road to replace the mule trails. A wagon pulled by four mules could bring as much to market as twenty mules could carry, and in half the time. Antônio Paes de Barros proposed such a road, to extend as far as Rio Claro, and funds were authorized in 1851. It seems, however, that the project was beyond the capacity of the province. Repair work on the road down the coastal escarpment absorbed most of the revenue collected on the post roads. Greatly improved in the 1790's, that road was re-paired twice more before a general reconstruction between 1841 and 1846. The funds allocated for the wagon road, therefore, were spent on a fifth rerouting of the cliff road, between 1856 and 1864. The contracting of this road was undertaken by José Vergueiro, Nicolau's son. The widening of the trail to Campinas was finally effected sometime after the first railway reached Jundiaí, appar-ently after work on the extension to Campinas had begun. The exporting economy of Rio Claro, after 50 years of primitive trans-port, leaped almost directly into the age of the railroad.[25]

In 1865 a British-owned 1.6-meter line was opened between Santos and the capital. In 1868 it was extended to Jundiaí. When the company proved unwilling to take up its option to build as far as Campinas and Rio Claro, a group of planters undertook the task on their own. Among them were 22 with plantations in Rio Claro, including the count of Três Rios, the Vergueiro family, and the viscount of Rio Claro. Capital raising was slowed by the Para-guayan war, but the Companhia Paulista de Estradas de Ferro brought the line as far as Campinas by 1872. Strong pressures

from Rio Claro and Limeira forced the company to continue laying tracks to Rio Claro, and the section was completed in August
1876 at a cost of 5.8 million milreis. Thereafter the Paulista sought
to cut toward the east, in order to draw off traffic from a competing
line, the Mogiana. When a Liberal government was installed in
1878, the count of Pinhal, boss of São Carlos, and his father-in-law,
the viscount of Rio Claro, extracted from the ministry approval of
a trace that passed through the viscount's lands in Ajapi and Cuscuseiro (Analândia). The Paulista, challenged to carry out the project, desisted. Its directors wanted a different trace to the west that
would have extended the company's privileged zone to Brotas and
Jaú.[26]

In response the count of Pinhal organized his own company,
with heavy participation by the viscount and his sons and other
planters of Rio Claro. This 1.0-meter line was opened to traffic in
1881. The count of Pinhal had no special interest in running a
railroad. Although it was as profitable as the Paulista, he sold it
to a British company, which resold it to the Paulista two years
later at a stunning profit. In 1914 the Paulista built a 1.6-meter line
along the trace they had originally favored, but ran the narrow-
gauge route for many years. The Rio Claro Railway was unquestionably the largest enterprise ever attempted by the planters of
Rio Claro. The section that ran to São Carlos cost nearly 2.5 million milreis, and was not allowed a profit guarantee by the province. The political effort required to gain approval of the trace
was enormous, and was crucial to most of the planters north of the
town center, since the Paulista trace, although shorter and less
graded, cut through poor land. The clear connection of local Conservatives with the Paulista scheme discredited them and preserved
Liberal control through the beginning of the Republic.*

The railroad reduced the cost of transporting coffee, but not
much. By 1884 the tariff amounted to .81 milreis per arroba, or .20

* Companhia Rio Claro, *Relatorio da directoria relativo ao semestre de julho
a dezembro de 1886* (São Paulo: Typographia a Vapor de Jorg Seckler & Comp.,
1887); Museu Paulista, Arquivo Aguirra, Rio Claro, May 16, 1881. The sale and
resale of the Rio Claro line are quite a mystery; the English investors deliberately ran the line incompetently, so as to cause a general public demand for Paul-

milreis per ton kilometer to Santos. Carting and loading, however, might double that figure, depending on the distance from the station. It was reported in 1882 that Rio Claro planters were paying about a quarter of their gross sales for transport. The railways helped to preserve concentration of property. Political influence decided the location of stations; both the viscount of Rio Claro and the count of Três Rios had their own sidings. The companies were allowed 12 percent profit before the province would act to lower rates. Therefore the largest planters, all of whom had invested heavily in the lines, received extremely secure profits that were, in effect, a kind of rebate. The companies usually favored stockholders with contracts to supply wood for ties and fuel and other supplies.[27]

Railways were essential to the spread of coffee plantations. The use of mules was not only more expensive; it was impracticable. In the last year before the Jundiaí station opened to traffic, more than a half-million mules passed the toll bar at Santos. The planters no longer suffered higher charges for transport when the harvest was abundant, and were free of the need to finance mule drivers and turn over pasturage to them. The railroad enlarged trade in other goods and reduced travel to the capital from a week to a day. Rio Claro was both a railhead and a junction between lines of differing gauge, and thereby gained some additional commercial functions, but the railroad also permitted increasing concentration of urban functions in São Paulo. The provincial capital grew rapidly in comparison with other towns along the rail lines, from 1872 onward.[28]

The railroad transformed the operation of the plantations. Before, travel had been so slow and communication so uncertain that it was quite difficult for a single owner to supervise two or more

ista acquisition. Their profit was £1,950,000 on an initial £850,000! Diana Maria de Faro Leal Diniz, "Rio Claro e o café: desenvolvimento, apogeu e crise, 1850–1900" (Ph.D. dissertation, Dept. of Social Sciences, Faculdade de Filosofia, Ciências e Letras de Rio Claro, 1973), pp. 165–66. Complaints regarding service are in University of São Paulo, Dept. of History, Setor de Documentação, Records of Palmares Plantation, letters of Jorge Whitaker, Oct. 29, 1891, and Jan. 14, 1892.

plantations at any great distance apart. The planters of Rio Claro lived on their estates or in town, where many of their mansions, imposingly second-storied, were constructed by the early 1870's. The railroad brought the capital of the province within a day's travel of Rio Claro, and it offered telegraph service and daily mail deliveries. Over the next two decades the planters departed, leaving town houses to fall in ruins. County politics were abandoned to the local pharmacist, drygoods merchants, notary, and other middle-class notables.

The larger plantations were put in the hands of hired administrators. The richest planters came to own strings of estates, all supervised from their mansions in São Paulo. The administrator mailed daily reports to the owner, in a form that appears to have been standardized. First, a report on the previous day's activities, which included all expenditures of money. Second, a copy of the day book, which listed the workers' names, the work they performed, and illnesses. Finally, a description of the work to be undertaken the next day. Generally the administrator kept a running account of the expenses and income from coffee. The owner usually kept a set of accounts—not necessarily double-entry—copies of contracts, and copies of directions sent back to the administrator. These seem to have been limited to advisements concerning the persons upon whom drafts might be drawn and to whom shipments of coffee should be sent.[29]

The coffee of Rio Claro was forwarded to *comissários*—brokers—in Santos, for sale to exporters in both Santos and Rio de Janeiro. In Rio Claro, Nicolau Vergueiro and Manuel Rodrigues Jordão, two of the largest planters, were principally brokers and exporters, and several other planters were at times associated with Santos firms. Others could claim some blood or marital kinship with the brokers they dealt with. There were lesser brokers in town. They accepted smaller shipments, mainly from smaller growers who did not own their own processing machinery. The Santos brokers operated with far more resources than even the largest of the planters. They dealt with their clientele avuncularly, often buying and selling with power of attorney. They kept better accounts than the planters, and were better informed concerning the market.[30]

At harvest time the owner and his family came to one or more of their plantations, or stayed by turns at several. Close attention was paid to the processing of the coffee, and the state of the groves and of the slave gang was carefully assessed. Maria Paes de Barros records that her mother attended the slaves in a clinic, an activity that the family regarded as an act of charity and kindness rather than as plant maintenance or workers' compensation. Dismissals and hiring of free workers took place at the end of harvest, just before the family's return to the city.[31]

The plantation houses were generally spare and unornamented, since the planters preferred to decorate their mansions in São Paulo. The *sobrado*—second-storied house—of the Santa Ana plantation was probably typical. A town contractor built it in 1874 for 11,000 milreis, with all materials supplied by the owner. It was of plastered brick, 53 meters in front and 17 deep, with wattle-and-daub interior walls. The three salons in the center were carefully paneled and floored; the rest—five bedrooms and six other rooms—were merely plastered. Furnishings were quite modest until the turn of the century. Inventories of the 1850's and 1860's list few household goods of value. Always the first item is the conjugal bed, of jacarandá, symbol of the patriarchy that bred for serious purposes; sometimes some silverware, a few pieces of gold and jewelry, and a clock; a little culture, for the planters were not much given to literature—"three books, one of domestic medicine, a work by Jesus Christ, and *Duas horas mariannas*."[32]

The rest of the estate buildings were even more starkly utilitarian: storage buildings, processing sheds, a machine shop, sometimes a chapel and a clinic, and the *quadrado*, the square compound where the slaves were penned at night, in stalls arranged around an open square. Flower gardens and shade trees were rare, but there were often citrus orchards and sometimes vegetable gardens for the owner's table.[33]

In the province of Rio de Janeiro the expanding market for coffee bestowed riches on a new elite that came to power with the Conservative Party in the late 1830's. In São Paulo, it has been asserted, "The latifundium dates only from the nineteenth century, with the cultivation of coffee." Indeed the coffee trade was

TABLE 2.6

*Concentration of Coffee Production, 1860*

| Size of harvest, in arrobas | Number of producers | Percent of producers | Arrobas produced | Percent of production |
|---|---|---|---|---|
| 10,000 and over | 1 | 2.3% | 12,300 | 10.4% |
| 4,000–9,999 | 10 | 22.7 | 61,300 | 51.5 |
| 1,000–3,999 | 13 | 29.5 | 21,100 | 17.7 |
| 999 and under | 20 | 45.5 | 24,300 | 20.4 |
| TOTAL | 44 | 100.0% | 119,000 | 100.0% |

SOURCE. APESP, OD/RC 397, "Quadro dos estabelecimentos de cultura, 1858–1860."

to provide far more wealth than sugar, enabling another group of planters to surpass, by the 1880's, the influence and power of the Conservatives of Rio de Janeiro. The coffee-planting group grew more stratified (Table 2.6 indicates concentration in 1860). In Rio Claro there were a few whose possessions were far greater than the rest. They were persons of influence at court, holders of important offices, the deciders of policy in the empire. Among them, in Rio Claro, three of the most important were Antônio Paes de Barros, José Estanislau de Oliveira, and Nicolau Vergueiro.

By 1835 Antônio Paes de Barros was working 73 slaves on two plantations in Rio Claro. Barros was the son of one of the wealthiest of Itu planters, Antônio de Barros Penteado, whose initial capital had come from gold mining in Mato Grosso. With landholdings in Itu and Piracicaba as well as Rio Claro, Barros was prominent in provincial politics. He was sent by São Paulo to the Portuguese revolutionary Cortes of 1821, and he participated in the provincial Council of Government after independence. Among his brothers and brothers-in-law were an appellate judge, a baron, a senator, and a marquis. He was styled baron of Piracicaba for his political services in 1854. Representative of a new elite in the province that emerged with independence, Barros was to become involved in roadbuilding, railroads, and cotton factories as well as plantations. His first purchase of land in Rio Claro seems to have taken place in 1823, when he bought a piece of the Pereira sesmaria, "a quarter and a half of frontage with half a league toward the *sertão*," that is, 816 hectares, for 600 milreis in cash and "thirty-two unbroken beasts, etc." The planting of cane began on that land three years later. By 1855 Barros had four adjoining plantations in the area east of the town.[34]

José Estanislau de Oliveira was also the possessor of a fortune in land, with political connections and honors, but his social position was a little lower than that of Barros. Whereas Barros was directly the heir of an aristocratic family, Oliveira was the son of a Portuguese schoolteacher who had come to Campinas in 1785, married into a prominent family there, and somehow accumulated land and slaves worth about 70,000 milreis by the time of his death. José Estanislau, one of four sons, had joined the army, but he resigned his ensign's commission when he married the daughter of the garrison medical officer, on the ground that army pay was insufficient for a man with a family. In 1836 he bought a piece of land in Rio Claro in what had been the sesmarias of Goes Maciel and the Lopes family, but was by then in the hands of third parties. Lacking further funds to buy slaves (it is said that he had sold his wife's piano for his first land purchase, although he must have also had some share in his father's estate), Oliveira returned to Campinas. There he bought salt, which he took to the market of Sorocaba and bartered for mules. These he drove to Rio Claro and sold to planters for the Santos trains. After three years of this triangular traffic, Oliveira had enough to establish his plantation. By 1855 he reported that the original tract had grown to three-quarters of a league (3,267 hectares), and a reserve of 11,600 hectares more was in his name in the part of the county later to become Analândia. Although Oliveira also was ennobled later in life—he became viscount of Rio Claro, in recognition of his leadership of the local Liberal Party—he seems the perfect self-made bourgeois. Lacking elevated origins, he did not scruple to become a tradesman, and once established in Rio Claro, he became its most important moneylender.[35]

The third of Rio Claro's leading planters, Nicolau Pereira de Campos Vergueiro, represented still another source of capital. He was a Portuguese immigrant who arrived in São Paulo in 1802 or 1803 with no other resource than his law degree. Professionals like lawyers, medical doctors, and schoolteachers were then so scarce that their degrees immediately admitted them to the highest level of the elite. Vergueiro was, in fact, one of only two lawyers in the captaincy. He was made Judge of Sesmarias in 1813 and obtained a sesmaria for himself in Piracicaba. For the next several years he acquired other properties in partnership with the richest merchant of São Paulo, Brigadier Luis Antônio de Souza. When the partnership was dissolved in 1825, Vergueiro received two plantations, one on the southern edge of Rio Claro, purchased in 1818 from the sesmaria owned by Joaquim Galvão de França; the other, north of the townsite in what is now Ajapi, was purchased the same year from the Goes Maciel sesmaria. Both of these holdings were expanded by later purchases. By 1855 the plantation in Ajapi, called Angélica, was nearly three square leagues (130 square kilometers) in size. At the same time that the partners began planting cane, Vergueiro opened an agency in his own name to export sugar via Santos. He was also the province's largest dealer in slaves. These commercial interests were more important to Vergueiro than his two estates in Rio Claro and Limeira.[36]

Vergueiro was an enthusiastic advocate of independence. He accompanied Antônio Paes de Barros to the Portuguese Cortes and when he returned he took part in the Constituent Assembly of 1823. An astute politician, he was a leading figure in the Liberal Party and held posts in every government until 1842. Vergueiro was extremely interested in the central problem of manpower and, as will be discussed, was the first planter in Brazil to test the feasibility of immigrant plantation labor.

It is important to notice that Oliveira and Vergueiro were self-made only in a restricted sense. They were of families affluent enough to provide them with an education or at least a stake. Their wives' connections were valuable, and still others were formed when their children married, for indeed all elite marriages were arranged. Furthermore, the inruption of the planter-capitalists into the Rio Claro area was not carried out single-handedly. Typically, there were relatives settled in the neighborhood who lent mutual economic and political support. Oliveira's brother, João

Batista, owned a plantation nearly as large as his, and Oliveira married off his daughters to the political bosses of São Carlos and Dourados. Vergueiro's father-in-law was his partner in his first sesmaria, and it was managed by his brother for several years before Vergueiro transferred to Piracicaba. Two of his sons married the daughters of important political figures, and a daughter married into the Souza Queiroz family, with whom Vergueiro shared business interests.[37]

Coffee enlarged the fortunes of Vergueiro and the rest and secured the plantation system. Plantations, on the other hand, were not essential to the development of an export trade in coffee. Unlike sugar, coffee does not have an unrelieved history of large-scale cultivation. The plant responds to extra labor inputs and skillfulness of tending with greater output and higher-quality berries. Thus in Jamaica, Puerto Rico, and Colombia in the nineteenth century coffee was the salvation of a smallholding peasantry. The exporters of Santos, therefore, necessarily directed their coffee to a mass market unable to pay for better quality and inured to an undistinguished product. A great paradox: the freeholding peasants of the Caribbean raised their superior coffee for an affluent European middle class, while their factory- and farm-working counterparts in the United States drank the product of slave-driving latifundists.

# CHAPTER 3

# Slave Labor

Rio claro's coffee planters conformed to the system of labor exploitation that prevailed everywhere in Brazil where there were great estates and the possibility existed of engaging in export production. By 1800 about a third of Brazil's population of three million was enslaved. That ratio was maintained for the first half-century by importing more than a million Africans from the Portuguese possessions of Angola and Mozambique. Slaves were present on every estate; in Rio Claro, they engaged in every stage of cultivation, from the clearing of forests to the operation of the processing machinery. Until final abolition there were no free plantations in the county; all depended heavily and constantly on forced labor to maintain production. The persistence of slavery in this area is remarkable, since the coffee boom in the Paulista West took place after slavery began to decline in the rest of Brazil. The prohibition of the African slave traffic in 1850 had doomed the institution to extinction—the slave population did not reproduce itself. The coffee planters were therefore obliged to regard their labor system as transitional, justifiable only as an economic expedient.[1]

From the beginning of the coffee cycle, the planters were experimenting with the system of labor exploitation that they thought might successfully substitute for their diminishing supply of slaves —contracted European laborers. Free European wage labor was increasingly employed from 1849 onward in Rio Claro; it was introduced by Vergueiro shortly after his first employment of Swiss and German "colonists" on his plantation in nearby Limeira. The two systems coexisted in Rio Claro for nearly 40 years on the same plan-

TABLE 3.1
*Slave Population, 1822–88*

| Year | Number of slaves | Percent of total population | Year | Number of slaves | Percent of total population |
|---|---|---|---|---|---|
| 1822 | 489 | 32.1% | 1882 | 4,852 | — |
| 1835 | 598 | 20.6 | 1883 | 4,866 | — |
| 1856 | 1,426 | — | 1884 | 4,980 | — |
| 1872 | 3,935 | 26.2 | 1885 (June) | 4,709 | 20.5% |
| 1874 | 4,182 | — | 1887 (March) | 3,304 | 14.7 |
| 1875 | 4,429 | — | 1888 (March) | 1,663 | — |
| 1876 | 4,467 | — | | | |

SOURCES. 1822, 1835: APESP, População Piracicaba. 1856: Paulo Pestana, *O café em São Paulo*, p. 13. 1872: Census. 1876: Brazil, Directoria Geral de Estatística, *Relatorio*, 1878. 1874–88: APESP, Escravos 1, 2, and SP(P), President of Province, *Relatorio*, 1883–89.

tations. All the participants in this imbroglio, including the slaves, were aware that slavery was decadent and free labor was its inevitable successor. Nevertheless, the number of slaves in Rio Claro continued to increase, almost to the year of abolition (Table 3.1). Paradoxically, the Paulista West, where free wage labor found its best rewards and the planters were least committed to slavery as a social system, was also the area that could afford to buy the slaves of less prosperous regions. This internal traffic in slaves lessened the urgency of devising alternatives, it provoked the planters to a fear of losing their heavy and recent investments, and it gradually eliminated slave ownership in the rest of Brazil. The plantations of the Paulista West, therefore, were at the same time the most progressive and the most retrograde sector of Brazilian society.*

By 1872 there were 2,496 slaves employed in full-time agricultural labor in Rio Claro, or 55.4 percent of the total agricultural work force (Table 3.2). Most of the rest of the slaves of working age were either domestics or day laborers, a category that probably involved a good deal of part-time agricultural work. Slaves comprised 32.8 percent of persons, free and slave, thus listed. There were nearly 200 slaves engaged full time in crafts. Male slaves formed about a third of the craft work force, and were present in

* One author states that Indian slaves were used on the plantation of Estevão Cardoso de Negreiros; J. Romeo Ferraz, *Historia de Rio Claro* (São Paulo: Typographia Hennies Irmãos, 1922), p. 19.

TABLE 3.2
*Slave Occupations, 1872*

| Occupation | Female | Male | Total | Percent of slave force |
|---|---|---|---|---|
| Agriculture | 912 | 1,584 | 2,496 | 76.4% |
| House servants, day labor | 327 | 257 | 584 | 17.4 |
| Crafts | 65 | 122 | 187 | 6.2 |
| *Clothing* | *65* | *17* | *82* | |
| *Carpentry* | — | *46* | *46* | |
| *Construction* | — | *38* | *38* | |
| *Metalworking* | — | *12* | *12* | |
| *Hides and leather* | — | *9* | *9* | |
| TOTAL | 1,304 | 1,963 | 3,267 | 100.0% |

SOURCE. 1872 Census (Itaqueri omitted). The census also contained a category—"without professions"—that appears to include mainly children under ten years of age (a total of 328 persons).

every activity except textiles and shoemaking. It is likely that some of the craftsmen were resident on the plantations, where inventories occasionally identify two or three of the gang as stoneworkers, carpenters, tilers, or smiths. The others were either apprentices of free craftsmen in town or simply journeymen for hire, who paid their wages to their owners. Female slaves were absent from the crafts, save needlework, in which they competed with eight times their number of free women. Some of the slave women on the plantations, although listed as domestics, were probably engaged in making clothes, nursing, and cooking for field gangs. No slaves listed in 1872 were in any commercial or other non-manual occupation. In 1835 nearly 90 percent of the slaves had been engaged in full-time agricultural work, and of those exempted only nineteen were not day laborers or domestics—five craftsmen and fourteen mule drivers. It seems, then, that there was a tendency to employ slaves in semiskilled occupations, and that tendency was growing somewhat faster than the urban nucleus, in spite of the shortage of slave field hands.[2]

The profitability of slavery has been questioned in American historiography, but not in Brazil. The Paulista planters thought the employment of slaves was profitable, right up to the day of abolition. The records of Rio Claro provide the basis for calculat-

TABLE 3.3
*Yearly Cost of Maintaining an Adult Slave, 1857*

| Item | Milreis |
| --- | --- |
| Depreciation and interest, original cost of 1500 milreis, 20-year straight line, 12 percent on undepreciated balance | 165 |
| Transfer tax of 5 percent, amortized with 12 percent interest | 8 |
| Supervision: one *feitor* for each 25 slaves at 250 milreis each; one administrator for each 100 slaves at 1000 milreis each | 20 |
| Housing, clothing, medicines | 12 |
| Tools | 28 |
| TOTAL | 233 |

SOURCES. Prices, Table 3.4; interest and other expenses, RC/C-1, Inventories and Livros de Notas, 1857.

ing the yearly cost of maintaining an adult slave (Table 3.3). The slave owners did not figure depreciation; hence they had an exaggerated idea of the profitability of slaves. There were, it should be noted, contingent expenses, such as the rewards that had to be provided for catching runaways, and the increased rate of interest on any loan secured by a slave, if he died unseasonably early. The other costs of upkeep were trifling because the slave was expected to shift for himself or do without. It never occurred to the planters that free labor might be more profitable simply because they observed how much more intensely they could exploit slaves. Whereas a slave provided for his own subsistence with one day's work a week, the free tenant, they assumed, would render no more than one day's work to the owner, even with all his powers of eviction. It was this analysis, and not any sort of cost accounting, that confirmed the planters in their commitment to slave labor.[3]

During the sugar cycle, Rio Claro's slaves were obtained mainly from the same places that furnished the free population. The new planters arrived with gangs inherited from parents, or borrowed from relatives, or perhaps transferred from other estates they owned. Purchases of slaves were few and casual, often only one or two at a time, and usually the sellers were planters from counties farther from the frontier where the prospects of sugar were less promising. Until the beginning of the coffee trade, this desultory trade was sufficient.

The sudden shift to coffee in the late 1840's required heavy inputs of labor in clearing secondary growth, planting seedlings, and laying out terraces. Unfortunately for the planters, this critical period coincided with the effective abolition of the African slave traffic. (It had been declared illegal in 1831, without any enforcement.) The price of slaves tripled in the next ten years—while the general price level doubled (Table 3.4). The planters of Rio Claro complained bitterly. Amador Lacerda Rodrigues Jordão, the owner of Santa Gertrudes plantation, declared in the provincial assembly in 1857, "Today to buy a slave, not only are there none, but also the few that appear in the market are at an excessive price. The planters struggle with difficulty to keep their properties." In a report to the provincial president, another lamented that "Many beginning to farm . . . are downcast to find that their resources are insufficient for the purchase of slave labor." This scarcity was in striking contrast with the plantations of the Paraíba Valley. There the inflow of slaves had been on a large scale and had increased up to the time of the prohibition of the traffic. The planters of that area were to a degree reimbursed by the rise in the value of slave stocks on hand, which enabled them to borrow money to purchase still more slaves. They were also consoled by the thought that the scarcity of slaves would slow down competition from the newer plantations of the Paulista West.[4]

Well into the 1860's the supply of slaves continued to come from nearby counties. Nearly all the sales recorded in the local notarial offices were for lots of fewer than five slaves, whose owners were resident in places like Jundiaí, Bragança, or Mogi das Cruzes. The new clearings continued to attract the resources of planters' relations. In 1861, for example, Joaquina Nogueira de Oliveira, widowed sister-in-law of José Estanislau de Oliveira, signed a contract with her son-in-law, Francisco da Cunha Bueno. Francisco, who owned a plantation in Indaiatuba, was to bring his twenty slaves to her short-handed plantation and manage it for her. He was required to obtain another twenty within a year, so that his gang would equal hers in size. Probably he accomplished this by selling his Indaiatuba estate and picking up loans from other relatives,

TABLE 3.4
*Prices of Male Slaves, Aged 15–29, 1843–87*

| Year | Number of cases | Ave. price in milreis | Year | Number of cases | Ave. price in milreis |
|---|---|---|---|---|---|
| 1843 | 6 | 550 | 1866 | 4 | 1,500 |
| 1844 | – | — | 1867 | 3 | 1,700 |
| 1845 | – | — | 1868 | – | — |
| 1846 | – | — | 1869 | – | — |
| 1847 | – | — | 1870 | – | — |
| 1848 | 5 | 460 | 1871 | 17 | 1,770 |
| 1849 | – | — | 1872 | 3 | 1,920 |
| 1850 | 6 | 650 | 1873 | 8 | 1,600 |
| 1851 | 4 | 610 | 1874 | 1 | 1,000 |
| 1852 | 5 | 870 | 1875 | 16 | 2,200 |
| 1853 | 5 | 960 | 1876 | 11 | 2,270 |
| 1854 | 3 | 980 | 1877 | 15 | 2,130 |
| 1855 | 3 | 1,200 | 1878 | 20 | 2,070 |
| 1856 | 1 | 1,700 | 1879 | 78 | 2,080 |
| 1857 | 4 | 1,450 | 1880 | 3 | 2,300 |
| 1858 | 4 | 2,000 | 1881 | 1 | 2,000 |
| 1859 | 6 | 1,800 | 1882 | 1 | 1,400 |
| 1860 | 3 | 2,030 | 1883 | 8 | 1,080 |
| 1861 | 13 | 1,750 | 1884 | 1 | 1,000 |
| 1862 | 10 | 1,860 | 1885 | 26 | 870 |
| 1863 | 8 | 1,920 | 1886 | 3 | 1,000 |
| 1864 | 4 | 1,970 | 1887 | 1 | 885 |
| 1865 | 1 | 2,000 | | | |

SOURCES. RC/C-1 and C-2, Livros de Vendas de Escravos, Livros de Notas, and Inventories. Excluded were donations, transfers *inter vivos*, and forced sales to creditors. No significant difference in prices was found between sales and inventories. The 1887 source was from a registration listed in APESP, Escravos, 1.

among whom was a brother Tomaz, the richest merchant in Limeira. Within five years he was sufficiently in the black to open a new plantation on land belonging to his wife in Itaqueri. That move was described by the historian Alfredo Ellis, one of his descendants, as a heroic trek: wagons bearing his wife and children, the mules loaded with household goods, and the entire slave gang afoot, patiently in tow; and Francisco, this time a pioneer patriarch, rashly laying out plantations far beyond the range of pack transport, in the hope that rails would soon arrive.[5]

Another manner in which slaves were introduced to the new estates was to let out the planting and tending of the trees for the first three to five years to "entrepreneurs," a system already described; this brought into Rio Claro more than 300 slaves. The movement of slaves into the county through "location contracts" and the migration of planters with their own gangs continued into the 1880's. Meanwhile the transfer of slaves through purchase grew to larger proportions, and changed in character. Special books to register slave sales were kept in the notaries' offices beginning in 1861. From that year until 1872 the average sale numbered only 1.7 and most of the slaves were bought in nearby counties. The 1872 census listed only 463 slaves born in other provinces, out of a total of 2,918 Brazilian-born (the figure does not include Itaqueri). Usually these early sales were direct, but sometimes they were made through agents, who often appeared to be relatives of either the buyer or the seller. The sales recorded from 1873 onward were larger—an average 3.7—and nearly all the slaves were from other provinces (Table 3.5). The sellers acted through persons who were clearly professional itinerant salesmen. The most important of these agents were Antônio José Simões Viana, of Rio de Janeiro, José de Souza Leite Cabral, José Guilherme da Costa Negrão, and José Duarte da Costa Negrão, the last three of a firm called Cabral and Negrão, located in Minas Gerais, and its successor Guilherme, Negrão and Company. These persons rarely acted as principals; most often they sold on commission.*

The sales were occasionally on credit, as in March 1877, when Manuel Alves d'Oliveira Doria bought 36 slaves from Rodrigo Marques dos Santos, a "merchant and proprietor" of São Luis in the province of Maranhão, for 60,700 milreis. Doria gave dos Santos a mortgage on the slaves and a plantation with 90,000 coffee trees. He was to repay the principal in two years. Almost all of the other sales, however, were for cash. Thus the local landowners did not become the debtors of the northeastern elite. Planters in Rio Claro

---

* Sales of slaves, RC/C-1 and C-2, Livros de Vendas de Escravos. Profits may have been high. The average price in Salvador was half that prevailing in Rio Claro. Katia de Queiroz Mattoso, "A propósito de cartas de alforria, Bahia, 1779–1850," *Anais de Historia*, 4 (1972): 50. Cleveland Donald's study of slave prices in sugar-growing Campos, province of Rio de Janeiro, shows that the market, even in the south, was quite localized. "Slavery and Abolition in Campos, Brazil, 1830–1888" (Ph.D. dissertation, Dept. of History, Cornell University, 1973), p. 65.

TABLE 3.5
*Provenance of Slaves*

| Place | 1872 census | Percent | Sales, 1873–83 | Percent |
|---|---|---|---|---|
| North-northeast | 339 | 73% | 160 | 63% |
| *Maranhão* | — | | *39* | |
| *Pernambuco* | *96* | | *16* | |
| *Bahia* | *133* | | *73* | |
| *Other provinces* | *110* | | *32* | |
| Center-east | 124 | 27 | 74 | 29 |
| *Minas Gerais* | — | | *56* | |
| *Rio de Janeiro* | *124* | | *12* | |
| *Other provinces* | — | | *6* | |
| South | — | | 18 | 8 |
| *All provinces* | — | | *18* | |
| TOTAL | 463 | 100% | 252 | 100% |

SOURCES. 1872: Census. 1873–83: RC/C-2, Livros de Vendas de Escravos, 1–7. The 1872 census probably is defective; it is extremely likely that slaves from Minas Gerais should have been listed. Note that the sales data are very incomplete: 1,571 slaves were brought into the county, 1874 to 1885, of whom nearly all were from other provinces.

who could not afford cash mortgaged their property to the dozen or so banks located in São Paulo and Rio de Janeiro, or to individuals in the local area who loaned money as a sideline. A few of these "capitalists," principally Francisco de Assis Negreiros, a planter, and Joaquim Teixeira das Neves, a merchant and dealer in real estate, also bought slaves on their own account, as a speculation. The size of the slave trade was considerable. From the general slave registration in 1874 until 1885 a total of 2,668 were brought into Rio Claro and 897 were sent out—indicating that the town was something of a minor entrepôt in the trade.[6]

The interprovincial trade in slaves was an inevitable result of the prohibition of the African traffic in 1850 and the growing disparity, from about 1830 onward, in the prospects of export production in the north and the south. The sudden increase in volume of trade in Rio Claro was caused principally by the arrival of the railroad to Campinas in 1872, but the passage of the Law of Free Birth, in September of 1871, was possibly also an important factor. That law, which declared all children henceforth born of slave mothers free, obliged the mother's owner to feed and clothe these *ingênuos* until they turned eight—or until they reached twenty-one, if he wished to take advantage of their labor until that age. For landowners in the stagnant north—and townspeople everywhere—the ownership of pubertal slaves thus became a potentially expensive risk, with uncertain compensation. The upkeep of a slave child in the 1870's cost roughly 40 milreis a year, and no more than half the ingênuos could be expected to survive for eight years. The sales of slaves recorded in Rio Claro from 1872 onward consisted largely, it is interesting to notice, of boys ten to fifteen years of age. They were rarely accompanied by parents, and were declared to be—probably nearly always falsely—of unknown or deceased mothers.[7]

The prices of slaves did not vary with their color. Apparently mulattos and blacks were considered of equal value in the fields. Nor was any distinction made between Africans and creoles. Females were sold on the average for three-quarters of the value of males. Children at age two were sold for about a tenth of the adult price; by age eight they were valued at about half. Because of the inflow of slaves from other counties and provinces, the local landowners were able to minimize the inevitable aging of the slave population and to maintain a majority of males (Tables 3.6 and 3.7).

A tendency toward creolization of the slave population is noticeable even before the abolition of the African traffic (Table 3.8). This is attributable, like the rise in the female ratio, to the appearance of an urban center and also to the relatively slow growth of the county during the sugar cycle, which made purchases of slaves directly from the port towns unlikely. The origins of the Africans are quite obscure; only the first census of 1822 indicates points of origin, but these are the names of African ports, not of tribal membership. Nearly all of Rio Claro's Africans were identified as arrivals from places controlled by the Portuguese south of the equator: Congo, Cambinda, Benguela, and Mozambique followed the names of 81 percent of the 344 Africans counted. In 1835 no particular provenance was noted for any of the slaves *da nação*— "of the tribe." By the 1880's African birth made so little difference to the registrars of the slave population, so it would seem, that it

TABLE 3.6
## Aging of Adult Slave Population

| Year | Total slave population, 16 and over | Ages 16–40 | Percent | Ages 41 and over | Percent |
|------|------|------|------|------|------|
| 1822 | 580 | 522 | 90.0% | 58 | 10.0% |
| 1835 | 460 | 419 | 91.1 | 41 | 8.9 |
| 1872 | 2,941 | 1,722 | 58.5 | 1,219 | 41.5 |
| 1887 | 3,374 | 2,369 | 70.2 | 1,005 | 29.8 |

SOURCES. 1822, 1835: APESP, População Piracicaba. 1872: Census (Itaqueri not included). 1887: SP(P), President of Province, *Relatorio*, 1888, p. 58; APESP, Escravos, 2, "Resumo geral dos libertos ... até ... 1887." The 1822 total includes slaves in two wards that were not part of Rio Claro.

NOTE. Population age 15 and under are not comparable, since the ingênuos begin to be recorded in the 1872 Census. The 1887 figures include bonded sexagenarian freedmen, ages 60–63.

TABLE 3.7
## Sex Ratio of Slaves

| Year | Female | Male | Percent male of total |
|------|------|------|------|
| 1822 | 133 | 356 | 72.8% |
| 1835 | 221 | 364 | 62.2 |
| 1850–51 (partial) | 32 | 36 | 52.9 |
| 1861–62 (partial) | 64 | 81 | 55.9 |
| 1872 | 1,621 | 2,314 | 58.8 |
| 1876 | 1,758 | 2,709 | 60.6 |
| 1884 | 1,883 | 2,983 | 63.4 |
| 1887 | 1,250 | 2,054 | 62.2 |

SOURCES. 1822, 1835: APESP, População Piracicaba (1835 omits 13 slaves of unlisted sex). 1850–51, 1861–62: RC/C-1 and C-2, Inventories. 1872: Census. 1876: Brazil, Directoria Geral de Estatística, *Relatorio*, 1878. 1884: APESP, Escravos 1, 2, and SP(P), President of Province, *Relatorio*, 1885. 1887: SP(P), Comissão Central de Estatística, *Relatorio*.

TABLE 3.8
## Ratio of African to Creole Slaves

| Year | African-born | Brazilian (creole) | Percent creole of total |
|------|------|------|------|
| 1822 | 359 | 122 | 25.4% |
| 1835 | 337 | 254 | 42.9 |
| 1859–61 (partial) | 45 | 99 | 68.7 |
| 1872 | 687 | 3,248 | 82.5 |
| 1885 | 704 | 2,670 | 79.1 |

SOURCES. 1822, 1835: APESP, População Piracicaba. 1859–61: RC/C-1 and C-2, Inventories. 1872: Census. 1885: estimate—70 percent of slaves 40 years old or more, i.e. born before 1846, and therefore conceivably of African birth. Eight slaves in 1822 were of unlisted origin.

was disregarded—even though the proportion of Africans had probably not declined since 1872. In fact, recording of African birth would have been in many cases embarrassing. There were quite a few Africans in the province too young to have been transported before the legal end of the traffic in 1831. Although the fact of illegal entry was often openly recorded in Rio Claro in the 1870's, by the last decade of slavery public statements might have invited legal action by abolitionists.

The appearance of mulatto slaves in the 1872 census is quite striking: there were almost none at all in 1822 or 1835, but the later census shows that more than a quarter of the slaves were of mixed race (Table 3.9). This might suggest a new reluctance on the part of slave owners to manumit a category of captive that had seemed peculiarly worthy of freedom as long as fresh levies of Africans were available. There was in the same census, however, a contrary tendency: for the first time a considerable number of free men were listed as being black—609, or nearly 30 percent of the free population of color. It appears that in 1872 for the first time the census takers made a distinction between slave status and ethnicity. The changed perception that a free man might be a black or a mulatto a slave, it might be hypothesized, may have been in accord with a changed reality. There is also the possibility that both the socially defined categories of black and mulatto slaves might have contained, by 1872, persons less biologically Negroid than before. Occasionally a sale or inventory noted a *fulo*—"tawny" slave—or listed a slave as *pardo* when others on the same list were defined as mulatto. These were probably quadroons. In 125 sales from 1871 to 1883 in which color was noted consistently, twelve were listed as fulo, nearly 10 percent. No fulo slaves were found in the sales or inventories before 1871. It is likely that any preexisting tendencies to manumit slaves of mixed ancestry had largely benefited this group. As a whole, mulattos were, during the last two decades of slavery, less likely to be manumitted than before, and nearly all the increase of mulatto free persons may be attributed to self-reproduction.

The inflow of slaves from other counties and provinces was

TABLE 3.9

*Apparent Racial Composition, Slave Population and Free*
*Population of Color*

| Category | Number | | | Percent | | |
|---|---|---|---|---|---|---|
| | 1822 | 1835 | 1872 | 1822 | 1835 | 1872 |
| Free total of color | 153 | 795 | 2,372 | 24.2% | 57.1% | 37.6% |
| Blacks | 1 | 7 | 609 | 0.2 | 0.5 | 9.7 |
| Mulattos | 152 | 788 | 1,763 | 24.0 | 56.6 | 27.9 |
| Slave total of color | 479 | 598 | 3,935 | 75.8 | 42.9 | 62.4 |
| Blacks | 463 | 581 | 2,867 | 73.3 | 41.7 | 45.5 |
| Mulattos | 16 | 17 | 1,068 | 2.5 | 1.2 | 16.9 |
| TOTAL | 632 | 1,393 | 6,307 | 100.0% | 100.0% | 100.0% |

SOURCES. 1822, 1835: APESP, População Piracicaba. 1872: Census.

necessary not only because of the spread of plantations, but also because the slave population did not reproduce itself. The unequal proportion of the sexes does not account for that fact; that in-equality—on the coffee frontier at least—was a result of the slave trade, not its cause. The European immigrant population of the succeeding generation was even more skewed toward the males. From 1876 to 1908, never did females account for as much as 25 percent of the Italian contingent. Yet the immigrant population swarmed in São Paulo. The ratio of surviving children to child-bearing women was more than three times higher for the free group (Table 3.10). The discrepancy was even greater, in fact; it will be shown below that the death rate of slave women was sub-stantially higher than that of free women, so that the cohort of slave childbearers was originally larger. It is possible that the ap-parent higher rate of births among free women may be partly attributable to manumissions of children at baptism. Baptismal records, unavailable for the period, were a sufficient legal instru-ment. If half the apparent difference in birthrates between whites and free women of color is due to manumission at birth, 52 chil-dren should be added to the slave cohort, which increases the ratio, but only to 60.7.[8]

It might be supposed that the lower ratio of surviving children was mainly the result of lower fertility. In Rio Claro there is no

TABLE 3.10

*Surviving Females of Childbearing Age Compared to Surviving Children, by Apparent Racial Group, 1872*

| Class and color | Females 16–60 | Children 3–15 | Children 3–15 per 100 females |
|---|---|---|---|
| Free: | | | |
| White | 1,500 | 2,467 | 164.5 |
| Mulatto | 250 | 453 | 181.2 |
| Black | 50 | 205 | 410.0 |
| Subtotal Mulatto + black | 300 | 658 | 219.3 |
| TOTAL FREE | 1,800 | 3,125 | 173.5 |
| Slave: | | | |
| Mulatto | 217 | 279 | 128.5 |
| Black | 783 | 276 | 35.2 |
| TOTAL SLAVE | 1,000 | 555 | 55.5 |

SOURCE. 1872 Census. Note that ingênuos do not appear in either section of this table.

evidence that slave owners discouraged sexual contact among slaves. Although segregation by sex was practiced in other places, it seems inconceivable that this measure would have effectively enforced continence on a population already tightly restrained in every other way. Unfortunately age at first conception is lacking in the Rio Claro data, but Table 3.10 suggests a very high proportion of sexual contacts with white and mulatto males. Among the slave children there were as many mulattos as blacks, even though there were three-and-a-half times more black than mulatto female slaves! Considering, indeed, the competition for slave women's "favors," their frequency of intercourse may well have been higher than that of free women. It is possible that slave males practiced *coitus interruptus*. Married slave partners may have sought to prevent what both must have regarded as a disaster—the conception of a slave child. They may also have practiced infanticide, for that reason. It is unlikely that casual contacts, especially with free males, would have involved any precaution. The 1822 census provides an opportunity to gauge the relative fertility of free and slave women, since it recorded all births, including stillbirths. It shows fifteen children born to 114 slave women between the ages of fifteen and

44, and 38 children born to 282 free women in the same age range, thus a fertility rate of 130 per thousand among both groups.*

Apparently fewer of the slave children survived. There are no accurate counts of infant deaths, not even for the free population. There was a registry, however, of all ingênuos in the county, including deaths, from September 28, 1871, onward. The ingênuos were not slaves, but they shared slave quarters and rations, and were probably assigned the same tasks that they would have performed had they not been freed. According to the 1871 law, they could not be separated from their mothers, and probably they were not dealt severe corporal punishment; therefore their mortality rate may have been somewhat lower than that of the previous generation of slave children. By June 1886, 2,421 ingênuos were registered, including 179 who had been transferred into the county. Of these, 998 had died. Assuming a steady rate of births for this period of fourteen years and nine months, deaths averaged 67.6 per year, or 55 per thousand, which might be compared to an age-specific rate for a population aged 0–15 years.[9]

This is certain to be too low, however. The report of ingênuo deaths was not as complete as that of births. Although there was a penalty for not advising the authorities, it is evident that reports were not prompt, nor were they always forwarded for compilation. Even more serious, infants who died within the first month were usually not reported at all. Slave owners had 30 days within which to register births to slave mothers; if the child died during that period, the owner felt no obligation to report. Municipal correspondence contains police inquiries concerning alleged failures to register ingênuos. When the owner replied that the infant had died, the matter was invariably dropped. Assuming that no more

---

* Adolphe d'Assier, *Le Brésil contemporain* (Paris: Durand et Lauriel, 1867), p. 140, notes access to slave women. Emília Viotti da Costa, *Da senzala à colônia* (São Paulo: Difusão Européia do Livro, 1966), p. 268, remarks that the "masters closed their eyes to what happened in the *senzalas.*" The local registry of ingênuo births lists 147 born during the first 12 months, to Sept. 1872, which compares with the census count of (approximately) 720 slave women, aged 15–44, hence a fertility rate of 210 per 1,000. This was a low count because the registry underreported births. APESP, OD/RC, Vicar to President of Province, 1873.

than a quarter of the neonatal deaths were listed, and that infant deaths represented 60 percent of all deaths among ingênuos in this group to age 15, then there were 125 deaths per thousand, for the group as a whole, and infant mortality reached 470 per thousand.[10]

It might be objected that so high a death rate would not fail to be noticed by the owners, who would certainly design effective countermeasures. In fact, they did observe it, but they did not attribute it to the lethal conditions of the *quadrados*. The memoire of plantation childhood written by Maria Paes de Barros contains vivid reconstructions of the self-justifications of the slave owners. She recalls her mother, wife of the owner of the Santo Antônio plantation, chiding the slave mothers for permitting their children to die. Her conception was that they were careless and neglectful, and had failed to provide the proper nourishment. The mothers, then, were obliged to beg her pardon and promise to do better with their next pregnancies! In this way the perpetual holocaust of slave infants was defined as yet another sign of the incapacity of the slaves, impossible for the benevolent but despairing planters to overcome.[11]

It may be said that work in the coffee groves was by its nature less exhausting than most other plantation regimes. Its most wearying task was the incessant weeding between the rows, carried out with long-handled hoes. This was gang labor, supervised by *feitores* who were sometimes slaves themselves, who maintained discipline mainly with insults and threats, with the whip as a last resort. The planters typically understaffed their groves; therefore they pressed as much hoework as they could out of the field hands and eliminated released time for subsistence activities. Subsistence crops, mainly corn and beans, seem to have been raised by gang labor in large fields, not in individual patches. These fields supplied free day workers as well as slaves. The work day was sun to sun, and after dark during harvest. One day of rest was granted. This was a regime far more severe than any free man in Rio Claro experienced, and it was entirely unremunerated. No incentive was offered except freedom from the lash, and promotion meant the obligation of applying the lash to one's fellows.[12]

The slaves were housed in long barracks called *senzalas*, which were aligned to form quadrados, or squares, entirely closed and facing on a dirt-surfaced courtyard, whose sole ornament was the flogging post. The quadrados were, according to a visitor to Ibicaba plantation in the 1880's, dirty, smoky, and without furnishings. The slaves supped on cornmeal mush and beans, served, like slops, from wooden troughs. In the morning they were wakened with coffee ladled from a pot, sweetened with raw sugar. In winter a measure of cane brandy might be served as well. Meat was very rare except for bacon. Diverting cash resources or field labor to feed the slaves must have been approached in a miserly fashion, and was undoubtedly held to a minimum. It is not possible to assert that the caloric intake of the slaves was less than that of free day laborers, or even of the free smallholders. It is certain that their diet contained less protein, however, and probably—because it was not as varied—less vitamins and minerals.

Slaves were provided cotton yardage once a year with which to make their clothing, and they were given a blanket at less frequent intervals, which also served as a cloak in cold weather. The cash outlay for these goods was quite modest. The heirs of the baron of Porto Feliz spent 1,437 milreis to outfit their 81 slaves in 1879, while in the same year their own clothes cost 4,118. It should be noticed that shoes were not provided the slaves, for they were a mark of the free man. Lack of covering for the feet left the slaves more vulnerable to parasites and insects and snakes.[13]

The slaves' contacts with the planter were stylized to resemble that of lord and peasant. At dawn, before heading to the fields, they were assembled before the owner's window. They removed their hats and bent slightly at the knees, and he blessed them. The planter held audiences at which punishments were imposed and favors were granted. The arrival of the planter and his family was marked by the distribution of the new supply of cloth and blankets, and sometimes individual gifts of ribbons, buckles, and the like. The slaves were expected at Ibicaba plantation to participate in festivities arranged by Vergueiro. A visitor in 1884 witnessed a torchlight religious procession of slaves led by a brass band, with

banners, a crucifix, fireworks, and the firing of a cannon. He
thought it was a "weird spectacle."

There was no mirth. I could not perceive a single indication of cheerful-
ness. Everything seemed of an opposite character. The air was cold, almost frosty, and when at length the procession returned and marched into
the yard of the slave quarters, little fires were kindled in different spots
for warmth. As I was looking out of a window on the scene and heard the
gate shut, and a heavy bolt turned after the procession had all got in, the
thought struck me, rather sadly, that these people were like prisoners.

The next day he attended a mass for the slaves in the chapel, cele-
brated by the Italian priest from Rio Claro. He performed the
ceremony in just twenty minutes as those present, mostly women,
knelt on the floor, chanting plaintively the while, "a sad look on
every face."[14]

Slavery required legal incapacity. It could not be otherwise. Because the slave was chattel, the law's contradictory implication that
he had a personality was without effect. What was punishment for
free men was often reward for him. Although young men of the
county were terrified of army recruitment, it was a lucky chance
for the slave, even during the Paraguayan war. Although the provincial jail was bleak and unhealthy, slaves were rarely sent there
lest such a relatively mild regime become an incentive for criminal
acts by other slaves. The slave was under curfew—he could not
appear in town at night under any circumstances and was invariably detained until morning. He often wore a metal dog collar for
identification. He was given no schooling. He was allowed no
choice—where he would live, whether he would work or not, what
he would eat, what he would wear. His master could sell him, rent
him, mortgage him. He was subjected to indignities and criminal
acts which were defined as legal. He could be cheated, violated, and
brutalized with impunity, and in the normal course of events, he
was.

It is not necessary, in order to condemn slavery, to recount atrocities, which were even contemporaneously regarded as criminal acts
and occasionally denounced. Yet there were many, and not to recount them would distort this description, since, although seem-

ingly fortuitous, they could only have gone unpunished within the legal and social framework of slavery. Murders of slaves by their masters were almost never reported to the authorities. According to the Swiss agent J. J. von Tschudi, in 1857 only two had been discovered in the whole province in six months. Both of these were denounced, he thought, only because the planter-murderers had personal enemies who sought to embarrass them publicly. Evidently the killing of a slave would be brought to light only under unusual circumstances. It was not the habit of police delegates to make inquiries, or for small-town newspapers to print accusations. Slave murders were often disguised as suicides. Complaints that reached the police unsolicited were likely to be ignored. In 1876 Luiz Gama, a lawyer in São Paulo, himself a mulatto freedman and well known as a defender of the slaves, forwarded a letter to the provincial chief of police, who took no action on it:

If the chief of police had knowledge of the inhuman and horrible acts practiced by a certain kind of person in these backlands, he would certainly take urgent measures, since the victims of these barbarities, besides the misfortune which pursues them for being slaves, also suffer punishments so barbarous that they are at the point of extinction.

A planter of São Carlos do Pinhal [the county bordering Rio Claro on the north], named José Estevão de Torres, is one of those who can be called cannibals, for those unfortunates who have fallen in his hands have been reduced to a twentieth part. At least for those who may be alive, in the short time that is left, they would give thanks to be free of the fury of that assassin . . .

I do not intend to sign this letter, not because I cannot prove what I have stated above, but only and solely because unfortunately I live among these perverted creatures in human form.

The wanton murder of slaves would seem in a radical sense "dysfunctional" for the system itself. Indeed, Luiz Gama remarked in his covering letter on the "necessity of rigors . . . to maintain a legal monstrosity" but which should never be permitted the extremity of murder. There was nothing within the system that prevented its occurrence, however, and much that encouraged it.[15]

For some people, undoubtedly, the institution of slavery was license to indulge their desires, no matter what form they might take. The hired gunman of the baron of Grão-Mogol, a black freed-

man from Bahia who continued to live in the plantation great
house long after the baron's death and the estate's dismemberment,
would astonish the immigrant family who cared for him in his declining years with tales of sadistic orgies presided over by the baron
in his cellar, his invited guests all honorable members of the town's
elite, and the baron's slave women, chained to posts and railings,
their *pièce de résistance.* *

Until the last decade of slavery, there was only one circumstance,
besides elite vendettas, under which violence against slaves might
be noticed: if the slave responded violently while outside the
boundaries of the plantation. The records of two trials during the
1860's are preserved in Rio Claro in which slaves, terrified of beatings with which they were threatened, attacked their keeper rather
than return to the estate. In one of these cases the slave had escaped
and was being brought back to the owner, Rita Benedita de Camargo, when he broke loose on a public road and wounded the
slave catcher with the latter's own knife. The slave told the police,
when he was recaptured, that he had received many beatings and
was threatened with more. In the other case a slave named Tolentino had been sold to the heirs of J. E. Pacheco Jordão, whose
plantations were well known, according to the deposition of a
policeman, to be places where "the slaves are punished and mal-
treated badly." Discouraged and frightened, Tolentino decided to
beat up the slave foreman who was conducting the gang to the
plantation, in the hope that he would be refused by the owner as
a troublemaker. Unfortunately he miscalculated and killed the
driver, and was captured by the rest of the gang, who must have
feared punishment as accomplices. The first slave was condemned
to 200, the second to 400 lashes.[16]

Beatings, and even murders, carried out within the plantation,
were not subject to notice by public authorities. Slaves were buried
on plantations, and there was no requirement for death certificates
until 1875, when a law on death registration for the general popu-

* Statement by Mr. and Mrs. Pedro Rossi, Rio Claro, Dec. 13, 1968. The
baron, falsely claiming that his wife was insane, kept her locked in the attic.
He was, nevertheless, well regarded in the county and was once president of
the county council.

lation was put into effect. Indeed, even after that date, all that was needed was a friendly physician, perhaps a relative of the owner. Nevertheless, occasionally violence against a slave took place away from the plantation, which had to be made to appear accidental. Thus a local newspaper printed this curious notice of a slave death in 1880:

> Accident or suicide? The black woman Marcelina, slave of Dona Gertrudes Tereza Ferraz de Andrade, was walking in the direction of the plantation, accompanied by another person who was conducting her as a prisoner. Owing to a small inattention, the said slave managed to escape, and three days later her body was discovered on the Piracicaba road.
>
> Being informed of the fact, the authorities undertook an official autopsy, and determined that her death was caused by the blast of a shotgun, which was discovered near the feet of the victim, with the wound received in the stomach, traveling upward.
>
> It is not known whether the wound was produced by the slave accidentally placing her left foot on the trigger of the shotgun, or if, on the contrary, she decided to put an end to her existence.

The newspaper did not explain how the slave came into possession of a shotgun, or to whom it might have belonged, nor did it remark on the peculiar choice of locale. Notice also that the name of the slave catcher went unreported.[17]

In another case the slave survived and bore witness against his attackers. A slave named Fausto, who belonged to José Vergueiro, was examined by police for "diverse injuries." Another slave informed them that Fausto was accustomed, like other slaves, to work on his day off for other planters. He had gone to the plantation of João Lopes for six milreis which was owed him. Instead Lopes and his *capangas*—hired gunmen—beat him up and left him unconscious on the Paulista railroad track. He was seen in time by the engineer and returned to his owner. The police collected depositions from Lopes's hands that Fausto had never worked there and from a Paulista employee that Fausto had declared he wanted to commit suicide and that the bruises were caused when the cowcatcher passed over him—a close call indeed. The police accepted this version—ignoring a deposition by another slave that Fausto's off-hours employer had been *Manuel* Lopes, not João—and closed the case peremptorily. This investigation had been undertaken at the request of Vergueiro, who must have been displeased at the treatment his slave had suffered. It may be that he pursued the matter no further, lest face be lost by another planter, or simply because he disliked the practice of free labor on the day of rest and this was a cautionary example for the rest of his gang.[18]

If Fausto had been attacked by his own owner, there would have been no need to make his injuries appear to be accidental, because the police would not have interested themselves in such a case. In May 1886, Amaro, a slave of João Evangelista de Toledo, whose plantation was in nearby São Carlos, fled to the chief of police in São Paulo because he feared being flogged to death. The complaint was within the jurisdiction of the police chief, because Brazilian law forbade unnecessary cruelty. Nevertheless, slaves were also legally disqualified from testifying against their owners, and the police were quite incapable of undertaking investigations that, it can be imagined, would prove endless and provocative to the landowners. Amaro, it should be noticed, did not bring his complaint to the county police delegate, whom he probably could not imagine to be powerful enough to act upon it. At any rate, Amaro got no satisfaction in the provincial capital either. He was jailed like an ordinary runaway and Toledo was notified of his capture. Six days later the planter appeared at police headquarters and deposed that he had never punished Amaro too harshly, nor, he said, "did he ever give an order to his foreman to punish him barbarously, much less would he be killed if he rebelled against any such punishments." The chief remanded Amaro with no further formality.[19]

The slaves of Rio Claro endured an everyday regime of unremitting labor and vile living conditions, subjected on some plantations to barbarities occasionally, on others frequently. Their fate was not a public concern. It had been shown that in other regions of Brazil the planters sought to substitute patriarchal direction and manipulation—to a degree at least—for threats and violence. Their intention, it seems, was to economize administrative overhead and reduce personal risk to themselves and their property, and possibly to ease the slaves into a state of serfdom during periods when falling export prices rendered the purchase of additional slaves uneconomic. It is also likely that the planters were not wholly calculating; they were imperfect bourgeois who admitted occasionally to longings of a very traditional sort: a peasantry that would perform its endless tasks gladly in return for protection, benevolence, and tenure.[20]

In Rio Claro there were signs of a blurring of distinctions between agregados, so frequently mulatto and sometimes black, and those slaves who occupied special positions: slave drivers, mule skinners, and capangas. The capangas are especially interesting, since they were used against agregados, as well as runaways and even against other proprietors. Still more surprising was the employment of a slave by Nicolau Vergueiro as his administrator on Ibicaba plantation in the 1830's, although Vergueiro was frequently absent from the estate. Such slaves undoubtedly enjoyed greater power over their fellow slaves, thereby providing all at once an intrinsic reward, an incentive to maintaining discipline, and a barrier to cohesive social relations among the slaves. Yet there is some evidence that these special slaves were sometimes rewarded in accordance with ideas of prestige that held good among the free agregados. The supervisory slaves, as can be seen in the early censuses, were often older than the rest of the gang. Perhaps they simply survived longer by being drivers, but it is more likely that the owners were recognizing seniority within the gang. These slaves were also more often married than the other slaves. The offer of the possibility of contracting a single stable relationship would have an effect distinct from the alternative of offering indiscriminate access to the women of the gang. In practical terms, it would lessen the slave supervisors' control over the gang, but it would provide an incentive of emulation. Most interesting, the nuclear family must have been a strong incentive to the eventual establishment of tenure in the form of yearly contracts, thereby enabling some freedmen to bypass a peasant relationship and to join immigrant laborers in the transformation of the plantations in the 1880's.*

---

* Paes de Barros' father remarked of one insubordinate slave, "We'll have to marry off that negro and give him a piece of land [i.e. make him a tenanted agregado], to straighten out his life and improve his judgment." Maria Paes de Barros, *No tempo de dantes* (São Paulo: Brasiliense, 1946), p. 76.

Manumission, frequently assumed to be evidence of a liberal tendency in Brazilian slavery, was—in Rio Claro at least—a very clear expression of paternalistic control. The formula of the *cartas de liberdade* terms the act a "grace" which the slave merited on account of his "great loyalty" and "obedience." Records were found of only nine unconditional, immediate manumissions in Rio Claro up to 1888. Almost all of the *cartas* before 1880 were conditional upon the owner's death. A carta of 1857, for example, written by Ana Veloso de Anhaia on her sickbed, gave freedom to a slave named Catarina, but provided that if Ana Veloso recovered, the act was void! (A curious essay at gaining heaven, which is reminiscent of a will discovered in the coastal town of Ubatuba that provided for the sale of a slave to pay for masses for the repose of the departed owner's soul.) While the owners remained alive, the slave was enjoined to continue to provide services "always with love and tenderness." A slave freed in this fashion was legally a sort of ward, free but not yet allowed to exercise freedom. From 1846 to 1856, 43 slaves gained this conditional sort of freedom, fewer than four per year. Of these, seven were children. Twenty-two were males, fourteen females. Most appear to have been domestic servants or artisans. Only three were African-born. In the 1872 census only eighteen of the 695 Africans in Rio Claro were free! Almost all of the free blacks and mulattos in the county, it must be concluded, were the result of natural increase, not manumission.[21]

The possibility of revocation of freedom was quite real. The law allowed it until 1871, and the cartas sometimes included the threat of it, "should the said [freedman] turn ungrateful and scornful of this proof of esteem, by failing to provide services [to the former master], or behaving himself in such a way as to be unworthy of this grace." The notaries preserve a few acts of revocation in Rio Claro. One, dated 1857, is a malediction that goes on for two pages of fury and lèse majesté. The owner, Mariana Cándida das Neves, had granted Marcelina freedom four years before, conditional upon her death, but now she complained of the slave "having ceased to comply with the determining conditions of the said act of manumission, and having even turned very ungrateful toward the bestower of her liberty, for which the said Lady repents of having freed her." One imagines the scene in the notary's office, to which the slave had undoubtedly been brought, so as to be awed by the ceremony—four years of cowering and shuffling gone for nought under the dictated incantations of a vile woman's rage: "and therefore let the said *carta de liberdade* be revoked, from today and henceforth, so that she shall be once again a slave, as though she never were free, and a captive she becomes through this document, because the letter of manumission that freed the said slave is now without effect . . . and I want my signature to serve as witness."[22]

Even the fate of Marcelina is evidence of paternalism, because only a real psychological interaction could have provoked such a storm of resentment. Marcelina had somehow or other gotten at her mistress. Yet this sort of interaction seems confined to a small segment of the slave population in Rio Claro. The decadence of slavery in the Paulista West did not engender either peasants or lords. The overriding problem was to create an underclass that would work as hard as the slaves; the expansion of the agregado tenants would not answer that demand. Besides, as long as a price tag was attached to every slave, there would always be a strong temptation to treat him as a piece of merchandise, rather than as a faithful servitor. In 1857, for example, João Joaquim Lopes de Figueiredo Brasil was given no other property in his father's will but two aged slaves. The slaves, in the same will, had been bequeathed one hundred milreis, however. João Joaquim, therefore, entered in the notary's office a *carta de liberdade* in favor of the slaves and pocketed the bequest, declaring that it was evidently his father's intention that the slaves should use the cash to buy their freedom. This transparently guileful transaction also enabled the son to rid himself of the cost of maintaining two old people who could no longer be expected to return a profit. (One wonders, was this the same João Lopes whose capangas beat up Fausto 27 years later? If so, the moment of primitive accumulation is observed, and as Balzac would have relished it.)[23]

Another act of revocation provides an example of self-interest outweighing paternalistic obligation, although the owner tried to justify himself on both counts. In 1848 Salvador Pires Pimentel declared to the notary that he was obliged to cancel an act registered ten years before in Bragança in behalf of a young man named Manuel, to take effect upon the owner's death, because "his [Salvador's] circumstances had changed entirely, to the point that he could no longer grant such a favor, since he owes a good deal, and since he wants to pay his debts off quickly, which he can't do without selling the said *mulatinho*, and besides he no longer much deserves such a grace, since he has displayed some causes for offense."[24]

The custom, very frequently to be found in the notarial records, of giving slave children as gifts to relatives seems, at first, to partake of a sort of patronal relationship: one woman of means, "desiring to give a sincere demonstration of esteem and friendship," would dress up an unpromising daughter or son of one of her house servants, and send the child across the county to a granddaughter or niece who was just setting up her household. It was sometimes recorded in the act of donation that the slave was worth so many milreis, a way of leaving the price tag on, no doubt, and it is always an exaggerated value. The gift may have been both well intentioned and well received, the child often pampered and favored. Yet what a horror that a little girl should be treated exactly as though she were a mechanical doll; and while the vapid gentleladies in the parlor screeched their customary pleasantries at each other (one thinks of the overweight mistresses of ceremonies on Paulista television) over the person of the five-year-old living birthday present, in the kitchen how did the child's mother stifle the pain of separation?[25]

Meanwhile the husbands of these ladies did not display any tendency to recognize their offspring by slave women. The ratio of mulatto slave children to slave women, displayed in Table 3.10 (p. 62), suggests quite strongly that white males had frequent intercourse with slave women. Had there been no sexual contacts between slave women and free men, and had all contacts with slave males been entirely random, then less than 5 percent of those 555 slave children would have been markedly mulatto in the eyes of the census takers—only 27 children. Nevertheless, of numerous declarations of paternity registered by free men in the notarial office, only one—in the course of 42 years—referred openly to the legitimation of a slave child. The landowners of Rio Claro were quite ready, on the other hand, to acknowledge liaisons with free women, even extramarital ones. To this single case of generosity should be added a half-dozen more in which slave women were freed along with their children, an alternate form of recognition, perhaps, yet one that avoided the danger present in declarations of paternity: the right of inheritance. Although there is no local record of it, the baron of Grão-Mogol, it is said, did recognize fifteen of his children by slave women, all of whom shared in his estate, the Angélica plantation. No other cases of this kind were encountered.*

The survival rate of the slaves is usually considered a consequence of the working and living conditions provided by the owners; that is, as a measurement of the benevolence of the masters. It might as well be offered as evidence of the internal organization of the slave community, since survival was largely in spite of the arrangements the planters provided for them. Slaves trapped, fished, and farmed on their own account on days off, in order to supplement their diet. They worked for hire in order to add to their meager stock of clothing and blankets. They cared for each other in sickness, employing their own remedies, which were sometimes African cultigens. The planters made little effort beyond the isolation of contagious cases. Slaves were generally not admitted to hospitals during epidemics. The town doctors ministered almost

* RC/C-2, Livros de Notas, June 18, 1866: Francisco Franco de Arruda, bachelor, recognized his son, João, two-and-a-half months old, "of his mulata slave named Dominiana," and gave him freedom. On the baron, an interview with Oscar de Arruda Penteado, Oct. 27, 1968. Emília Viotti da Costa (*Da senzala à colônia*, p. 272) provides some evidence against the claim that manumission of offspring was common. F. J. de Oliveira Viana, a penetrating analyst of Brazilian society, although an unabashed advocate of the plantation elite, wrote lyrically of the planters as the *garanhões fogosos da negralhada* (fiery stallions of the negress-gang), *Populações meridionais do Brasil* (3d ed.; São Paulo: Companhia Editôra Nacional, 1933), 1: 86.

exclusively to the free population. The records of the baron of Porto Feliz, for example, show four visits by a doctor in 1879 and 1880, to treat the baron and his family, and during that period three slaves died.[26]

The duration of slaves in the field has been variously estimated from seven to fifteen years. This is meaningless without a knowledge of the range of ages of the slave population in the field. The censuses of 1822 and 1835 provide an opportunity to calculate slave survival and hence, indirectly, life expectancy. In Rio Claro there were ten estates that remained in the hands of the same persons in both of the censuses. Of the 131 slaves in the first, 38, or 29 percent, were found present thirteen years later (Table 3.11). It is likely that nearly all the slaves who did not appear on the later list had died. Escaped slaves would probably be reported present, even several years after their disappearance. It does not appear that any were manumitted. The slaves of the first census were sought among the agregado and day worker population of the second, but none were located. It may be that freedmen found it distasteful to remain in the county where they had been slaves, but there were few freedmen in Rio Claro who had migrated from other places—only seven persons in 1835 can definitely be identified as freedmen. None of the planters in Table 3.11 owned plantations farther toward the sertão, to which slaves might have been transferred. None had children who set up their own plantation during this time. Only one, Pedro Vaz de Campos, declared a decline in the size of his gang, suggesting that he may have been failing and was obliged to sell some of the slaves. Even so, an epidemic could have caused their disappearance, and the death of a large part of a slave gang would have been a major reason for business failure and the need to sell the rest.[27]

Even if Vaz de Campos' slaves are removed from consideration, only 36 percent of the rest survived for thirteen years. The average age of this group was 23 years. It is not possible to convert this into life expectancy because the ages of the group are quite spread out, and are somewhat inaccurately reported in any case. A comparison with Arriaga's life table, based on the 1872 census, however, is very suggestive. In 1872, 76 percent of males aged 23 would survive the

TABLE 3.11

*Comparison Log of Slave Survivals, 1822–35*

| | Number of slaves | |
| Name of planter | 1822 | Remaining 1835 |
| --- | --- | --- |
| Pedro Vaz de Campos | 27 | 0 |
| Estevão Cardoso de Negreiros | 21 | 8 |
| Alexandre Goes Maciel | 17 | 8 |
| José Ferraz de Camargo | 17 | 3 |
| Manuel Paes de Arruda | 16 | 7 |
| Francisco de Goes Maciel | 13 | 7 |
| Antônio Ferraz de Camargo | 10 | 0 |
| José da Cunha Castanho | 5 | 1 |
| Antônio de Goes Maciel | 4 | 3 |
| José Moreira | 1 | 1 |
| TOTAL | 131 | 38 |

SOURCE. 1822, 1835: APESP, População Piracicaba.

next thirteen years, and their life expectancy was calculated at 29 years, i.e. to age 52. It seems likely that the life expectancy of this group was less than half that.[28]

In this sample there was no significant difference in rates of survival of mulattos compared with blacks, of married slaves compared with unmarried, or of females compared with males. The ages of those who survived were an average four years lower than those who did not, all of which may be taken as measures of the validity of the inference that the missing slaves were dead. Of the children in the group, only four of the ten aged five and under and none of the seven between six and thirteen survived, which suggests a higher mortality than that of the ingênuos, already noted. In that case the lack of profit in breeding slaves is underscored.

In Rio Claro in 1822 and 1835, more than a third of the adult slaves were recorded as married (Table 3.12). The sharp apparent decline in 1872 was probably due principally to a legalistic definition of "marriage," since there was also a sharp decline in the proportion of the free adults listed as married. Assuming a reduction of about 10 percent in the real proportion of married slaves (an estimate that will be explained below), it can be inferred roughly that one slave couple in four obtained church sanction,

TABLE 3.12
*Slave Marriages, 1822–72*

| Category | 1822 | | 1835 | | 1872 | |
|---|---|---|---|---|---|---|
| | Number | Percent | Number | Percent | Number | Percent |
| Slaves, 16 and older | 138 | 34.1% | 150 | 39.5% | 214 | 7.3% |
| Male | 71 | 23.2 | 79 | 34.3 | 122 | 7.0 |
| Female | 67 | 69.1 | 71 | 47.3 | 92 | 7.7 |

SOURCES. 1822, 1835: APESP, População Piracicaba. 1872: Census. Fifteen persons whose marital status was not recorded were not counted in the calculation of the 1835 percentages. NOTE. Percentage is percentage of all slaves age 16 and older.

compared to two out of three of the free couples. A very few slaves were married to free persons—four males and two females in 1822, and one male in 1835. This was probably the result of one partner obtaining liberty after acquiring a mate. In one household in the 1822 census, two free female spouses were listed among the slave gang! The size of the gang influenced the incidence of marriage. Slaves in the smallest and largest gangs were most likely to be married.

It is possible that the marriages were to a degree arranged. In one household with four slaves, Antônio was married to an Antônia and Francisco was married to a Francisca. The acquisition of mates for single slaves in a small household was not uncommon; there are records also of purchases or exchanges by owners so that a couple might be reunited. Again, the patriarchal style is evident and suggests control through the bestowal of favors. It may also be that the practice resolved suspicions that would the more easily have arisen between the owner and his wife concerning the sexual favors of slaves who lived under the same roof. The wide variation in the incidence of marriage—in 1822 two large gangs had no married partners at all—further raises the possibility of arrangement and control, since the main variable would have been the policy of the planter. This is not the most likely explanation, however. The plantations with no married adults were those most recently established; relationships among the slaves may not have formed. In 1835 none of the plantations holding females were without married couples.

Slave marriages resembled the male-dominant and monogamous marriages of the free population: the older and higher-ranked male was more likely to be married and usually his mate was younger than he. The marriages appear creole, rather than African, in other ways. Brazilian-born males were more likely to be married than Africans, and almost all of them married creole, not African, partners. Among the African-born slaves, there was no tendency to marry persons listed with the same tribal-port designation. The slaves may have achieved some marginal gains through marriage, but they were quite unable to replicate the family arrangements of the free population. The male was not a member of a wider kin group; he did not possess a family name, and only rarely a second first name. His birthplace was not nearby. Since the male slave was more oppressed and controlled than the agregado, his control of his family was even more precarious. It can be seen that the sexual aggression of the free males was not limited to unmarried female slaves. In the two early censuses there were eight plantations that listed mulatto children and infants, although all the slave women who might have borne them were recorded as married. One of the plantations was Nicolau Vergueiro's, where there were seven mulatto children in 1822. In 1877 the slave Joanna was accused of poisoning her husband with ground glass. Her defense was that she had been given the substance by a feitor, Manuel Gomes, with whom she had been having intercourse, but that she had not known it was poison. Gomes had fled, thereby convincing the jury of the truth of Joanna's statement. On other occasions, complaining slave husbands were probably silenced with less inconvenience to the good order of the estate.[29]

Slave children were frequently sold away from their parents. The books of slave sales show that they were separated from their mothers from eight years onward, at which age they were able to begin a reduced work load. A horrifying example is a sale in 1878 by Francisco Gomes Botão of two children, eight and eleven, the offspring of a *freed* couple! The separation of slave partners was undoubtedly the cause of the anomalous "married" persons without spouses in the censuses. Table 3.12 conceals the true number

of these forced separations. In 1835 there were twelve males and
five females "married" but without partners, or 4 percent of the
adult slaves. By 1872 the number of anomalous married males without females had increased—one out of four slave husbands was
apparently without a wife. The free population experienced a
similar phenomenon, but not to the same degree—one out of nine
free husbands was without a wife—clearly because of the shift of
unaccompanied males to the agricultural frontier. Slaves whose
separation was of longer duration, having passed, perhaps, through
the hands of brokers, were probably not listed as married, hence to
some degree the apparent decline in the proportion of married
adults may have been real. For the province as a whole, including
areas not in the coffee zone, the proportion of married adults in
1872 was 19 percent. The rapid growth of the coffee plantations
was causing, it can be seen, dislocations among the slave population that would limit their chances as freedmen.[30]

The formation of a stem family, with ties of blood-relatedness
and ceremonial kinship, was essential to the emergence of a freeholding class of color, since the society's legal and economic institutions were founded upon the family. A man who did not have at
his disposal the skilled labor of a wife and the unskilled labor of
numerous children would be quite unable to exploit a small farm
effectively, much less put aside a surplus for the purchase of a legal
title. To the degree that the slave family was interfered with by
the planter, abolition would engender only a mass of rural *jornaleiros*—casual day laborers—not a class of small farmers. It cannot be
supposed that the planters' interventions had that deliberate outcome in view; possibly, as has been suggested before, the deliberate
acts of the planters were designed to create a dependent peasantry,
in spite of the disabilities such a group would present for the con-
tinuation and aggrandizement of the plantation system.

It is likely that social organization beyond the level of the slave
couple existed among the captive population, yet hardly any evidence remains. In 1884 the vicar of Rio Claro, Nery de Toledo, reported that his predecessor had "tolerated for many years" a
brotherhood—that of Saint Benedict—whose members were slaves

and freedmen, probably mostly town residents. It had maintained in the parish church a cash fund, obtained through solicitations, which was spent on a yearly celebration. Religious brotherhoods were a significant social and political institution of small towns, conferring status and cementing neighborhood relations. Yet the vicar had suppressed the society, along with all the others in town, "until it goes through the proper formalities." There had been a reaction against the decision, which he imagined darkly to be instigated by personal enemies. Implicitly he assumed the brotherhood was the instrument of persons at a higher social level. It is difficult to credit this belief fully. The manipulation of lower-class groupings is a common element of elite control, on the other hand the easy generalization that all lower-class associations are manipulated is a myth both useful and comforting to the elite.[31]

The local Catholic church, although established and favored by the civil authorities, scarcely encompassed the slaves. It was, after all, run by whites, mostly for the benefit of the townspeople. It is quite likely that slaves never attended mass in town, unless accompanying their owners. The priest excluded even free persons who arrived poorly dressed, or who were not respectable, saying that "even God in heaven establishes distinctions." Slaves newly arrived from Africa and slave children born on the plantation were supposed to be baptized, but it appears possible that that essential ceremony was not always performed. The vicar, as long as he controlled the town cemetery, refused to bury slaves, on the suspicion that they were heathen. This attitude must have related to his own lack of diligence in proffering the prerequisite sacrament. The vicar, like the other town professionals, approached the plantations only when called. His correspondence with the provincial government never included any mention of the slave population. The Protestants in Rio Claro had ministers of their own from time to time, but proselytization—even of the free—was legally not permitted them. Nor would they have engaged in it, judging from their lack of interest in the freedmen after the separation of church and state in 1890. Occasionally the vicar was also a slave owner. In the censuses of 1822 and 1835 he possessed a male house servant.

Sometimes priests came into the ownership of plantations through inheritance. Possibly they dealt with their slaves less harshly than others, but they did not manumit them.[32]

The slaves possessed other organizations set against those imposed by the planters and the white townspeople, but they were necessarily hidden and obscure. There were warlocks secluded in the forest who practiced African medicine and sorcery—*mandinga*. The slaves held religious observances of their own and played *batuque*, not brass instruments, and danced the lascivious *lundu*, all contemptible to the whites and therefore not for their eyes, but all invested with meanings beyond the comprehension of their captors. In the months before abolition they brought the forbidden drums defiantly to town, set bonfires, and terrified the burghers with their dancing.[33]

The slaves of Rio Claro resisted their fate. The frequent advertisements in newspapers for escaped slaves suggest that they ran away often, but it is difficult to determine the rate of permanent desertions. The jailer reported to the provincial chief of police in 1885 a year's total of 47 recaptured slaves, at the time one percent of the total slave population. Most of them were brought in by professional *capitães-do-mato*—slave catchers. There were usually at least three persons in town with that occupation. The standard fee, according to provincial law, was 20 milreis if captured in town, or 50 milreis outside of town. Advertisements offered a good deal more, as much as 200 milreis. Still other slaves may have come back voluntarily, after trying unsuccessfully to earn the price of their freedom, or compelled by family ties, or simply because the fugitive life was precarious and solitary.[34]

Some remained uncaptured. The 1872 census lists the "absent population," an intriguing datum, since the possibility is strong that many of the absent slaves had escaped permanently (Table 3.13). The figures for portions of the population are demonstrably incomplete. It is likely that there were more absent adults of color and caboclos. The recording of whites was probably more accurately accomplished, since they were more often persons of social standing whose temporary departure would be remarked.

TABLE 3.13

*Absent Population, 1872*

| Class and color | Males | Females | Total | Percent of adults |
|---|---|---|---|---|
| Free whites | 22 | 10 | 32 | 0.8% |
| Free of color | 13 | 4 | 17 | — |
| Slaves | 29 | 16 | 45 | 1.5 |

SOURCE. Census, 1872. Itaqueri not included. There were no absent persons under 16 years reported, and no caboclos were reported absent.

It is also likely that only those slaves would be listed who were permanently deserters, since recent escapees would be listed as still present. It is possible that all of the absent adult slaves, nearly twice as many proportionately as whites, had permission or were away on rental. But that is very unlikely, since wages and rentals in Rio Claro must have been at the time as high or higher than anywhere else in Brazil. The large number of unaccompanied males, both free and slave, in the census of Rio Claro is strong evidence that the flow of rented labor was into the county, not out. It can therefore be hypothesized that half the absent number, at least, were permanently escaped. If so, then in any given year 2 to 3 percent of the slaves departed, of whom about half were never brought back—odds that were better than waiting for manumission.

Most of the notices of recapture, forwarded by the chief of police in São Paulo, were from the cities of São Paulo, Santos, and Rio de Janeiro, probably because the police were more effective there. Some of the slaves went to the edge of the wilderness, to join the mestizo pioneers. There were a few more or less temporary settlements of escapees in the region. The word *quilombo*—runaway colony—is encountered frequently as a rural place name. The part of town now called Vila Nova was once named Quilombo, and one of the smaller plantations in the area that is now Ipeúna was also called Quilombo. Another place on the road from Campinas to Piracicaba retained that name as late as the 1860's, and there is still another place, in the county of Artur Nogueira, 50 kilometers southeast of Rio Claro, where the name survives to the present. The quilombos, like the other squatter settlements, were regularly swept aside by the arrival of the plantations. Sometimes escaped slaves found employment as agregados. Their irregular status made them ideally loyal, but the planters had to disguise their origin from other slave owners and from their own slaves as well.[35]

Another form of resistance was theft. The slaves, well acquainted personally with the money economy since they often worked for wages on their free day, smuggled plantation supplies and coffee to itinerant pack traders and to other workers. A number of contracts between owners and entrepreneurs forbade the latter to deal without permission with the plantation's slaves. These acts of reappropriation were regarded sympathetically by the free workers, who were quite willing accomplices in the traffic.[36]

Slaves sometimes murdered their captors. Three slaves were convicted of homicide in the courts of Rio Claro. Romão killed his owner, José Ferraz de Campos, in 1860, and Guilherme, along with four companions, killed a feitor on the plantation of Antônio José Vieira Barbosa in 1877. Romão was hung. Guilherme, probably because his victim was lower-class, merely received 300 lashes and was soldered into an iron vest, which he had to wear for three years. A third conviction, for the murder of a slave feitor in 1866, has already been noted; the punishment was also flogging. Since Rio Claro was for a time the seat of a criminal court district, other murder trials were held there. In 1849 a slave was condemned to life imprisonment for the murder of his owner in Descalvado, and in 1860 another was executed in town for the murder of his owner in Araraquara. There were more murders than trials. At least one other killing was committed openly, that of a feitor on the plantation of José Ferraz de Sampaio, in 1871, but the attackers were never apprehended.[37]

The slaves more often resorted successfully to covert violence. Alfredo Ellis, Jr., accused a woman house slave named Dita, African-born, owned by Ellis's grandfather, Francisco da Cunha Bueno, of poisoning on separate occasions her owner's mother-in-law, brother-in-law, and wife! The poison, the venom of a snake or scorpion, was supplied by a hermit warlock. Although the physician suspected murder, the police took no action, possibly for lack of evidence. Ellis does not explain why an assassin was allowed to remain in the kitchen, but possibly she was not suspected until the third of the mysterious deaths. Ellis exhibits a degree of the planters' paranoia in this tale, perhaps, and certainly when he goes on to claim that such murders occurred by the thousands. Other historians have passed along similar tales: a snake in the mattress, a scorpion in the boot, ground glass in the corn meal, all accidental in appearance or impossible to discover. An immigrant druggist in Araras remembered that he had to be extremely careful that prescriptions to be picked up by slaves could not be opened without breaking the seal, for the slaves were masters in the art of herbal poisons and vengeful enough to seize the opportunity. Even when these stealthy acts were uncovered, the slave would not face public justice. The owner might do away with him personally, but just as stealthily to avoid spreading the knowledge that a slave had duped him. He might also simply sell the slave to someone else, avoiding thereby the loss of his investment. Owners known to be harsh in their treatment of slaves were probably presented with their match in this fashion, on occasion.[38]

The owners were constantly aware of the dangers that surrounded them. They went armed always. José Vergueiro kept two large hounds, which followed him everywhere, and his manner before the slaves was that of the lion tamer. The slaves responded to this provocation with utter impassivity. Lamberg witnessed the shape-up at Ibicaba plantation: Vergueiro shouting over and over again the simplest instructions, mingled with threats and curses, while the slaves stood motionless, denying him the slightest sign of recognition or understanding. A display of fear would have made them vulnerable, anger would invite reprisal, but impassivity was a mirror in which the owner could read his own terror and frustration. How strange it seems that a man would choose such a career for himself, since only rage could sustain it.[39]

Of course the owners feared uprisings. More than once beatings administered to feitores were the work of a whole gang, who then fled the estate together. What if these fugitives should come across others? What if some conspiracy should be joined, not mere coincidence but the result of a plan? To avert this danger, the planters

forbade drums, and staggered the day of rest, so that the slaves
would not all be idle at once. Another breach of the Catholic faith:
"On this plantation, I am the pope," boasted many a planter. No
general uprising occurred in Rio Claro until the year before abolition—that uprising was a major cause of abolition and will be
discussed later—but the unease of the free population at the
awakening sense of injustice among the slaves long preceded that
final crisis.

The slave owners had reached this impasse because they were
never capable of defending their position on moral grounds. A
letter of manumission by Maria Severina Borges in 1857 may have
been the only written expression of the moral contradiction of
slavery, but no one would have had the temerity to disagree: "I
see that slavery is altogether born out of the order of violence and
despotism, and is entirely incompatible with the laws of Our Lord
Jesus Christ." And Maria Paes de Barros, when presented for the
first time to her new husband's slaves as his bride and their new
mistress, cringed and thought to herself, *"Ai de mim!* if only I
could say to them, go along, you're free, all of you!" Moral order
within a slave society was unavoidable; it had to be fostered within
the slaves themselves, for amoral slaves would be unpredictable
and uncontrollable workers. The moral qualities of the slaves—
grudgingly, condescendingly, and incompletely recognized and
rewarded—were, as everyone realized, essential to the survival of
the slave system.[40]

Two dramatic episodes are worth mentioning. According to a
newspaper account of 1885, a slave of Rio Claro, whose name was
omitted, saved a child from death by abandonment. The act impressed the townspeople so strongly that they began to raise a fund
to free him. A police report of 1877 tells of a slave on the Palmeiras
plantation (there were several of this name, so that it cannot be
known who was involved) who had run after his master's drunken
son when he observed him leave the house with a shotgun. "Hoping
to avert a conflict in the neighborhood," the slave asked for the
weapon, but the son refused, "and furthermore took it as an im-
pudence that he, with the quality of a slave, should make such a

demand." The son then beat the slave with the gun butt. One slave rewarded, the other gravely injured, but both for effective acts of moral concern. It is altogether likely that the police interested themselves in the latter case with foreknowledge of the facts: the inspector may well have been demonstrating a desire to protect a slave who had preserved the peace, lest other slaves be discouraged from similar acts. The police did not under ordinary circumstances come to plantations to take depositions from slaves. In the long run, a deeper awareness must have been operating in that slave society—an awareness that society would benefit from the acceptance by slaves of a community of interests in which they would be encouraged to behave as moral men and women, and not merely as beasts, though neither their owners nor the rest of the free population would openly admit their sacrifice or give them the just reward they merited—freedom from their bondage.[41]

# CHAPTER 4

# An Experiment in Free Labor

IN 1845, Nicolau Vergueiro, foreseeing the gradual depletion of the slave labor force if the prohibition of the African slave traffic was made effective, decided to attempt the importation of free European field hands. Through his influence the Liberal ministry of the viscount of Macaé inserted in the imperial budget an authorization of 200,000 milreis for loans by the provincial governments to any private persons who desired to introduce immigrant plantation workers. As it turned out, Vergueiro was the only taker in all of Brazil. He received a three-year loan from the province of São Paulo, at no interest, to cover the cost of transportation of 1,000 immigrants. The first levy of 64 German families, 432 persons in all, from Prussia, Bavaria, and Holstein, arrived at Vergueiro's Ibicaba plantation in Limeira in 1847, just as his coffee groves were beginning to bear.[1]

The introduction of Europeans to serve as field hands was a considerable triumph for Vergueiro. Although the imperial government was already engaged in fostering the immigration of Europeans, hitherto it had followed a policy of smallholding colonization on crown lands, mainly in the border province of Rio Grande do Sul. This effort was more or less deliberately designed to initiate the transformation of Brazilian agriculture to a freeholding peasantry, which was considered to be more productive than plantations, and to lessen the importance of the African element of the population, which was regarded as culturally and racially inferior. The official colonies had not been very successful, however. They were located for the most part remote from town markets, and the settlement itself was underfinanced. Rio Grande do Sul, furthermore, was exposed to border wars and civil conflicts that did not end until 1852. Nevertheless, the prospect of a solidly installed yeomanry, even in a frontier province, was alarming to the planters of Rio de Janeiro and São Paulo. Vergueiro, in a memorandum to the government as early as 1828, had elaborated a justification of a quite different method of encouraging immigration. Official colonies, he complained, were contrary to liberal economic doctrine; the government should interfere as little as possible in a process of immigration that should be spontaneous. Crown colonies wasted public funds on administration, surveying, and roads, from which no taxable revenues could be realized in the short run. The plantations would be a better locale for the assimilation of the immigrants. There they would acquire local agricultural techniques, they would adjust to the climate, they would absorb Brazilian ways and intermarry with the native population. On the great estates they would earn in a few years enough cash to repay the cost of their transportation and to buy smallholdings of their own.[2]

Thus the transformation of Brazilian agriculture would be achieved at no cost to the state and, assuming a constant flow of new arrivals, with considerable profit to the planters. The proposal could not be dismissed by the government because it promised an immediate increase in exports, which were the government's principal source of revenue and thus the source of the planters' growing political influence. Vergueiro's agents in Hamburg, Zürich, and other cities did, in fact, receive assistance from Brazilian consuls, who, it might be mentioned, were instructed to avoid recruiting "socialists, or Young-Germany veterans who may have belonged to the free-corps; none of those officers who talk politics, or discourse on the forms of government."[3]

Vergueiro offered the immigrants an indenture contract. He traced its origin to an earlier attempt he had made to employ contracted Portuguese laborers on the Ibicaba estate in 1841, while he was still growing cane, but it is possible that his was not the only experiment with a harsh and primitive regime of Portuguese

indenture in the Paulista West. References to at least two other
cases were found, apparently comparable to Vergueiro's attempt.
According to Swiss Commissioner Tschudi, some of the Portuguese
were day workers, who lodged in dormitories not unlike the *quadrados* and were fed slave rations. They paid off the cost of their
transportation and first year's keep with their entire wage, 12
milreis per month—three-quarters the going rate for day labor.
Others were tenants of a sort, apparently families, quartered in
separate houses with their own subsistence plots, upon which they
paid rents. They worked in the fields in gangs, like slaves, under
*feitores*. Vergueiro mentioned vaguely that his first settlement of
Portuguese had scattered during the Liberal rebellion of 1842, in
which Vergueiro had been involved, implying that the government's repression had been to blame. It is more likely, since the
troops never came within 50 kilometers of Ibicaba, that the Portuguese simply seized the chance to escape, or may have fled an attempt to recruit them. Of the 70 families introduced in 1841, seven
remained in 1847.[4]

Vergueiro offered the Germans what appeared to be a fairer and
more lucrative arrangement. They were to be assigned their own
grove of mature trees, and although they would receive some supervision, they were to be more or less independently responsible for
tending and harvesting them. According to the contract they signed
before departing Hamburg, they were to bring the harvested
berries to the terraces, and contribute proportionately to the work
of processing them. They would be paid on shares, receiving half
the proceeds of the sale of the crop, after costs of transport, taxes,
and commission had been deducted. If the worker produced more
on his subsistence plot than his family could eat, half the surplus
was also due Vergueiro. Although Vergueiro called this contract
*parceria*—sharecropping—it differed from the European versions
in that the selling of the crop was undertaken by the landowner,
not by the worker. Vergueiro also called the workers *colonos*,
thereby blurring the distinction between indentured laborers and
freeholding settlers such as those in Rio Grande do Sul. Ever
since, the term has been applied in the Paulista West to various

kinds of rural proletarians, and never to smallholders, who are called *sitiantes*, after *sítio*, a small farm. The contracted workers were, in fact, indentured servants, because the full cost of their transportation was owed the planter, just like their Portuguese predecessors. Vergueiro was to withhold a minimum of half the worker's share each year, in order to retire the debt. Meanwhile the worker was charged 6 percent on his first year's subsistence advance and, after two years' grace, on his transportation as well. The entire family was collectively responsible for the debt of each member. Thus if the husband died, the widow and children would be obliged to serve out the contract, as would the orphans if both parents died.[5]

The immigrants, after a voyage of nearly two months, were put ashore at Santos. There they rested for a few days, and then were conducted, on foot, with the trunks, the children, and the infirm loaded on two-wheel carts, up the coastal palisade and cross-country. Two weeks more were spent in this agonizing march. At Ibicaba they were greeted by the Vergueiros, who, although maintaining considerable social distance, gave demonstrations of sincere welcome and concern for their well-being. Vergueiro's sons had been educated in Europe and were able to address them in German. They were taken to a place more than a kilometer from the great house and its slave quarters and installed in a cluster of one-room huts with straw roofs, wattle-and-daub walls, and dirt floors. A German long resident in Brazil was appointed director of the "colony."[6]

The Germans must have been shocked by the primitiveness of these arrangements, although they were somewhat better than the housing of other landless free workers in the region. They also had to accustom themselves to a different diet, but Vergueiro did not limit the amount they might borrow from the plantation store. A German physician who resided in Rio Claro was contracted, and each family was billed six milreis per year to cover his retainer. One of the immigrants was paid a stipend, to which parents contributed, to teach the children their letters. There were, it seems, many deaths and illnesses in the first years, especially of older immigrants.

The prices of every article except the barest necessities were much higher than in Europe. What they could not make for themselves they had to do without—even paper and pencils for the children. The spareness of their existence, the extreme isolation, and the strangeness of their neighbors all caused them unease.[7]

Yet they were able to carry out the terms of the contract, and the land provided abundant harvests. They acquired pigs and goats, cows, and even a few horses. They ate better than in Germany, and they began to furnish the town dwellers of Rio Claro and Limeira with produce never seen in the market before—milk, cheese, eggs, honey, and vegetables. They formed a singing society and a beneficient association. Observers remarked on the absence of crimes and illegitimate births in the colony. The families managed to improve their rented housing; they tiled the roofs, laid floors, and built furniture. Evidently the culture of a German peasant village was being successfully reconstructed in that prodigiously remote place.[8]

Vergueiro was disappointed to find that the consular agents had not troubled to make certain that prospective immigrants were in fact experienced farmers. He put some of the craftsmen to work when they proved unadaptable to the groves. Ibicaba had wheel-wrights, coopers, harness makers, stonemasons, and blacksmiths. Fifteen of the families were released to carry out their trades in Rio Claro and Limeira, and to another twelve he advanced further funds so that they could buy land. Vergueiro saw no way to eliminate the problem, except by importing the workers in larger numbers.[9]

At any rate, he was not discouraged, and in the second levy of 65 Germans and 50 Portuguese, who arrived in 1849, there was only one family that could not adjust to farming. Of the first group, eighteen families were free of debt by the third year (Table 4.1), and their total indebtedness had been reduced from 32,220 to 9,754 milreis. Vergueiro reported to the imperial government that it was his "most profound conviction" that the colonies would be "of great public utility" in acclimating immigrants to Brazil under favorable conditions.[10]

TABLE 4.1
*Accounts of Indentured Workers, Ibicaba Plantation, 1851*

| Category | Number of families | Credit or debit per family in milreis |
|---|---|---|
| Families with credits | 13 | 392 |
| Families with zero balances | 5 | — |
| Families with debits | 54 | −196 |
| Families who left, owing debits | 27 | −158 |
| TOTAL | 99 | −98 |

SOURCE. Arquivo do Museu Imperial, Petrópolis. Nicolau Vergueiro to Nabuco de Araujo, June 6, 1852. Note that the accounts of 1852 were not yet settled.

Vergueiro's neighbors began to take an interest in his scheme after the passage of the Queiroz law in 1850 effectively ended the slave trade. The indentured workers seemed to be making money for Vergueiro, who told a visitor that he found the "labor of a man who has a will of his own, and interests at stake, vastly more profitable than slave labor." (He did not abandon slave labor, however. A force of 250 of them continued to tend other groves on Ibicaba.) Vergueiro therefore began to act as agent for other planters. In Rio Claro several asked for indentured workers, and Vergueiro decided to establish a second "colony" on his Angélica plantation. In 1852 he signed a second contract with the provincial government, again at no interest, but this time covering only half the cost of transport. In Germany and Switzerland, however, several municipalities put up the rest of the cost for any of their citizens who wished to emigrate.[11]

Within six months 600 more immigrants were delivered, mainly from Thuringia, Pomerania, and Holstein. By 1857 there were 60 colonies in the Paulista West. Ten of them were in Rio Claro, where more than 1,000 indentured workers tended the groves (Table 4.2). Some Portuguese and native Brazilians signed *parceria* contracts, and a few Belgians were recruited, along with additional Germans and some Swiss. Vergueiro, reporting to the provincial government in 1853 shortly after signing a second renewal, declared that within ten years he would be importing 10,000 a year.[12]

TABLE 4.2

*Indenture Colonies in Rio Claro and Limeira, 1847–57*

| Plantation | County | Owner | Founded |
|---|---|---|---|
| Ibicaba | Lim | Vergueiro & Cia. | 1847 |
| São Jerônimo | Lim | F. A. de Souza Queiroz | 1852 |
| Boa Vista | RC | Benedito Antônio de Camargo | 1852 |
| Morro Azul | Lim | Joaquim Franco de Camargo | 1852 |
| Biri | RC | J. E. Pacheco Jordão | 1852 |
| São Felipe | Lim | F. A. de Souza Queiroz | 1852 |
| Corumbataí | RC | M. R. de Carvalho Pinto | 1853 |
| São João do Morro Grande | RC | J. Ribeiro dos Santos Camargo | 1853 |
| Tatu | Lim | C. J. da Silva Serra | 1854 |
| Cresciumal | Lim | F. A. de Souza Queiroz | 1854 |
| São José de Corumbataí | RC | Domingos José da Costa Alves | 1854 |
| Morro Grande | RC | A. Joaquina Nogueira Oliveira | 1854 |
| Angélica | RC | Vergueiro & Cia. | 1855 |
| Cauvitinga | RC | J. E. Pacheco Jordão | 1855 |
| Sertão de Araraquara | RC | Domingos José da Costa Alves | 1855 |
| Santa Barbara | Lim | F. A. de Souza Queiroz | 1856 |
| Bom Retiro | Lim | Joaquim da Silva Diniz | 1856 |
| Espandonga | Lim | F. A. de Souza Queiroz | 1856 |
| Palmira | Lim | Lourenço Franco da Rocha | 1856 |
| Itaúna | RC | Ignácio Xavier de Negreiros | 1857 |

SOURCES. SP(S), Secretaria de Estado dos Negócios de Agricultura, Comércio e Obras Públicas, *Relatorio*, 1893; APESP, Colônias, 2, "Mappa das colonias visitadas e examinadas . . ." [Jan. 1857].

The first indenture contract was modified by Vergueiro to permit him to transfer it to another planter, as long as the worker had no "just or well-founded motive" to refuse. He also tightened somewhat the landlord's control by extending the required notice of departure to one year. Furthermore, possibly to reduce his initial outlay for transport since the province had reduced its advances, the later contract specified that the accumulation of 6 percent interest would begin when the immigrant signed it in Hamburg or Antwerp. Interest on the advances was added, not on the average balance, but on the entire year's debt, and before calculating the credits earned by the worker.

Several of the clauses of the earlier version were markedly ambiguous and had already been the subject of dispute, but Vergueiro did not bother to alter them. It was not clear, for example, who was to pay the cost of transport from Santos to Ibicaba. The contract stated that the planter would "furnish" it, but Vergueiro intended all along that he would charge the immigrants for that service. Since the transport of trunks or persons in carts might cost half as much as an ocean voyage, and since the Europeans had no experience of such exorbitant overland rates, it was to a degree guileful of his agents neither to have pointed them out nor to have advised the immigrants to reduce their baggage. Nor did Vergueiro make explicit in the second contract that he thought it reasonable to add to the worker's indebtedness the commission of 10 percent he paid his recruiting agents.[13]

The manner of calculating the worker's earnings also caused heated arguments. The worker brought his coffee to the terraces in containers by measure of volume, called *alqueires* (36.27 liters—distinct from the *alqueire* that was a surface measure). The contract stated that a worker who did not carry out the task of turning and drying his own berries would be charged by his companions for it at the rate of three alqueires for one *arroba* (at the time 14.69 kilograms) of processed beans. The planters insisted that this formula applied equally to their calculation of the harvest accounts. That is, for every three alqueires picked, they would credit the workers with one arroba of processed beans. In later labor contracts it was generally stipulated that an arroba was the equivalent of two alqueires. Vergueiro justified himself with the excuse that there was some wastage in processing. This was undoubtedly true, yet one measure lost in three is unbelievable. Furthermore, it was unfair to charge the loss entirely to the worker, since the planter took part in the operation and should have shared the risk equally. The extent of the waste in processing can be quite accurately calculated, in fact, since the Santa Gertrudes plantation kept accounts for several years of the volume of the harvest and the output of beans in arrobas. Translated back into the earlier nonmetric equivalents, one arroba was derived from 2.44 alqueires. The workers, then, should have been credited with an arroba for that amount at least, and might well have been credited with more. The real shares under the parceria contract, as Vergueiro administered it, were not 50-50, but 60-40 in his favor.[14]

The immigrants, once parceled out among the plantations, discovered that the contractual requirement to submit themselves to the regulations of the colony implied renouncing to some extent their civil rights. The worker was forbidden to absent himself or to invite guests except with permission. The planters, as was their custom in dealing with agregados, quite often punished drunkenness, laziness, or wife beating as though they were justices of the peace. They were especially careful to put an end to grumbling among the workers that might lead to organization. Vergueiro expelled from the first group two "socialists," one of them the schoolteacher, for "indiscipline" of this sort. The penalties were ordinarily in the form of fines, which could easily amount to a year's salary if repeatedly applied, and which on most estates were pocketed by the planter, rather than put at the disposal of the colony. The planters understood quite well that the most likely source of replacements for their workers was their relatives and former fellow townspeople; therefore optimistic reports were encouraged by various means including bribes, and finally, since they had access to the mail on their estates, the planters began to censor correspondence surreptitiously.[15]

Any disputes arising out of the contract were to be decided, without appeal, by county authorities—that is, by the county council–appointed justices of the peace. In Rio Claro and Limeira the presiding judges were themselves also planters. They followed the harsh Employment Law of 1837, especially designed for immigrant contracts. A worker fired for cause was obliged to pay on the spot the entire sum owed the planter. If he could not, then he was liable to summary condemnation to public works "for as long as necessary," or, if none were at hand, then to jail at hard labor for a maximum of two years. A worker who quit without notice was to be seized wherever he was found and put at public works until he had earned twice the amount owed the employer. These provisions might be the equivalent of a life sentence, and beggary for the rest of the family. The law also stated that a worker who had completed his contract was to be given a certificate by his employer. Anyone who employed a foreigner without such a certificate was liable to double the worker's indebtedness to former employers, and the worker was subject to arrest for absconding.[16]

In spite of early enthusiasm for the indenture system, Vergueiro turned out to be wrong in his prediction. Only a few more planters were to hire immigrants, while others soon desisted and returned to slave driving. The immigration of Europeans did not increase; indeed, fewer arrived in Santos during the 1860's than had in the 1850's. Not until the late 1880's did the flow of immigrants provide a work force sufficiently large to allow the planters to dispense with their slaves. In this sense, the indenture system was a failure. The most varied reasons have been advanced to account for it. In retrospect, it can be seen that the immigrants were perfectly suitable field workers, more efficient than slaves, and capable of transforming not merely the labor relations of the plantations, but the entire economic structure of southern Brazil. Why their arrival was delayed in the most prosperous and propitious region of the country is therefore a momentous question.

The immediate cause of the planters' sudden loss of interest in Vergueiro's parceria regime was a series of labor disputes arising out of the contracts, culminating in 1856 and 1857 in widespread strikes and desertions. The crisis was immediately the effect of an internal inflation combined with stagnation in the export price of coffee. The workers saw themselves falling further behind in their accounts with the plantation store while their earnings from coffee remained at the same level. At the same time they were driven by the discrepancy in prices to pay more attention to their food cash crops than to their coffee groves, making it still more difficult to pay off their indebtedness, and ruining the planter's chances of making a profit. The prospect of perpetual debt peonage for one and bankruptcy for the other hardened the demands of both sides. In the eyes of the former, the unwillingness of the planters to revise the terms of the contracts seemed part of an implacable design. It became easy therefore to discern fraud in all the planters' dealings—the account books, the set of weights and measures, and the rates at which they exchanged their German and Swiss currency. The prices at the plantation stores, they noticed, were usu-

ally higher than those in town, and the policy of freely granting
not only subsistence but cash advances seemed in retrospect to be
a form of entrapment.[17]

The planters began to cut their losses as the prospect of profiting
from their workers faded. Joaquim Franco de Camargo, owner of
the Morro Azul plantation, with 204 workers, reported in December 1855 that he had fired fourteen families—for idleness, thievery
(like the slaves, some workers stole coffee they considered theirs
and sold it in town), or "intrigue." Meanwhile, three more families
had run off, "led away by others," and three had departed with his
permission to try to work off their debts as artisans. Only one of
the remaining families had paid off its debts. At Francisco Gomes
Botão's plantation, after a year of trouble, 30 of his 40 workers
disappeared. Benedito Antônio de Camargo lost 34 of his 253 workers in less than a year, and complained to the president of the
province in October 1856, "It is my duty to tell Yr. Excy. that the
colony doesn't do well, because, of the 40 or so families I have,
there isn't one that carries out properly the obligations of their
contracts[;] what they do know how to do is Steal, [and be] disrespectful of others, in short the way it is going now it is very
costly to keep it up."[18]

A few of the planters did not limit themselves to summary dismissals. They sent for the police and had the workers jailed, sometimes along with their families. If the workers had abandoned their
groves, the police were sent after them as though they were runaway slaves, and they were brought back, either to tend the trees or
to be put to public works. It was a distasteful business for the police
and the townspeople, who were sympathetic to the immigrants.
Most of the planters, seeing how little use it was, desisted and
suffered the considerable loss of their advances. Others, attempting
to avert the disappearance of their remaining workers, or else in
order to make it easier for them to find another employer, "pardoned" part of their indebtedness.[19]

At Ibicaba the workers found a reluctant but intelligent and
articulate spokesman in Thomas Davatz, a Swiss from the canton
of Graubünden, who emigrated with his wife and children along

with more than 200 others from the Prätigau Valley in 1855. Davatz's account of his experiences in the Paulista West is one of extremely few in Brazilian history written from the point of view of the worker. Before he left, Davatz had been commissioned by the cantonal government to send back a detailed report on the conditions at Ibicaba. This was known to the Vergueiros, who gave him preferred treatment on the plantation—possibly, Davatz thought, in hope of favorable treatment. Instead he wrote a somewhat pessimistic account, which somehow was read by one of the administrators. Davatz was immediately called before Luiz Vergueiro, one of Nicolau's sons, who threatened obliquely to have him murdered. Shortly after, one of the administrators made it clear that they would not let him leave the property and would keep an eye on him to make sure he did not attempt to post his report. In despair, Davatz returned to tending his trees so as not to give the Vergueiros cause to imprison him. Meanwhile, he found ways to smuggle letters off the plantation containing pleas to the cantonal government to bring him back to Switzerland, where he intended to present his report in person.[20]

The Vergueiros, supposing Davatz under control, restored his job as schoolteacher, apparently in the hope that a favorable report could be extracted from him eventually. Meanwhile, the other immigrants were growing increasingly apprehensive of their situation. During the harvest of 1856 the management predicted high prices for their coffee and the workers anticipated the removal of much of their indebtedness. When the accounts were presented, however, the result was far below their expectation. Furthermore, the committee appointed by the colony to examine the accounts was allowed only a brief glimpse at the ledger and was shown no vouchers of sale. When a Portuguese worker insisted that coffee was going for a better price in Santos than the management alleged and demanded to see the bills of sale, he was fired on the spot.[21]

Davatz, until then isolated and fearful of communicating with the other workers, was finally approached by several of them. They met in his house and drew up a list of complaints for in-

vestigation by the Swiss consulate in Rio and by the imperial government, which the immigrants trusted and imagined would provide them a fresh start on one of the official colonies in Rio Grande
do Sul. For several months they waited for a reply. In December
Luiz Vergueiro, in an effort to reassure the authorities concerning
rumors of discontent among the colonists, decided to arrange an
expensive celebration of his father's birthday, to which all the
political and bureaucratic lights of the region were invited, so that
they might form a favorable opinion of the relations between the
Vergueiros and their employees. The immigrants divined the significance of the affair, however, and most refused to attend. When
the administrators of the colony tried the next day to use the non-
appearance of the men's chorus as a pretext to purge its officers,
the meeting became an occasion for the men to voice their general
anger at the management. The next day 45 of the workers appeared
spontaneously at Davatz's house, where they drew up and signed
a list of complaints to be presented to Vergueiro, along with a
statement that they desired an official investigation. Later, some
40 of the Germans appeared to express their support for the Swiss.
Meanwhile, one of the workers was fired by Luiz Vergueiro for his
speech at the meeting, in which he had called the elder Vergueiro
a cheat.[22]

An administrator, Schmid, was presented with a copy of the
complaints, and he invited Davatz to deliver it to the Vergueiros.
Davatz confronted, in the salon of the great house, the old Senator,
Luiz, another administrator named Jonas, a German named Al-
scher, who tutored the family's children, and—somewhat apart
from the rest—the physician, Gattiker, contracted to attend to the
workers. Davatz could not understand Portuguese, nor the Senator
German; therefore Jonas interpreted the Senator's imprecations:
he accused Davatz of being a revolutionary, withdrew the school-
master's job, and prohibited him from any further attempts at
communication with higher authority. When Davatz attempted to
reply, the exchange became more heated, all the others shouting
in Portuguese and forwarding the Senator's commands in German.
Then they insisted on hearing the specific complaints. Davatz re-

plied that there were many but that the workers wanted them investigated as a whole. Finally he mentioned several. When he voiced the general belief that the price of coffee in Santos was higher than that alleged by the firm, the Vergueiros exploded in fury. The accusation touched on their honor. Gattiker, horrified, grabbed Davatz's arm and pulled him out of the room.[23]

Meanwhile, a couple of the workers who understood Portuguese had managed to slip up to the front porch, and clearly heard the Vergueiros deliberating loudly whether they should have Davatz killed. Terrified, one ran back to the colony to warn the others, who immediately rushed from their houses with whatever weapons they possessed. Halfway down the road, this angry parade encountered the surprised Davatz, who did not yet know of his peril. He and a few of the other workers managed to pacify them, but not before they had in turn threatened the frightened Jonas, who accompanied Davatz, and fired two random shots in the air. The workers, nevertheless, returned to the colony and made no further show of anger.[24]

These events of December 24, 1856, have been referred to as the "uprising," although there was nothing more to them than this, a mob of workers fearing that one of them was in danger of being murdered, yet whose basic demand was merely an official investigation into a matter of contractual obligations. The provincial government quickly sent a detachment of 30 soldiers to Limeira, where they found the town militia already on patrol but not interested in taking the side of the Vergueiros. The immigrants received the soldiers with great enthusiasm, since they continued to regard the provincial and imperial authorities as their defenders. The commander of the troops was much impressed by their attitude and reported sympathetically to the president of the province.[25]

Not until January 29, however, did an investigator appear at Ibicaba, and his efforts were compromised and ineffective. The provincial president was an appointee of the Conservative ministry of the duke of Caxias. He was probably pleased at the embarrassment of the Liberal Vergueiro and his friends, and saw no need to end it abruptly. In the provincial assembly Liberal members complained that the president did not inform them of his intentions in the affair, and hinted that he sought indirectly to pressure Vergueiro out of trying to influence an election in Santos.[26]

Meanwhile the colony, still frightened of an attack by Vergueiro, kept sentries posted and remained armed. Davatz received many workers' deputations from the other colonies in Limeira, Rio Claro, and Piracicaba. The Vergueiros, observing all this with alarm, became convinced, as they wrote the president of the province on February 10, that the immigrants were part of a vast conspiracy of "clubs," determined to overthrow society, with the help of the slaves. In the Limeira area alone they numbered 5,000 armed men! The whole plot was directed by a Swiss named Oswald, a "communist" living in São Paulo, who possibly was a mere front for even higher conspirators lodged in Rio. What was needed was a show of force, Vergueiro insisted: the government must send immediately a full battalion of troops! The basis of this paranoid construction was, it seems, a letter written by Davatz, but stolen by Vergueiro, in which he had asked Oswald, a man known to be hostile to the parceria system, for information about colonies in other provinces. At any rate Vergueiro's fantasies were generally shared by other planters in the region. An appeal by the county council of Rio Claro, dated two weeks later, stated that "it is an incontestable fact that the Swiss colonists . . . under the direction of a secret society have armed . . . ; they speak of forming a Free State. We do not fear that they will achieve their damnable ends, but we fear the destructiveness of an outbreak." They therefore joined Vergueiro in demanding soldiers.[27]

By then, however, the Swiss commissioner, J. C. Heusser, had already arrived, accompanied by an aide from the consulate in Rio. His investigation, which took three weeks, confirmed, to a degree, all of the eighteen points raised in the petition drawn up by the Swiss in December, and also provided proof of charges outside the contractual specifications, which Davatz had not been allowed to raise, such as the opening of mail by the administrators. Davatz's attitude and actions he characterized as honorable and selfless.

Nevertheless, he was unable to effect any redress for the immigrants. His settlement merely called for the restitution by the planters of debits that were improper, but he did not specify, family by family, exactly how much was due. Nor did he provide for any further legal action in case Vergueiro reneged, as in fact he did. As part of the settlement, Luiz Vergueiro was removed from the management, and a new director of the colony was supposed to be appointed. Davatz was excused of his debts and dismissed summarily. The consulate paid for his return to Switzerland.[28]

There were several more investigations in the area, notably that of Manuel de Jesús Valdetaro later in the year on commission of the imperial government, and in 1860 those of Sebastião Machado Nunes, and of J. J. Tschudi, a Swiss agent with long experience in South America. Valdetaro's report disputed few of the facts, but he assumed that the planters had in some cases merely made honest mistakes in their application of the contract and in other cases—the charge for the recruiter's commission, for example—had acted perfectly equitably. The director of the General Department of Public Lands asserted that the report showed how unfounded were criticisms of the parceria system, and assumed that immigration would resume when the facts became known.[29]

Meanwhile, the situation of the indentured workers at Ibicaba and other plantations in the area remained unchanged. Although the planters had been instructed to make amends for specific irregularities noted by Valdetaro, they were not compelled to do so. Benedito Antônio de Camargo, for example, simply replied to the president of the province that Valdetaro had been in error concerning prices in his store, and that his rents were entirely reasonable. Tschudi, who arrived in the region nearly two years after Heusser, found that the indentured workers were raising the same complaints. José Vergueiro refused to allow him to enter his plantations. This seemed highhanded to the Swiss commissioner, who doubted wryly that "the power of the ministry goes as far as Ibicaba." Vergueiro was still opening mail, and paid off the workers in scrip. Furthermore, although the Swiss municipalities had excused all their advances, Vergueiro had pocketed the payments he had already received, including those forwarded to him by other planters, claiming that they were due him for "damages" to his plantation in the "uprising." Tschudi was unable to extract any of these funds from him.[30]

The publication of Heusser's report, however, and of Davatz's impassioned memoire provoked an immediate reaction in Europe. The Prussian ministry forbade further recruitment, and the Swiss federal government strongly recommended the same measure to the cantons. There were also protests in Portugal and Italy. In São Paulo the consuls of these countries often became the advocates of the remaining indentured workers. This was not surprising, since the immigrants found it difficult and expensive to plead on their own for redress from the local justices of the peace. A few of the consular agents made themselves quite unpopular with the planters, notably the Prussian agent in Campinas, G. H. Krug. The planters preferred to think that they were motivated by a desire to rise in the consular service rather than by sympathy for their fellow countrymen. Their reports to their governments were generally hostile to the planters. Travelers in the Paulista West in the 1860's, such as Avé-Lallement, Expilly, and "Jacaré-Assu" (an Englishman evidently once resident in São Paulo), denounced the planters roundly.[31]

It is easy to recount the circumstantial manner in which the planters lost their chance, for 30 years, to replace their slaves with free labor. Yet the basic reasons for this failure are not clarified thereby: was the system not viable economically, or was there in the relationship between the planters and the workers some other insuperable obstacle to the arrangement of a deal acceptable to both?

Machado Nunes, after his inspection carried out in March 1860, pronounced the parceria contract incapable of producing enough income for the workers to allow them to clear their indebtedness. Emília Viotti da Costa, in her account of the Vergueiro experiment, was led to the same conclusion. The planters desisted and the Europeans stopped emigrating because parceria did not provide enough profits to the former or enough cash income to the latter to enable them to cancel their debts in any reasonable amount of time. Indeed, Viotti da Costa calculated that the immigrants would tend to fall further in debt. If this is correct, then it is not surprising that the planters returned to the employment of slaves, and they may be exonerated from responsibility for the great delay, insofar, of course, as a sheerly capitalist standard of judgment is applied, and contempt is withheld from any line of action as long as it is demonstrably more profitable to the property owner than any other course at his disposal.[32]

In this case, however, the plantation owners cannot be freed of the charge. They made a mistake in abandoning free labor, because both parties would have improved their gains had they persisted. Scattered evidence of workers' earnings and expenses show that the typical family *was* able to free itself of debt within a reasonable period. The cost of transport of a family of five would have amounted to about 338 milreis, and one year's subsistence would have added another 374 milreis (Table 4.3). In addition, under the most disagreeable of contractual interpretations, the worker would have to pay 6 percent, or 43 milreis, the first year on the entire sum before any allowance was made for earnings. This estimate of total indebtedness accords with the accounts presented in all the official

TABLE 4.3
*Estimated Initial Indebtedness of Indentured Family, 1856*

| Item | Cost in milreis | Item | Cost in milreis |
|---|---|---|---|
| Transportation: | | First year's subsistence: | |
| Ocean passage | 280 | Food | 250 |
| Commission | 28 | Rent | 12 |
| Overland transport | 20 | Clothing | 45 |
| Baggage | 10 | Tools | 28 |
| TOTAL | 338 | Doctor and medicine | 36 |
| | | School contribution | 3 |
| | | TOTAL | 374 |
| | | GRAND TOTAL | 712 |

SOURCES. Thomas Davatz, *Memórias de um colono no Brasil*, pp. 95–110; food and clothing allowances in APESP, Colônias, 2, Nicolau Vergueiro to President of Province, Feb. 29, 1856, and APESP, OD/RC, 396, Subdelegate to President of Province, Jan. 1856 (day illegible). Transportation confirmed elsewhere, e.g. Charles Expilly, *La traite, l'émigration et la colonisation au Brésil*, p. 115.
NOTE. The family consisted of husband, wife, two children under 12 years, and one infant.

investigations. Initial indebtedness rarely exceeded this amount, and was often lower because the immigrant applied personal savings to it, or was able to begin immediately to earn cash by day labor, so as to keep down his bill at the plantation store. Notice that this estimate is for an entire family. Viotti da Costa assumes that family indebtedness was unbearably greater, because children and wife were unproductive. This is not correct. The planters themselves recognized that family units were more productive than individual laborers; that is the reason they preferred to contract them. The output of children was proportionate to the cost of maintaining them because their parents put them to work in the grove and subsistence plot when they were seven or eight. Although the wife was obliged to spend part of her time at household tasks, she also tended the subsistence plot and animals, and produced most of the homecrafts sold in the towns.[33]

In order to eliminate the initial debt calculated in Table 4.3 within five years, the worker would have to put aside 164 milreis each year. Yearly earnings would vary widely because of fluctuations in the yields of the trees, and family earnings varied still more because of differing productivity of the groves assigned, and individual differences in diligence, skill, and health. It can be taken at an average that the male adult could handily tend 1,500 trees, even though he was sometimes given fewer, and his wife and children could tend another 1,500. Mature trees on superior soils might yield more than 100 arrobas per thousand trees, especially if they were frequently hoed and carefully picked. Nevertheless, the average would be less in Rio Claro and Limeira, perhaps 225 arrobas from 3,000 trees. Davatz provided accounts for the year 1856 at Ibicaba (Table 4.4), showing a net return to the worker of not quite 1.4 milreis per arroba. The calculations may have been fraudulent, as some workers alleged, but the average sale price of coffee in Santos that year *was* somewhat lower than the price Vergueiro claimed he got. It is necessary to discount the worker's putative earnings, however, because of Vergueiro's insistence that three alqueires of berries were the equivalent of one

TABLE 4.4
*Shares of the Coffee Harvest, Ibicaba Plantation, 1856*

| Item | Milreis per arroba |
|------|--------------------|
| Average sale price, delivered in Santos | 4.400 |
| Less: | 1.602 |
|    *Freight* | *1.040* |
|    *Processing* | *.400* |
|    *Sales commission (3 percent)* | *.132* |
|    *Tax* | *.030* |
| Net shares | 2.798 |
| Shares to indentured worker (50 percent) | 1.399 |

SOURCE. Davatz, p. 101.

arroba of beans. Thus the worker received only 180 arrobas' credit for delivering 225 arrobas' worth of berries.[34]

Nevertheless, in 1856 183 arrobas earned 252 milreis. Thus, assuming an average grove of trees, an average yield, and a price somewhat below average, the indentured worker could obtain the cash to retire his debt from coffee earnings in five years or less. For additional cash, the worker and his family might perform casual labor, or they might sell the surplus of their subsistence plot and dairy animals. Day labor was paid .50 milreis, and skilled labor was worth 1.50 milreis. A half alqueire (land measure) of corn required about 24 days' labor and yielded 47 milreis worth of corn, less the cost of carting.

These estimates accord with the findings of the government investigators. In spite of the panic of 1856, most of the indentures were worked off in three to seven years. During their indenturement, nearly all the families acquired animals worth 50 milreis or more, and usually were able to sell improvements made on their dwellings to workers who replaced them. A few of the families were extremely successful and had managed to accumulate as much as 1,000 milreis in credit with the planter. A few, on the other hand, were completely swamped in debts almost as large as slave prices. Some of these were families who had suffered the death of one or more members, and were obliged to pay off, *solidàriamente*, the debts of all. That most were able to buy out of their contracts accords with logic and the later experience of the Paulista West. Free labor *was* more efficient than slave labor. If the planters were willing to resume the exploitation of slaves, they could not have been losing money with indentures.[35]

It is not possible to counter this argument by asserting that European indentured labor, although more efficient, had to be so generously rewarded that it did not yield a profit. The planters charged the going rate of interest on every conceivable advance to the workers, and generally paid no interest on credits the workers accumulated with them. The official reports scarcely show to what extent the planters overcharged their services to the workers—processing of the berries, sales of foodstuffs, tools, and other equipment, and house rentals—but there are a few signs that the planters profited hugely. Valdetaro's report, for instance, shows that Benedito Antônio de Camargo was charging a yearly rental of 12 milreis per family for plantation housing. Camargo claimed that was merely 6 percent interest on the cost of construction; yet the inventory of his property carried out upon his death two years later evaluated the shacks at an average worth of just 30 milreis![36]

It cannot be maintained that free labor, although profitable, was less profitable than slave labor. The slave had a price tag attached to him that was five times higher than the cost of passage of an entire immigrant family, and his first year's keep was at the owner's expense as well. The slave had to be driven, clothed, housed, and cared for, at some minimum expense, and he had to be written off in twenty years (see Table 3.3, p. 53). These costs added up to nearly as much as the share of profits awarded an entire immigrant family. Indeed, the comparison is apt, for a single adult male slave was usually thought able to tend as many trees as an indentured family, that is, 3,000. This was certainly a mistaken impression, which must have been based on a ferocious assumption concerning the effectiveness of the lash in extracting an ultimate degree of exertion from the slaves. The result of assigning so large a number of trees to the slaves was quite certainly a lower yield and a shorter productive life for the trees. By demanding extra effort from the slaves and reducing the amount of time they might devote to their own subsistence, the planters also jeopardized their investment in the slaves. Slaves who died prematurely, furthermore, or ran away, represented a greater loss than the indentured worker in arrears, because mortgages secured with them were either called or doubled in interest.[37]

This exposition is no proof that the employment of slaves was unprofitable. It is true that the slave owners did not calculate depreciation, but it is not likely that they were running generally and unknowingly into bankruptcy. It is much more likely that the calculations of indentured workers' debts and earnings that have been presented are too conservative because they are based on representations by the planters biased in their favor. The relationship between the costs to the planters of the two forms of labor exploitation is reasonably accurate, however: even under parceria, slavery was less profitable to the planters than free labor.

Another sort of argument has never been raised, but ought to be. If the workers were rebellious and uncooperative because they were burdened with excessive charges, why couldn't the planters have improved the deal? What costs were they put to, in settling immigrants on their plantations? Only these: the depreciation and interest on the formed grove, and the administration of the "colony." It has been estimated that the capital investment in the groves and processing equipment came to about 1,500 milreis for 3,000 trees (Table 2.3 and accompanying discussion, pp. 33–34). This would have to be written off in 40 years, at a cost of 127 milreis a year, including 12 percent interest. At Ibicaba there was one director for 62 families, who was paid no more than 1,000 milreis a year in cash and probably received some perquisites, worth altogether about 20 milreis per family. The planter's yearly cost of installing an indentured family, therefore, was about 147 milreis. Yet the parceria contract, in the hypothetical case described above, awarded him 449 milreis in shares on a family's output of 225 arrobas (net shares shown in Table 4.4, less 180 milreis to the worker). The profit, therefore, was about 300 milreis per family-sized plot of 3,000 trees, or 20 percent on capital invested.

These calculations lead to the conclusion that underlying the crisis of 1857 was the necessity of liberalizing the terms of the contracts, brought on by the spread of the system to a larger number of competing plantations and the growing sophistication of the workers regarding local wages and price levels. If the demands of the workers were not to be satisfied, only the application of force could keep them on the job. This was one reason why Vergueiro's fantasy of imminent revolution found so ready a hearing among the other planters. The problem, according to them, was only that they had been too liberal with "men who, having lived in their countries subjected to a very heavy yoke, find themselves here very unbridled." The government, however, faced with the ineluctable necessity of attracting further immigrants, refused to apply the massive force that would be required, and the planters retreated to the employment of slaves.[38]

Another line of analysis has customarily been followed by historians overly ready to credit the complaints of the planters. It was their opinion that the indenture system collapsed because the immigrants were of inferior quality. The Swiss and German towns had allegedly dealt underhandedly with their own citizens. They had impressed the undesirable among them—drunks, idiots, crippled, and senile—in some cases obliging families to claim them as members before they would advance the passage money.[39]

It happens that the parceria system was undertaken at the moment that emigration was suddenly a matter of survival for millions of European peasants. The potato failure of the late 1840's ravaged central Europe and obliged not only the landless but even smallholders to emigrate—sometimes entire villages, bought out by nobles using cash paid them for the extinction of their feudalities. Elsewhere, as in Switzerland, the emigration was forced by the sudden surge in population among smallholders who could subdivide no further. The 1850 census records that 10,000 out of a population of 90,000 permanently emigrated from the canton of Graubünden. The refugees included, no doubt, criminals and other undesirables, but overwhelmingly they were simply the poor, both wage earners and peasants. There were town councils in Germany—but not, apparently, in Switzerland—that subsidized their departure in the hope of avoiding social disorders. Undoubtedly they rid themselves just as commonly of the most ambitious and energetic of their lower-class citizens. Overwhelmingly the Germans and Swiss sought the ports of Hamburg and Antwerp for passage to the United States, but some few set out for Brazil and Australia because the passage money was advanced. Migration studies show that selectivity is at a minimum when, as in central Europe in the 1850's, the push of local economic conditions is strong. The emigrants who chose the Paulista West, then, were probably on the average poorer than those who went to the United States and Canada, but there is no reason to suppose that there were any other differences. If the indentured workers were truly inferior human stock, it would be a remarkable historical exception.[40]

The manner in which complaints were raised against the workers awakens strong suspicion that they were merely justifications after the fact. In particular, Vergueiro's role as forwarding agent of supposed incompetents is oddly paradoxical. Tschudi implied that Vergueiro was a party to the fraud because he was only interested in collecting his commission from other planters. Surely, however, he would not have accepted misfits on his own plantation, and yet Davatz's account of his arrival at Ibicaba shows that the parceling out of the families among the planters was utterly random! The immigrants themselves would have had reason to become embittered and alienated from their home towns, had they really been dealt with as the planters afterward alleged. Instead they showed the Swiss agents and the German consuls complete trust and expected to be vindicated. In the case of the Swiss towns, the accusation of impressment appears to be quite unfounded, considering their strong evidences of concern: the commissioning of Davatz to answer an extremely detailed questionnaire on conditions in São Paulo, the quickness in canceling the repayment of advances they had made, and the immediate dispatch of an agent to investigate the complaints of the immigrants.

Davatz's account does not contradict the charge that some of the immigrants in Switzerland had been unemployed paupers, but this he laid to the hopelessness of their condition there. He insisted

that even these, as long as they thought they could clear their indebtedness and start life afresh, were industrious and self-confident.
On the other hand, some of the families had been in Switzerland
prosperous enough to have saved money. Those who came to Ibicaba and Angélica in 1855 possessed among them an average of 50
milreis each. Nearly all of the workers, however, lost interest in
the groves when it began to seem impossible to clear themselves
of debt. Indeed, Valdetaro contradicts his own analysis when he
mentions, as another reason for the inability of the immigrants to
pay their debts, their expectation of too high a level of consumption. Yet the neat houses, tiled and limed with their own hands,
full of furniture they had made, and utensils, tools, remedies, pre-
serves, and animals, all observed by Valdetaro, were evidences not
of their luxuriousness but of their industriousness. Valdetaro's
manifest distaste for prosperity among the peasantry was symptom-
atic of a counterproductive and malign ideology that obstructed
the evolution of Brazilian agriculture.[41]

More than half the immigrants in the levy that accompanied
Davatz were craftsmen of various kinds. This has frequently been
alleged to signify that they were therefore unacquainted with
farming. Since the Swiss had come from an extremely rural area—
the largest town in Graubünden contained only 6,000 inhabitants
in the 1850's—few of the immigrants could have been anything
but farmers exercising craft occupations part-time. Craft specializa-
tion in rural areas in Europe was indeed usually a sign of poor soils
and extreme subdivision of plots. It might be more logically inferred that as craftsmen the immigrants were as a group better able
to reconstruct their material culture in a primitive environment.
Indeed, Afonso d'Escragnolle Taunay contradictorily took that
position in regard to the later Italian immigrant group. Sérgio
Buarque de Holanda avoided it by denigrating the cultural contributions of the Germans and Swiss in the Paulista West compared
to a group of American Southerners who settled in the counties of
Santa Barbara and Vila Americana after the Civil War. The spoke-
wheeled wagon is always mentioned as an introduction of the
Americans, yet the American missionary Kidder found them at
Ibicaba, constructed by Germans, twelve years before the South-

erners arrived. The *tróli* maker in Rio Claro was a formerly indentured Swiss, João Jacob Meyer, who established his shop in
1854.[42]

It is sophistic in the extreme to examine the credentials of the
immigrants without examining those of the planters. At least as
many of them, proportionately, failed in their businesses, committed theft, got drunk, and beat their wives, not to mention their
slaves. Their eccentricities and personal shortcomings had greater
effect on labor relations than those of the workers. By some standards the workers may well be considered the superiors of the landowners. Unlike the planters, for example, the Germans and Swiss
were nearly all literate. They signed their names to contracts in
the 1850's while their employers scratched X's. Nine out of ten of
the Swiss and German women cosigning contracts were literate,
but eight out of ten planters' wives were not. These considerations
are not essential to an analysis of the parceria system, however.
At worst the incapacity of a few of the immigrants might have been
provided for by the planters with a small reserve to cover bad
debts. Clarifying and liberalizing the contract might well have
eliminated most of the need for it.[43]

On the other hand, the planters were not prepared to deal with
the indentured workers on a sheerly contractual basis. In a sense
the system presumed, as Sérgio Buarque de Holanda has pointed
out, absolute confidence of the worker in his employer. The onerous conditions of the contract were essential to the planter's style
of control: they could be selectively removed in reward for ex-
pressions of loyalty and respect. Increasing productivity or even
salvaging the contractual relationship were considerations of less
importance. Yet the paternalism of the planters could operate only
if the employees accepted the role of dependents. "In his dealings
with these people he, in my opinion, shows too openly that he
regards them as minors," observed the Dutch coffee expert van
Delden Laerne in 1881. The European workers, however, perceived
this manipulativeness as sheer intimidation. They responded by
appealing to the public authorities to reimpose the contractual
relationship.[44]

The planters, in turn, were first enraged, then terrified by this reaction. They had not imagined it possible that the workers would be capable of raising protests, organizing, and demanding investigations. Recourse to another authority was the supreme disloyalty, and it could only have been exercised by ingrates bent on subverting all of society, under the influence of outsiders with diabolical ambitions. The workers saw in the planters' consequent refusal to consider their demands a desire to subjugate them not merely to peonage but to slavery. Indeed, the usages of the planters encouraged this apprehension long before the crisis. One planter to whom Vergueiro had arbitrarily transferred a group of Germans told them, "I bought you from Senator Vergueiro; you belong to me." The mortgages of the planters show that they were using the debts of the immigrants as loan collateral, just as though they were the head prices of slaves. In a very late contract, dated November 1881, an *empresário* agreed to assign to "the tending of the aforementioned coffee groves three slaves and three *colonos* whom he at present possesses, the former leased and the latter contracted."[45]

This association of the roles of employer and slave driver in the minds of the immigrants had its counterpart in the planters' fear that the indentured workers and the slaves would somehow combine against them. "For the Brazilian planters," said Carvalho de Moraes, "it has always been and continues to be the motive of serious apprehension that simultaneously on his agricultural establishment exist free workers and slaves." This was simply a fantasy of bad conscience. Unfortunately for the social evolution of Brazil, the free workers maintained their distance from the captives. Davatz was obtuse enough to claim, in his memoir, that the indenture system was worse than slavery. Although the Europeans pitied them for their condition, after a fashion, they feared entrapment in it too much to see them as allies. It cannot be denied that they were intimidated by black skins and African culture, and thought of them as a sign of their estrangement from the familiar and longed-for Europe.[46]

In response to the events at Ibicaba, the imperial government published a regulation in November 1858 designed to mitigate the harshness of the indenture contract. Apparently it was effective in

its principal provisions, that no contract could extend more than
five years, after which time the cost of transportation was no longer
collectable, and that no transfer was valid without the worker's
consent. Other clauses were ignored. Housing, for example, was
to be free of rent, but most of the contracts in the notarial archive
continued to charge for housing. Members of the family remained
responsible for the debts of all, and the major deformity of the
Employment Law of 1837 was preserved—workers were still subject to imprisonment for noncompletion of contract. The relationship therefore continued to be essentially a form of peonage, since
the planter could not be imprisoned if he failed to carry out *his*
obligations. In 1879 a reformed employment law was passed, a
small forward step. Jail was still the fate of the worker who departed the plantation without leave, but only for a maximum of
60 days. Even then landowners in Rio Claro were still denouncing
recalcitrant workers to the court, which sometimes imprisoned
them without troubling to hear their testimony.[47]

For more than a decade after the "uprising" of 1857, the planters
showed little interest in reviving the importation of free laborers.
Their dismay long outlasted the crisis, and all began buying slaves
once again. A year later the county council of Rio Claro still
lamented that the "discouragement has been general, since the
rebels were not suppressed, and the proprietors consider themselves
to be without security, so that the planting will hardly or not at
all continue." Even more remarkable than the planters' estimation
of slaves as less dangerous than free workers was their willingness to
pay much higher prices for them than they had ever paid before.
Young males cost less than 1,000 milreis in 1854; by 1858 they sold
for 2,000, when they could be gotten at all.[48]

A few of the planters, in spite of their pessimism, continued to
maintain "colonies" under a modified regime. Parceria contracts
gradually disappeared and most of the tending of the groves came
to be carried out *por ajuste*. Under this contract the planter paid
the worker a flat sum in cash for each alqueire of beans delivered.
This arrangement, already in effect on a few plantations before the
strikes of 1856, ended effectively complaints and suspicions con-

cerning sale prices and measures, and eliminated the long delay between harvest and reckoning. The amount paid was usually .40 milreis per alqueire, or half that earned by the workers on shares at Ibicaba in 1856. Although the workers no longer suffered the fraud of calculating three alqueires to one arroba of beans, the result was still substantially in favor of the planter. By 1860 the price of coffee had risen from 4.40 to 5.90 milreis per arroba; thus the worker would have been earning twice as much if he had continued under parceria. Some of the contracts por ajuste kept the requirement of half the proceeds of sales from the subsistence plots; others charged rent for the plots.[49]

It is difficult to estimate how many free workers remained in the Paulista West in the 1860's because the provincial government no longer kept track of them. There were remnants of the original parceria group. The majority, however, were Brazilians from the local area and from Minas Gerais. These were agregados and day workers accepting a minor shift in status. Since tending the trees was more efficiently done by families and was less transient than camarada tasks like forest clearing, the por ajuste contract was sometimes a necessity for young men who had acquired a family. Nevertheless, on most of the plantations, day laborers and agregados remained the only form of wage labor employed. Since the agregados were useful mainly for the protection of the estate boundaries, their elimination coincided with settlement of most of the disputes and more intensive use of the land.[50]

Of the Europeans, only Portuguese continued to arrive, under indenture contracts as onerous as before, at prices lower than immigrants embarking from ports more distant. One of these indentures in Rio Claro came under police investigation in 1867, possibly at the instigation of political enemies. Five years before, José Elias Pacheco Jordão, owner of two plantations in the county, had personally contracted 23 Portuguese minors just landed in Rio de Janeiro. None were older than fourteen, and three were only eight. They were to serve three years (although agents in Portugal had told them their term would be only eighteen months) and to pay off their transport, and were to be properly fed, clothed, and cared for, and to receive one milreis a month in cash. The extremities of desperation and hard dealing displayed in the contract are shocking, but the planter did not intend to carry out even these small obligations. The depositions assembled by the chief of police showed, in his opinion, that "Doctor Jordão does not appear to be a planter kind to his slaves or humane, as, in general, are the masters in Brazil ... nor has he toward these [children] applied a treatment which his own interest should have counseled him." The children claimed that they had been fed only meager rations of corn and beans, they had been beaten and whipped, and when their three years were up, they were prevented from leaving. They said they had received no medical attention, and two, or perhaps three, had died. All but five had fled to Campinas.[51]

A report to the Minister of Agriculture in 1870 stated that the planters, hoping to work their slaves a while longer, were unwilling to experiment with indentures again. "Shifting between doubts and hopes, planning projects and delaying their execution, they turn their eyes from the future, or wait for events to propose or impose the solution that must put an end to their indecision." Only a few months later, slave unrest in the Paulista West caused great anxiety among the planters. The provincial assembly returned to the indenture scheme. A law was passed authorizing a fund of 600,000 milreis for loans to assist planters in importing workers. The loans were at 6 percent, but eleven years were allowed for repayment. A few planters in Rio Claro responded. Ignácio Xavier de Negreiros and Antônio Paes de Barros, the only planters still operating colonies, were joined by Silvério Rodrigues Jordão, inheritor of Morro Azul plantation, who refounded its colony. Meanwhile the baron of Pôrto Feliz established colonies on his Cafesal, Boa Vista, and Cascalho plantations, and the baron of Araraquara (another of the sons of the viscount of Rio Claro) began another on his São José plantation. Angélica, which the Vergueiros, whose fortunes were declining, had sold off to their creditors, the London and Brazilian Bank, resumed operations with an entirely free labor force. This was an extraordinary novelty —only two or three other free plantations existed in the province—

but unhappily it was not a successful one. The English managers were drunken incompetents who brutalized the workers and led the estate into bankruptcy.[52]

The contingent of Brazilian workers in Rio Claro was a motley one. It included migrants escaping the great drought of the northeastern provinces. Perhaps 3,000 settled in the Paulista West in 1877 and 1878; more than 600 of them were hired by the manager of Angélica plantation. There were also remnants of the pioneer squatting population, agregados brought in by the first planters, escaped slaves, freedmen manumitted locally or in other counties, second-generation refugees from failed official colonies in Rio Grande do Sul, Santa Catarina, and São Paulo, and—probably the largest group—unattached young males of smallholding or agregado families in Minas Gerais and other parts of São Paulo. These were classified as day workers or unemployed, and they had come to Rio Claro because of higher wages.[53]

Their relations with the planters were no doubt deferential and cast in those terms that were expected to lead to greater preferment, as they had formerly. But they were transients and the planters were increasingly absentee. Their most likely prospect, then, was not to attain the long-term unsalaried tenure of the agregado, a niche that was disappearing, but to obtain the sort of contract offered the Europeans, with cash payments and yearly renewal. The Brazilian workers, much less visible than the Europeans, were passed over in government reports because they presented no diplomatic difficulties, nor did they present the problem of credit for an initial transport indebtedness.

The in-migration of free workers from other provinces was so constant a factor in the growth of the plantations that it is surprising so little attention was paid to it. Possibly Brazilian workers might have resolved the labor crisis without resort to Europeans, had an effort been made to recruit them. This solution was indeed proposed by the provincial president, José Joaquim Fernandes Torres, in the wake of the failure of Ibicaba. By the 1870's sufficient regional wage differential may have existed to attract native workers from other parts of Brazil to temporary work on the plantations in preference to squatting, smallholding subsistence farming, or sharecropping in their own localities. The planters never sought them out, possibly because they disparaged the abilities of their mixed-race compatriots, or because the transfer of free workers presented potentially a greater political challenge than the interprovincial slave trade.[54]

Europeans continued to arrive in small numbers, mainly Italians contracted to lay railroad tracks, who then accepted work in the coffee groves. A few others, mostly Portuguese, were brought in directly. The contracts offered after 1871 were somewhat more favorable to the workers (Table 4.5). Payment per alqueire rose to .50 or .60 milreis, but this rate declined as a separate sum came to be paid for each hoeing of the trees, a task performed four or five times each season. The pay for hoeing, designed to prevent neglect of the groves between harvests, doubled the average income of the workers, but in the meantime the price of coffee and the general price level had risen about 30 percent. Reynaldo Kuntz Busch copied the accounts of 159 families on Ibicaba plantation for the decade beginning 1862 (Table 4.6). The real rate of saving may have

TABLE 4.5
*Wages in Contracts por Ajuste, 1856–80*

| Year | Milreis per alqueire harvested | Milreis per hoeing thousand trees | Estimated yearly family wages |
|------|------|------|------|
| 1856 | .40 | No pay | 220 |
| 1858 | .44 | No pay | 242 |
| 1863 | .40 | No pay | 220 |
| 1870 | .55 | No pay | 302 |
| 1874 | .50 | 10.00 | 395 |
| 1875 | .50 | 12.00 | 419 |
| 1876 | .49 | 5.00 | 329 |
| 1878 | .22 | 10.00 | 240 |
| 1880 | .55 | 11.00 | 434 |

SOURCES. 1856–58: Manuel de Jesús Valdetaro, "Colonias de S. Paulo," annex to Brazil, Repartição Geral das Terras Públicas, *Relatorio*, 1858, p. 19. 1863: APESP, Colônias, 1, Nov. 23, 1863. 1870: J. P. Carvalho de Moraes, *Relatorio*, Annex, RC/C-2, LN, Sept. 26, 1870. 1874–75: Domingos Jaguaribe, *Algumas palavras sobre a emigração*, pp. 29–40. 1876: APESP, Colônias, 3, Oct. 26, 1876. 1878: RC/C-2, LN, April 8, 1877. 1880: Visconde de Indaiatuba, "Memorandum sobre o início de colonização da fazenda 'Sete Quedas' no município de Campinas em 1852," in Campinas, Câmara Municipal, *Monografia histórica do município de Campinas*, p. 249. Family wage estimate assumes 3,000 trees per family, 225 arrobas yield, 4 hoeings per year.

TABLE 4.6

*Accounts of Indentured Workers, Ibicaba Plantation, 1862–72*

| Category | Number of families | Average number of years | Milreis credits per family | Credits per family per year |
|---|---|---|---|---|
| Families with credits: | | | | |
| Years on Ibicaba known | 76 | 4.46 | 318 | 71 |
| Years not indicated | 36 | 8.27 | 516 | 62 |
| Families with debits: | | | | |
| Years on Ibicaba known | 21 | 2.40 | — | — |
| Years not indicated | 26 | 5.25 | — | — |

SOURCE. Reynaldo Kuntz Busch, *História de Limeira*, pp. 192–95. From "Livro V de assentamentos," Ibicaba plantation. Two families whose debts were paid by relatives were omitted.

been different from that inferred in the table, because some of the families may have arrived with debts, including sea transportation. Most of the families, however, were probably not new immigrants, and most seem to have been the possessors of savings sufficient to offset at least part of the first year's advances. Some seem to have had large savings, which they kept with the administrator. As a guess, then, the initial indebtedness averaged about 100 milreis (compare Table 4.3), and consequently the real rate of yearly earnings above necessities was between 75 and 85 milreis for those 112 families with credits. This calculation is speculative, but it accords with the estimates made above concerning the earnings and expenses of indentured families under parceria contracts. It would seem, then, that the por ajuste regime did not represent an improvement from the worker's point of view, at least until the payments for hoeing were added in the 1870's.[55]

The apparent rate of saving displayed in Table 4.6 was barely sufficient to acquire a smallholding. The average family would need about 10 alqueires (24.2 hectares), assuming the soil was adequately fertile, to sustain a decent standard of living, including the ownership of a cow or some goats and pigs. Ten alqueires cost about 750 milreis, or the savings of at least eight years beyond the four or five needed by the immigrants to clear the initial indebtedness. Productivity, effort, and luck beyond the average were therefore necessary if an immigrant family was to be able to install itself as smallholders. The sale registries of Rio Claro show only 60 sales of rural property to persons with German surnames up to 1873. The average value of these plots was 700 milreis; eleven of them were less than 300 in value, and eleven were more than 1,000. Some of the owners were not originally indentured workers but had arrived as merchants or professionals. At least six of the holdings belonged to persons who had been directors of colonies, including the three largest: Guilherme Lebeis (4,000 milreis), J. Schmid and Carlos Koch (7,000 milreis), and João Vollet (12,000 milreis). These four had all married into planter families. At least ten of the properties were owned by persons whose savings were accumulated after leaving the plantations and setting up in trades in town. By 1872 about 10 percent of the population of Rio Claro was German or Swiss. Landownership, therefore, was slightly more common among them than among the general population—there were about 500 properties in the county at the time—but their area was a very small proportion of the total, and landholdings remained as concentrated as before.[56]

If, after an average twenty years in Brazil, nine-tenths or more of the indentured workers remained landless, it must be concluded that smallholding was difficult to achieve, or to remain successful at. Yet smallholding was the essential inducement to any program of unsubsidized immigration. Provincial authorities, and even some of the planters, recognized the great advantages in attracting workers who paid their own way and brought savings with them. José Vergueiro was quite frank in admitting that smallholding was not only a just and reasonable aspiration; it was necessary for the "social evolution" of Brazil. Carvalho de Moraes quoted an extraordinary letter by an anonymous planter in a provincial newspaper: "The great estates are only of advantage (if they are, which is doubtful) to their few lucky owners; the great mass of the people suffer on their account . . . ; the smallholders are those who provide the measure of felicity of a people, turning them energetic, hardworking, and rich." Official propaganda, therefore, always dangled the promise of eventual landownership to prospective immigrants. But optimistic pamphleteering was of practically no value com-

pared to reports sent back by relatives and fellow townsmen. Still
more effective would have been the transmittal of remittances,
or the return of at least a few of the workers to their home towns
after "making America." But there was none of this, evidently,
among the indentured laborers. Some of the town merchants may
have made remittances, but not until the turn of the century were
any of them to become prosperous enough to return to Europe
for retirement.[57]

By 1876, 45 plantations in Rio Claro employed some free as well
as slave labor, and there were several dozen small farms—sítios—
with a few thousand trees each, owned by townspeople and leased
out to a free tenant family or two. The transition had not been
achieved, however. There were still 22 other plantations with no
free hands at all. Many of the free workers were doubtless agregados
or day workers, hence merely auxiliary to the main labor force.
The slaves were in any case still in the majority. In 1872 about
1,700 free persons were employees or tenants on plantations and
sítios, compared to 2,753 slaves. The wage labor force had grown
not much more than half as fast as the slave force in the fifteen
years after the debacle of 1857.[58]

The domination of the county by slave-owning planters had
not abated; indeed, they were strengthened by gains from improvements in productivity that they had not distributed among
the labor force. Something of their preeminence may be glimpsed
in the obsequies observed upon the death of the viscount of Rio
Claro in 1884. Founder of the town, leader of its Liberal party
machine, several times president of the county council, co-organizer
of the Rio Claro Railway, and head of the largest landed clan in
the county, José Estanislau de Melo Oliveira was ennobled in 1867.
All of his twelve children, six male and six female, were provided
with plantations from his estates. Two of his sons and two sons-in-
law were styled barons, and a third son-in-law, the viscount's most
valuable ally in the Liberal party and the boss of neighboring São
Carlos, rose to the eminence of count.

The whole town joined the cortege; its leaders vied for the
handles of the coffin and bore the banners of the social clubs, hung

with crepe. The doors of all the merchants shut for three days. The viscount's obituaries called him a devoted father, a loyal and sincere friend, a true father of the poor, a Paulista of the old stripe, and a dedicated friend of hard-working men, whom he was always ready to help, with his influence and his money. The last referred to his loan business. Indeed, his will showed how thoroughly he had transformed into a capitalist. He divested himself of his lands before he died. The São José plantation, worth 260,000 milreis, was turned over to two of his daughters. Other plantations in Dourados and Analândia had been transferred earlier to his sons. The remainder of his fortune of 1,177,775 milreis was in loans, urban real estate, and stocks—principally railroad shares, which amounted to 798,310 milreis.[59]

Indentured European immigrants remained an inadequate source of labor on Rio Claro's plantations. While the proletarians of Europe flowed in ever greater number to the United States, Argentina, and other "new" countries, Brazil found itself unable to attract more than a few thousand a year. Attempts to reanimate indentures in the early 1870's had no more success than they had twenty years before. The planters procrastinated, not because wage labor was unprofitable but because they could not deal on a purely contractual basis with a real proletariat. Admittedly this was an immense paradox, for all the rest of their dealings, in land, in credit, in machine and transport investments, were altogether capitalistic. But the planters continued to fear, perhaps rightly, that competitively established wages would bestow on the workers the means of destroying their monopoly in the land, and thereby of overturning their society. Therefore, back to the dealing in slaves. All this appears lamentably regressive, and indeed it was. The planters were not capable of bringing about the great transformation through self-criticism. Their slaves had to persuade them to review their assumptions. The process required nearly twenty more years.

# CHAPTER 5

# The End of Slavery

IN APRIL 1871, 57 planters of Rio Claro demanded of the president of the province that he post a permanent military garrison in the county.[1]

At present the necessity grows in importance of a public force in the city at the disposition of the authorities when from the volcano on which we tread begin the explosions. On the 27th instant at 1:30 PM twenty slaves of José Ferraz de Sampaio, after having killed the *feitor*, departed in broad daylight from the plantation, passing through Limeira at 4 o'clock in the afternoon, and continued on, quite confident of not being pursued, since they harbored the conviction that they had exercised a right. The undersigned make no comment on the event, but they believe that it did not arise out of the same cause as others of an identical result, and only hope from Yr. Excy. the precautions necessary to free this city from the terror in which it finds itself.

Another petition had been sent two weeks earlier by 275 planters and merchants of Campinas with the same purpose. It cited the increase in size of the slave population and acknowledged the "perpetual divorce of the two races," which were "enemies treating each other not with embraces and tenderness," but there were, besides this, "peculiar circumstances" justifying "grave apprehension." An uprising was not alleged—the petition specifically discounted that fear as groundless. What worried the planters was more diffuse and more dangerous. Formerly, the petition stated, Brazil's slaves were nearly all African-born, in a state of "brutishness and limited understanding," therefore the slave owners were easily able to subject them. But now they had been replaced by creoles.

These, born and educated among us, and consequently participating in our nature, customs, and endowed with an intellectual horizon much broader than their primitive stock, tend toward aspirations compatible with their development and therefore toward liberating themselves from that passive subservience of their forebears.

Their promiscuous intimate relations [are] enlarged by crossing with the free population, [which] gives a type intermediate between the African and Latin races, and has enabled them to dispute the right of property that the law imposes on them and to doubt the legitimacy and logic of this same law. Their faculties achieve that which was unattainable by the Africans. Their spirit ill supports the yoke of slavery and seeks to free itself, as is revealed by facts repeated on all sides.

Thus it is that, questioning a slave of São João de Rio Claro, for what reason he had murdered his owner, he replied that *"he knew not the reason why he had to work his entire life for the exclusive benefit of a man no better than he."* [Italics in original.]

The permanent posting of soldiers was now even more necessary, the petition concluded, because the slaves had observed the panic of the free population in February and March, and had drawn the conclusion that the planters were weak. The planters' apprehensions were taken seriously by the provincial president. He sent an additional 50 riflemen from a battalion stationed in São Paulo.[2]

These extraordinary documents reveal a great deal about the transformation of the slave system after the abolition of the traffic. Although the petitions originated in the midst of the planter class, they admit the critical points of the abolitionist argument, before abolitionism presented any sort of political challenge. The slaves were undeserving of their fate, and their acquisition of Brazilian culture entitled them to freedom. Only force, the planters recognized, would henceforth be effective in maintaining an illegitimate law. Their only justification was the need to salvage the "prosperity, looming large in the eyes of the Province and the Empire," of the Campinas region—that is, the planters' prosperity. By 1871 the slave owners were morally bankrupt and were obliged to beg the central government to shoulder more of the greatly increased cost of repression.

These petitions shed light on the reasons for the passage of the Law of Free Birth, which was presented to the general assembly two weeks after they were written, debated all winter, and finally approved late in September. Although it has often been noted that the bill originated amid increasing slave unrest, engendered

indirectly by the Paraguayan war, and that the emperor pro-
pounded the possibility of slave rebellion as a motive for drafting
it, historians have been concerned mostly with the personal political struggles of the parliamentary chiefs, the altruism of the emperor, or tangential issues such as regionalism. This analysis appears ingenuous, considering the scale of the social crisis represented by the impending abolition. It could hardly have been the
work of a single man, or even of a few dozen, nor was it a side issue,
of a lesser size than others. More systematic analysis centers upon
the supposed development of the Brazilian economy—the growing
demand of the capitalist mode of production for greater specializa-
tion and the appearance of urban, in particular industrial, occupations. It is presumed that the planters perceived that free labor
was more productive than slave labor and that free labor was necessary for further growth. Yet none of these developments were
beyond the fetal stage in 1871, and surely the slave states of the
United States had proceeded a great deal further down the road
of capitalist development without ever sensing the need to renounce slavery, up to the moment of armed intervention from the
North. Abolitionist sentiment among the urban middle class was
insignificant in 1871, and the planters believed almost unanimously
that the abolition of slavery would result in mass flight from the
plantations, their financial ruin, and the collapse of class-based
society. Explanations that parallel ideologically the assumptions of
the slavocracy may be considered inherently defective. It is un-
acceptable to regard the slaves as inert, passive beings, whose role
was altered only when conditions beyond their reach or understanding had changed. Indeed, all of those conditions did vary
marginally over the course of the nineteenth century, but the slaves
changed much more.[3]

The petitions of Rio Claro and Campinas show that the slaves
had come to articulate questions of the legitimacy of their bondage.
It is also evident that the reason for the awakening of this revolutionary mentality was that the slave group had undergone a significant structural change. Before the extinction of the traffic, the
slave force was composed in the main of Africans of recent arrival,

members of different tribes thrown together indiscriminately, the whole mass controlled partly through the mediation of creole slaves, many of them mulattos, who were preferred in domestic and skilled occupations. For this latter group the escape valve of manumission was at least a possibility. It is not to be assumed that mulatto slaves were preferred out of sentiments arising from consanguinity. The mulatto gained his freedom, when he did, because his ambitiousness and aggressiveness were more effectively focused, making it harder for the owner to avoid rewarding him. Mulattos were probably less kindly regarded by the white elites than were the blacks; precisely because of their awakened desire for social mobility they were, and are, considered "pushy." The mulattos responded to the unease of the whites with heightened defensiveness, hostility, and guilt.[4]

Once the traffic ended, the African portion of the work force grew older and less numerous, while the native-born force was diverted from domestic occupations to fill gaps in the field gangs. Increasingly the slaves would be more mulatto as well as more creole. It took a generation for this process to produce a major block to the expectations of the slaves. In Rio Claro from 1846 to 1856, manumissions among a slave group averaging perhaps 1,000 had run about four per year. After the failure of the *parceria* system, they declined up to 1870 to little more than three per year in a slave population averaging about 2,500. Thus an 8.0 percent chance of manumission within the twenty-year life expectancy of the average slave had fallen to 2.4 percent. A lighter skin had ceased to be a guarantee of preferential treatment, and even a slave three-quarters white had lessened hope of manumission. Abruptly the rules had changed. The planters attest to the ability of the creole slaves to rationalize their grievances. They had absorbed the rhetoric of egalitarianism and citizenship. When a second-generation slave deposed, he did not refer to himself as a "creole" but as a "Brazilian." The Paulista West would be a main arena of the emerging struggle because there, more than anywhere else in Brazil, the planters had a strong market incentive to renege upon the incentives formerly available to the native-born and the mulattos.

The central provision of the Law of 1871 was not original, since the freeing at birth of all children born of slave mothers was a measure employed by gradualists elsewhere in the Americas. Yet it was remarkable as a response to the restiveness of the slaves. When the emperor's concern was expressed to the Council of State, its members considered at first the possibility of setting a terminal date for slavery. But an early date, they foresaw, would anger the slave owners and probably cause them to lose control of the slaves almost immediately, while a date set too remote in the future (one of them thought 1930 reasonable!) would, in the words of the viscount Rio Branco, "kill all hopes of the slaves." The councilors, significantly, were not in a position to kill the slaves' hopes, and therefore they abandoned setting a term and chose instead to proclaim the "free womb."[5]

The scheme had great attractiveness in a legal sense. Chattel slavery was abolished, since the slaves were no longer reproducible things like horses or cows, but were endowed with an undeniable attribute of personality: they gave birth to citizens. State power might thereby be extended much further into the *quadrado*. On the other hand, planters would be somewhat mollified by the abstention from interference with their rights of property. The state confiscated nothing already theirs. These advantages could be readily expressed in the debates of the general assembly. Unspoken was the thought that the bill also shored up the system in the eyes of the silent constituency of slaves, who not only acquired the wombs of human beings but were also recognized to have parental feelings, to be ambitious for the fate of their offspring, and to be worthy of the responsibility of rearing free citizens. The concession was not only timely, it was shrewd: the freeborn children—the *ingênuos*—would be daily reminders of the state's generosity and hostages to the continued good conduct of the parents. Within each gang the hierarchy of seniority, collaboration, and arranged marriages would be reinforced.

The law appeared to hold out the prospect of increased manumissions. Each province was to distribute funds to local boards, which were to see that all slaves in the county were registered for the purpose and to classify them according to certain criteria. Slaves were to be allowed to deposit their savings with local judges, who would determine their value and manumit them when the deposits were sufficient, whether the owner was willing or not. Furthermore, the law repealed the odious colonial ordinance which gave the owner the right to revoke acts of manumission in case of "ingratitude." Balancing these new opportunities, the law sought to guarantee continued submission by the slaves and to extract steady wage labor from the freedmen. Slaves who made attempts on the lives of owners or *feitores*, who committed any other crime, who tried to run off, or who were habitual drunks were to be struck from the classification. Freedmen had to produce valid work contracts for five years after manumission or they would be declared vagrants and set to work on public roads.

The planters of Rio Claro were hostile to the law, since the crisis of the 1871 harvest was already over, and they could count on the presence of a permanent army garrison. It seemed to them to be an arbitrary act of "improvidence," and the county council guardedly accused the government of "encouraging inertia and dissension, and by making work more necessary to supply the necessities of life, [it] increases the labor shortage against which we struggle in agriculture and industry." Their reaction, then, was to delay carrying out the provisions of the law, to evade them where possible, to use their local political power to avoid prosecution, and even to turn some of its provisions to their own benefit. Robert Conrad and Emília Viotti da Costa mention many instances of delay and evasion, especially in the setting up of the Emancipation Boards and the distribution of the funds assigned for the purpose, and in overvaluations of the slaves to be freed. In Rio Claro the first emancipation quota was not distributed until 1877. The complaints that appear in official correspondence can be assigned too great an importance, however. Nearly all governmental functions were carried out imperfectly at the local level, especially when they were unpaid. The valuations of slaves by the boards may have in individual cases provided neat profits to the owners who gave them up, but the existence of the boards probably contributed to the general decline in slave prices that is observable after 1880 (see Table 3.4, p. 55).[6]

In spite of the delaying tactics of the planters, the local bureaucrats were required by the law, and by a hail of regulations and circulars that followed—115 in all—to intervene in the relations between owner and slave, and occasionally, if only for their own political purposes, they could not resist doing so. One planter of Limeira, foreseeing officiousness and disrespect, swore he would rather have total abolition at once. The planters, he said, "ought not to delegate the examination of their affairs, of their lives, to the eyes of strangers, indifferent, or what's worse, hypocritically dedicated." The owners were aware that official intervention was eroding their control. They resented the fact that the emancipation boards, and not they, decided which slaves were selected for manumission, and that the slave now had the right, independent of their wishes, to contract for his own freedom.[7]

The planters' attempts to reassert their moral authority were sometimes ludicrous. When one was called to account for his failure to register an ingênuo, he replied that he thought it unnecessary, since he had personally freed him at baptism. The baron of Grão-Mogol, the same whose cellar orgies with slave women were local social events, in 1881 caused to be transcribed in the notary's book a statement he had made to a notary in Minas Gerais while he was still resident there, dated one month after the Law of Free Birth was passed:

I, the undersigned, having up to now kept in captivity not one child born of my slaves, for the pain I feel upon thinking of passing them from the tenderness with which I raise them to the rigor of an austere captivity, so much more so, considering the false base of property, I resolved for this reason to free the wombs of all the slaves I possess and of all I may come to possess, since the march toward the redemption of this part of humanity oppressed by slavery, by God's mercy, travels toward the point of equality established by the Redeemer.

Strangely, the baron appears to assert a private validation of a public law, and thought worthwhile to reaffirm it ten years later. He did not scruple to imply that he intended to go on buying slaves, and in fact when he transferred to Rio Claro, he brought with him a large gang of newly purchased slaves to Angélica plantation, which he had bought from the London and Brazilian Bank. He had great difficulty bringing them into the province without paying a prohibitive tax, and it may be that he was trying by means of this pious declaration to impress local bureaucrats.[8]

The slaves noticed the embarrassment of their owners. "After the Law of 1871," remarked a speaker in the provincial assembly on the eve of abolition, "relations of the master toward the slave shifted, which was more accentuated upon the abolition of the lash [1886]; and thus whenever the master departs from the legal conditions, he practices an action punished by the Criminal Code ... the effects of all the legislative acts breaking little by little the moral authority of the master over the slave." Another representative characterized the law a "disaster" because it "caused a fatal transformation in the spirit of the slaves." The municipal judges, "inexperienced and precipitate young men," were constantly calling planters into court "at the most trifling complaint of a slave or an ingênuo, for having received a simple light correction indispensable to maintaining the discipline of a plantation."[9]

In another way the Law of 1871 subtly undermined the slave regime. The ingênuos, being legally no one's property, could not serve as loan collateral. The emancipation boards, meanwhile, by setting low valuations on adult slaves, also limited the amounts banks would lend on the slave gang. The credit squeeze of the 1870's was at least partly the result of the failure of the planters to persuade the banks to write mortgages mainly on land and coffee trees. That reform was extremely unlikely to occur, however, until final abolition.

From 1871 onward the pattern of manumissions in Rio Claro was very clearly affected by conditions beyond the bounds of the plantation. A flurry occurred in 1871–72, when 30 were freed, doubtless because of the *grand peur* and the passage of the Law of Free Birth. Only one of those manumissions was a retroactive application of the law to a small child. The owner was a priest, João de Santa Caridade. One manumission was carried out with funds from a Masonic lodge, "Fraternidade," located in the capital. It has been mentioned by Emília Viotti da Costa as one of the first private organizations in the province to embrace abolitionism. Another manumission of a domestic worker and her four children was the first to propose "just remuneration" for her term of employment, but it also insisted on an indefinite term—the owner's lifetime—contrary to the law, which limited terms to seven years.[10]

A second wave of 38 manumissions took place in 1878–79 during the credit squeeze and a sudden heavy purchase of slaves in the interprovincial market. In that situation, it suddenly became necessary to raise cash quickly, and the first term transfers of slaves appeared. In Rio Claro the first manumission of this sort occurred in 1876. Maria Luiza Ferraz freed a slave named José, for whom she had been paid 2,000 milreis by Antônio Galdino de Oliveira, one of the sons of the viscount of Rio Claro, who then signed a separate contract with José to work for him at the rate of 600 milreis per year, until the amount was paid off. In the same years a number of slaves opened accounts with the Orphans Court for the purpose of purchasing their own freedom. Six of the slaves managed to pay their full price with their *pecúlios* (savings) in 1879.[11]

The term contract increased substantially the possibility of achieving manumission, and put the ex-slave immediately in the position of contracting his labor for a salary. It is not unlikely that the slave sought out in these term transfers the employer he preferred, and arranged the conditions with his owner himself. Obtaining freedom by means of savings was much more difficult (Table 5.1), but the receipt by the owner of a down payment constituted immediate manumission, and the rest was paid by agreement between ex-owner and ex-slave. Among the deposit records of *pecúlios* are two incidents that reflect the growing ability of the slaves to manage their affairs. Ângela, another slave of Maria Luiza Ferraz, withdrew 255 milreis on deposit because she was to be freed on other conditions. Upon examining the sum returned, she complained that the interest paid was insufficient, and the clerk corrected the record. On another occasion Antônio Galdino de Oliveira came in to deposit 138 milreis that had been left with

TABLE 5.1

*Slaves Freed, 1857–87*

| Manner of manumission | 1857–1870 | 1871–1884 | 1885–1887[a] |
|---|---|---|---|
| Immediate, without compensation | — | 6 | 3 |
| For services, including term | 46 | 88 | 181 |
| For cash payment, *pecúlios* | — | 19 | 58 |
| Law of Free Birth (*ingênuos*) | — | 1,138 | 285 |
| Emancipation Funds | — | 58 | 30 |
| Sexagenarian Law | — | — | 543 |
| TOTAL | 46 | 1,309 | 1,100 |

SOURCES. RC/C-1, C-2, LN; APESP, Escravos, 1, 2; SP(P), President of Province, *Relatorio*, 1883–88. It is likely that some manumissions were recorded in the notarial offices of the capital or neighboring counties. This list is therefore not complete.

[a] 1887 Jan.–Nov.

him by his deceased slave, Mariano, as a *pecúlio*. The amount was now applicable to the emancipation of Mariano's four orphans. Oliveira may have turned over the money wholly out of a sense of honor, but he may also have felt uneasy that other slaves in the gang might have reported the omission to the judge. In the same year an act of manumission by José Fermino Correa in favor of a slave named Lourenço stipulated a term of four years without pay. Lourenço then proposed a further condition, that "in the case of the death of his mistress, the provision in his favor should remain in force, and his obligations under the present contract would expire, which was accepted by the lessor." The provision referred to was evidently a clause in the woman's will that would free him. It would be unnecessary to insist on anything so elementary as the capacity of slaves to handle their affairs and to bargain with their owners, if the fact were not so generally neglected.[12]

The local distribution of the Emancipation Funds, which operated from 1877, freed fewer slaves than did private acts of manumission. A detailed list was preserved of slaves to be freed in 1882 (Table 5.2). It suggests that slaves were not overpriced by the Emancipation Board in Rio Claro, and shows that considerable errors accumulated in the provincial statistics, since three slaves, two already freed and one dead, are listed, and were included in the total in the report of the Ministry of the Interior. The listing also shows that two of the slaves applied their own pecúlio to the

TABLE 5.2

*Slaves Classified for the Emancipation Fund, 1882*

| Sex | Age | Marital status | Occupation | Value in milreis | Remarks |
|-----|-----|------|------|------|------|
| F | 61 | m | Farmworker | — | Freed by husband |
| M | 61 | m | Day worker | 20 | Not able to work |
| M | 60 | m | Farmworker | 300 | |
| M | 59 | m | Farmworker | 600 | Savings of 100 milreis |
| M | 51 | m | Farmworker | — | Died before freed |
| M | 50 | m | Farmworker | 800 | Savings of 50 milreis |
| F | 39 | m | Farmworker | 600 | |
| F | 34 | m | Farmworker | — | Freed by Fund in S. Carlos |
| M | 20 | s | Farmworker | 1,400 | |
| M | 18 | s | Farmworker | 1,400 | |
| F | 18 | s | Domestic | 1,100 | |
| F | 16 | s | Domestic | 1,100 | |
| M | 15 | s | Blacksmith | 1,400 | |

SOURCES. APESP, Escravos, 1, "Classificação dos escravos residentes neste municipio para serem libertados . . . 27 de setembro de 1882"; all these slaves were related to freed persons. None of the other lists included ages. This was the third classification of slaves for the provincial quota of funds.

fund. This was a forced contribution, since the law specified that a slave who did not render his savings would be dropped from the classification. The contributions of pecúlios to the funds are inconsistently reported, but seem to have amounted to 2 or 3 percent of the total value of fund manumissions.

Although manumission was given by the planters the appearance of private or public charity, it was clearly ceasing to be a method of manipulation and was becoming an expression of self-assertion on the part of the slaves. Term contracts were a sort of self-manumission on credit, and the pecúlios were composed mostly of money earned or borrowed, not donated. From 1877 to 1884 these forms of payment by the slaves for their own freedom constituted about half of the total of adults, and from 1885 to 1887, about two-thirds. Nevertheless, until the last months of slavery in Rio Claro, a slave's chance of dying remained many times greater than that of obtaining manumission. Between 1877 and 1884 roughly 80 slaves died each year in the county, compared to 12 who were freed (Table 5.3).

The ingênuos constituted almost 90 percent of the slaves freed

TABLE 5.3
*Slave Population, 1875–76*

| Population | Female | Male | Total |
|---|---|---|---|
| Population on Dec. 31, 1875 | 1,760 | 2,669 | 4,429 |
| Entered Rio Claro, 1876 | 66 | 124 | 190 |
| Less: | 68 | 84 | 152 |
| *Departed Rio Claro, 1876* | *30* | *32* | *62* |
| *Died, 1876* | *31* | *50* | *81* |
| *Manumitted, 1876* | *7* | *2* | *9* |
| Population on Dec. 31, 1876 | 1,758 | 2,709 | 4,467 |

SOURCE. Brazil, Directoria Geral de Estatística, *Relatorio e trabalhos estatísticos . . . 1878*, p. 136.

between 1871 and 1884. The Law of Free Birth provided that they were to remain with their slave mothers until they were eight years old, at which time the owner could turn them over to the state and receive a payment of 600 milreis in low-interest bonds, or he could continue to exploit their labor until they reached 21. Since the labor of a young person was worth a great deal more than the bond, which would sell at a discount in any case, the owners almost universally chose to keep the ingênuos. Their decision need not be considered altogether self-serving. The county had no establishments, after all, that could accept public wards, and the children were at least kept with their parents. In some respects the juridical status of the ingênuos was observed fully. Local records do not show the sale of any ingênuos, and when they accompanied their mothers, no higher price was charged. In one testament in which an appraiser had included ingênuos as part of the inventory, the court clerk had drawn a line through with the remark, "without effect." Ingênuos, like adult slaves, were all registered according to the Law of 1871. The ingênuo was able to cancel the service he owed his mother's owner fairly cheaply, by paying a pro-rated amount of the 600 milreis bond. A few quasi-manumissions of this sort took place in Rio Claro.[13]

Since the ingênuos were not paid, and remained subject to the discipline of the plantation, except that "excessive" punishment was prohibited, they were free only to the degree that the slave parents intervened, or caused the authorities to intervene, in the

children's behalf. It appears that there was a consciousness among
the slaves of the special status of the ingênuos, and a particular
resentment when they were punished. An instance was found of a
slave parent bringing his child before the police to protest mis-
treatment by his owner. None of the ingênuos was old enough for
labor until 1880, and until final abolition the great majority were
under the age at which slaves were burdened with an adult work
load. The exploitation that the ingênuos suffered, therefore, was
principally that of poor diets and unhealthy quarters. It cannot
be determined from the materials in Rio Claro whether they were
more neglected than slave children because the planter had no
permanent right to their labor, but it has been shown that their
death rate was extremely high (see turnover in ingênuo population in Table 5.4).[14]

The interprovincial slave traffic, possibly stimulated by the Law
of 1871, increased greatly in the 1870's in Rio Claro. By 1878 the
price of young males had risen almost 20 percent. Yet the increase
in the slave force added to the instability of the system. The slaves
imported to replace and enlarge the work force were coming from
farther away, and were more often persons unfamiliar with coffee
growing, and even with agricultural work of any sort. The census
of 1872 suggests that even at that date the formation of slave families had slowed down. It is possible that the planters were simply
discouraging marriages, in order to evade the legal requirement
of a law of 1869, repeated in 1871, that slave couples could not be

TABLE 5.4
*Ingênuo Population, 1875–76*

| Population | Female | Male | Total |
|---|---|---|---|
| Population on Dec. 31, 1875 | 227 | 199 | 426 |
| Registered, 1876 | 75 | 81 | 156 |
| Entered Rio Claro, 1876 | 17 | 21 | 38 |
| Less: | 33 | 36 | 69 |
| *Departed Rio Claro, 1876* | *1* | *2* | *3* |
| *Died, 1876* | *32* | *34* | *66* |
| Population on Dec. 31, 1876 | 286 | 265 | 551 |

SOURCE. Brazil, Directoria Geral de Estatística, *Relatorio e trabalhos estatísticos . . . 1878*,
p. 136.

separated. The planters were growing apprehensive that the slaves they were buying from other provinces were the most unmanageable and rebellious. In the provincial assembly it was alleged that as a result violent crimes were becoming more frequent: "bringing with them vice, immorality, insubordination, they place public order in peril. . . . Assassins, not workers, are what are harbored in the houses of those planters who buy slaves from the outside."[15]

The provincial assembly, considering the danger presented by this sort of immigration, decided in 1878 to stop it entirely. It debated a bill that imposed on each slave imported from other provinces a prohibitive tax of 1,000 milreis. This was an astonishingly draconian measure, since the flow of slaves had to be maintained even at the cost of violence and repression if the system were not to collapse. The sponsors of the measure were convinced that it was essential as a second step in the process of gradual abolition, which they regarded as inevitable and prerequisite to the attraction of European workers. Some ineffectual suggestions were made concerning the acquisition of coolies or European indentured workers, but it was clear from the character of the debate that political representatives of the planter class were still without a clear idea of whence the substitutes for the slaves were to come. One of them, João Romeiro, scoffed at the idea that the planters could do without slaves:[16]

Why then . . . do they go on buying them? Out of caprice, out of extravagance, would there be anyone in this province who would buy them? . . . It would suffice for them to obtain from free labor the same return they get from slave labor for them to prefer the former, no matter how routine-bound they might be. The enlightened planters who have signed the bill . . . show that among us, unfortunately, one cannot be a planter without owning slaves. If that were not the case, Mr. President, these planters, intelligent, enemies of routine, would try, certainly, to rid themselves of all the slaves they possess, to replace them with free workers.

Romeiro admitted that up to then the newly imported slaves had indeed been troublemakers, but that phase was past and more recently slaves were coming from entire northeastern plantations in liquidation. Undoubtedly the tax had some hidden gains for the planters who proposed it. Romeiro was from the decadent

Paraíba Valley and therefore was less able to conceive of the practicality of free labor. The bill's opponents also noticed that those slave owners who already had purchased heavily would find their gangs much increased in value, and consequently they would easily survive the still unresolved credit crisis.

The bill gained passage, 24 to eight, and two of the favorable votes were from Rio Clarenses, A. A. da Fonseca, a lawyer, and the count of Três Rios, owner of the Santa Gertrudes plantation. The former presented arguments during the debate to demonstrate the bill's constitutionality and agreed with another speaker that "it is not an agricultural question, it is a social question." The bill was vetoed by the president of the province, who admitted that he had been influenced by the reversal of opinion by the Agricultural Club of Campinas. Next year the bill was again passed, and again it was vetoed. The prospect of the extinction of the interprovincial traffic stimulated sales and kept prices high (see Table 3.4, p. 55). At last, in January 1881, the tax, by then raised to 2,000 milreis, was passed and signed by the president, apparently after a change of attitude by the Club. The new law was enforced. In Rio Claro sales of slaves from other provinces ceased. Unquestionably the interprovincial tax brought final abolition much closer. It is not possible to determine with certainty which of the motives expressed in the original debates was most decisive, since the bill was not discussed at all in the final passage. It should be noted that the credit problem had been alleviated, and the question of how to obtain free labor substitutes was still without solution. The restiveness of the slaves, on the other hand, was growing.[17]

The tax did not increase the trade in slaves within the province, if the records in Rio Claro are representative. With the exception of one large sale in 1885, dealings in slaves in the county virtually came to an end. Even more significant, the prices of the few slaves in the market dropped within two years to half the level of 1881. This is the strongest possible evidence that slavery was ceasing to be profitable. The Emancipation Fund could not have exerted much influence on prices; after all, it freed relatively few. The suspicion that an investment in a slave might well be money wasted must have been related to the increasing tensions in the quadrados. In late 1882, another cycle of violence appeared, including outbreaks in Campinas, São João de Boa Vista, and Araras. In their everyday resistance, the slaves were beginning to slow down at work and to run off in significantly larger numbers. Even though there was another flurry of manumissions in 1885—34, including 12 by pecúlio—there were more escapes, since the police managed to return 47 slaves to their owners.[18]

More and more the slaves turned on the feitores, and suffered ever severer punishments at the hands of the owners. In March 1885, a gang attacked and seriously injured a feitor on the São José plantation, and then walked to town and presented themselves to the police, who returned them to the plantation without preferring charges. A few days later the body of one of them, Liberato, was brought to town for burial. It was admitted that he had been "moderately punished," but an examining doctor reported only skin lesions. The cause of death, he decided, was a heart attack. There was considerable disbelief among the townspeople, and it was necessary to proceed to a second autopsy, which agreed with the first. Another death of a slave, in September 1884, was dealt with in the same way. The police carefully collected depositions from employees of the plantation, who confirmed the account of a heart attack in the first case, suicide in the second.[19]

The bare facts of the Liberato affair hint at changes in the relations of slaves and owners. That slaves would come to the police after attacking a feitor indicates that they believed they were acting in self-defense, and that they thought the police would intervene. But they were mistaken. The police, in effect, remanded them to their owner for punishment (as they did again, in May 1886, in the case of the slave named Fausto, who feared being flogged to death). The reopening of the case shows that at least some of the town middle class suspected murder and were ready to make accusations. This was also an element in the case, noted before, of a slave father who complained about the whipping of his ingênuo son. Yet the limits of middle-class abolitionism are visible in the reaction of the editor of the town newspaper, O Tempo. Although

he claimed to be in favor of abolition, and had alerted the public
to the alleged murder of Liberato, he was more concerned that
the word of "a distinguished gentleman physician of untarnished
character" had been questioned. The outcome of the second autopsy left him quite relieved and anxious to close the matter. Although "the tomb hides many scenes of horror" on the plantations,
he believed that "prudence is needed in making accusations";
otherwise they might "affect in a deplorable manner the discipline
necessary on an agricultural establishment of a certain importance." In the towns, distaste for slavery did not yet equal the combined strength of class solidarity and deferential dependency on
the plantations. As late as November 1884, the county council of
neighboring Limeira reported that overt abolitionist agitation was
"happily rare." In Rio Claro there was still no evidence of it.[20]

By 1885 the attitude of the slave owners, and of the local political
elite, had not changed from the time of the Agricultural Congress
of 1878. A questionnaire sent by Senator J. F. de Godoy to all the
county councils of São Paulo brought in 23 replies, none desiring
immediate abolition. Instead they preferred an extension of as
much as ten years, and demanded compensation to the owners as
a matter of the inviolability of property rights, and of the economic
survival of the plantations. As Robert Conrad has noticed, none of
the councils mentioned the possibility that free immigrant workers might be found to substitute for the slaves. It is exceedingly
important to focus upon that circumstance: the planters were re-
treating before the force of events *before* they had devised a solution to their labor problem. Apparently it was still their belief that
free workers would not yield a profit. Echoing João Romeiro's remarks of six years earlier, Martinho Prado asserted in the provincial assembly in February 1884 that this was an uncontestable fact,
and indeed nobody in the chamber did contest it.[21]

Later on that year the general assembly was obliged to consider
another bill intended to continue the gradual emancipation of the
"servile element." Brought before them by a strong Liberal op-
ponent of slavery, again at the wish of the emperor, the bill had
as its central provision immediate freedom for all slaves of 60 or
more years, with no compensation. The bill drew strong opposi-

tion from the coffee planters, partly because of its challenge to the
rights of property, and partly because many of the African-born
slaves had been registered with the Emancipation Fund under
exaggerated ages so as to hide the fact that they had been imported
illegally after 1831. The planters of Rio de Janeiro and São Paulo
managed at last to subvert the purpose of the bill and turn it into
a measure that supported their interests at the cost not only of the
slaves, but of the whole population. The slaves were to be registered a second time, and the sexagenarians were to compensate the
ex-owners with an additional three-year term of labor. The Emancipation Fund was to free slaves according to fixed valuations that
represented, at least in Rio Claro, the going rate for slaves, thereby
slowing down the deterioration in slave prices. A surtax of 5 percent was added to all government revenues except exports, for the
purpose of paying planters—via the fund—and also to support
provincial efforts to import Europeans for plantation labor.[22]

The revised bill compelled the freedmen to remain in the same
county for five years after manumission and to keep employed.
Habitually "vagrant" freedmen were to be exiled to "agricultural
colonies" to be established along the frontier, where they would be
subject to "military discipline." Persons who gave shelter to runaways risked fines and imprisonment, and runaways were declared
ineligible for any form of emancipation.

The freeing of the sexagenarians took place immediately in Rio
Claro. It appears, however, that the planters' declarations of the
ages of their slaves were not challenged, and they were left undisturbed in their possession of slaves too young to have been imported legally from Africa. Notarial records show that only two
of the 543 sexagenarians were excused from the obligation of three
more years of work. The former owners of four others accepted
cash payments in lieu of service. One of them, João Xavier de
Negreiros, who was owed only 33 milreis by a 63-year-old ex-slave,
made repeated trips to the tax collector's office to get his hands on
the money. The law was not effective in promoting the conversion
to free labor. None of the planters in Rio Claro took advantage of
the clause that promised a cash payment of up to half the value
of the slaves to anyone who shifted to wage workers.[23]

The social disorganization of the region was too far advanced to allow roundups by the police of freedmen on charges of vagrancy. They were already overwhelmed with the task of retrieving runaway slaves. The registry of slaves in June 1885 showed 4,709 slaves in Rio Claro; 21 months later, in March 1887, there were only 3,304 left. All sources of manumission, including the Sexagenarian Law, account for only 789 of the missing 1,405. It is not likely that the county suffered a net loss through transfers in and out, since it was continuing to expand its plantings. Deaths may be estimated at 145, the rate in 1878, when the population was about the same (the slaves had aged, but sexagenarians were no longer included). It is extremely unlikely that the owners would have failed to report the presence of their slaves, since nonregistration legally freed the slave; on the contrary, the owner would be likely to continue to report ownership for as long as he had any hope of getting the slave back. The unaccounted-for 471 slaves, 10 percent of those registered in the county, had escaped, and they probably departed well before March 1887. Still more slaves, it can be assumed, only lately escaped, were still being reported as present. The final blow to the planters was the refusal by banks and private lenders to accept slaves as loan collateral. The last mortgage in Rio Claro based on slave property was dated December 17, 1886.[24]

One of the destinations of escaped slaves was Santos. That town, isolated from the interior by the coastal palisade, a smaller-scale version of intensely mercantile Rio de Janeiro, full of freedmen and men of color working at the kinds of jobs that were later to be the first unionized—docking, warehousing, railroads, and even a few factories—was the scene of repeated violent demonstrations against police who tried to kidnap runaways. Finally, a municipal ordinance of October 1886 declared the few slaves remaining in the city free. Immediately it became a magnet for escaped slaves, who formed a squatter settlement on the edge of town, which gradually and peacefully grew to thousands of inhabitants.[25]

Some of the escapees were sheltered, given directions, and even led away by members of an abolitionist underground, many of them mulattos and freedmen. The police of Rio Claro leave no record of having encountered any of these activists in the county. There is evidence that wandering labor brokers led a considerable number of slaves away to other counties, where they signed wage contracts with planters no longer mindful of the responsibilities of class solidarity. The notarial records preserve several *termos de bem viver*, or promises of good behavior, signed by such persons, who are characterized as "seducers" and "speculators." One involved the disappearance of 40 slaves from Ibicaba plantation and their reappearance in Dois Côrregos. The commission amounted to five or ten milreis a head. It may be that the police did not make fine distinctions between brokers and abolitionists, since the abolitionists also sought jobs for their charges. It is hard to avoid wondering if slave catchers, who had interesting qualifications, might have been among those who turned to labor-broking, once their specialty became too dangerous. The planters who hired runaways could only have been newly established or marooned by their own slaves, already run off.[26]

In October 1886, the general assembly abolished lashing as a form of punishment for slaves convicted of crimes. Undoubtedly the measure reduced the effectiveness of the state as the wielder of repression of last resort. Jail at hard labor was no punishment at all for a slave; consequently, private violence had to be intensified. The abolitionist newspaper in São Paulo continued to publish reports of the use of the whip by planters in Rio Claro all through 1887.[27]

Antônio Leite Ferraz, follows his blacks with a rawhide whip in his hand and calls himself an abolitionist. [December 11, 1887]

José Luiz Borges, although he prays a lot, lays the lash on his slaves.... Speaking of whipping, Teixeira das Neves, a bad thorn for the slaves, in spite of being a Republican.... The demented Cândido da Rocha Campos, administrator of the plantation of the marquis of Três Rios [who] has put the black Anselmo in irons and punished him barbarously. [January 1, 1888]

In the first months of 1887 slave escapes continued and manumissions proceeded at a much faster rate. By October there were 40 more, including four through pecúlios. Most of the terms had been reduced to two or three years. In March the baron of Grão-Mogol promised to free all 70 of his remaining slaves, still mortgaged to the London and Brazilian Bank, at the end of five years. He told them that if he repaid the loan within that term, he would free them immediately. He also freed ten other slaves who were not encumbered, one female immediately, and the rest under term contracts, and promised to free two others who had fled, if they would return and accept contracts.[28]

In October, as the rains came and the time for planting arrived, the level of resistance to field work reached the proportions of a general revolt. The population of the fugitive settlement in Santos, 2,000 in July, swelled to 10,000 by December. There were uprisings in Itu, Campinas, Indaiatuba, Amparo, Piracicaba, and Capivári. For the first time, it appears, the slaves carried firearms, and instead of leaving the plantations stealthily, so as to avoid confronting the police, they seemed ready now to challenge them.

The sudden increase in the number of freedmen, many of them in fact escaped, further altered the structure of slave society. The suspicion with which freedmen had always been treated by the authorities, out of fear that they would fraternize with slaves, intensified very considerably in the circumstances. Indeed freedmen were present in the burgeoning *quilombos*. In late October they reacted violently in the provincial capital itself. A crowd of freedmen invaded a society gathering in the Largo de São Francisco, in front of the Law School, shouting "Death to the slavocrats!" The brawl was repeated the next day in the square before the presidential palace. The imperial ministry immediately dispatched a part of the Tenth Infantry Battalion and a company of marines. They were not deployed to chase runaways. A mass escape in Capivári had caused army casualties, and the enraged officers had ordered a massacre of escapees. Shortly afterward the Officers Association petitioned to be relieved of slave-catching duties. This has usually been remarked as proof of a changed consciousness on the part of the white officer class. They had had enough, it is assumed, of the distasteful repression and sought to recover their honor. But the officers readily accepted assignments, both before and after, that were equally repellent, such as the slaughter of the millenarians at Canudos, in Bahia state in 1897. It is more likely that they had come to fear the bullet in the back. Their troops, mostly men of color, were catching the same spirit of fraternization that had invaded the quadrados.[29]

Meanwhile the planters were devising a last formula for maintaining control yet a while longer. A group of them in Campinas proposed in September that the slaves be offered term manumissions to expire December 31, 1890. Their intent was to salvage the work force still on the plantations and to reduce the repressive effort to a scale the police could handle. Again, jail terms were proposed for workers who failed to complete the contract. The plan gained ground among the slave owners. In mid-November a planning committee was installed in São Paulo, which called a province-wide meeting for December. On November 28 the planters of Rio Claro discussed "the precarious state of agriculture," and decided to send delegates. Two hundred planters came together on December 15, adopting the name Associação Libertadora. The opening address by Leôncio de Carvalho congratulated the delegates on their decision to resolve the "social difficulties" without government intervention. "Time, liberty, capital, education, and charity well exercised" would cure the ill, not the "socialism of the state." A minority present doubted that term contracts would keep the slaves on the plantations and insisted on unconditional freedom. The majority bent somewhat: they accepted flexibility in the length of the contract and considered the advisability of offering some sort of wage, but in the end only 120 signed the declaration. Seven of them were from Rio Claro, including three members of the clan of the viscount of Rio Claro, and Antônio Paes de Barros. Together these planters owned nearly 600 of Rio Claro's slaves.[30]

The freeing of whole plantations had already begun. On December 12, Joaquim José Rodrigues Torres offered term contracts to his seven slaves. A day later Felisberto José Cardoso offered his eighteen slaves two-year contracts, with token wages—50 milreis

for the men, 30 for the women. The next day Joaquim da Costa
Correa freed four more. The returned delegates held another meeting in town, at which they decided to act in concert. Manumission
would be granted on Christmas day, in exchange for one more
harvest, that is, a nine-months term. On Christmas fifteen planters,
including José Luis Borges, Joaquim Augusto de Salles, Justiniano
de Mello Oliveira, Eduardo Bohn, and Alfredo Ellis freed their
slaves. All together about 550 slaves had been offered contracts.
The "liberators" were euphoric. Alfredo Ellis exulted in the local
newspaper:

I have just given full and total liberty to my slaves (41) and all continue
working with me and receiving wages; a wild joy reigns among all on the
plantation. Among the newly freed it is not just joy, it's utter delirium.
I feel happy to have, all at once, wrenched from the dark night of slavery
this handful of brothers who are now no longer mere things, but useful
citizens.

The manumitting of slaves continued through the holidays, including those belonging to Estevão Xavier de Negreiros, Antônio
da Costa Alves Ferreira, João Cordeiro da Silva Guerra—in all,
another 300 slaves.[31]

While the press in São Paulo received ecstatic telegrams from
the planters, the slaves continued to disappear. Most of the slave
gangs freed, it appears, were mere remnants. It is not clear whether
there was delirium on all the plantations or just mass departure
on the morning after. José Francisco de Paula Souza offered his
slaves term contracts, which were accepted by those on his São
Bento plantation, but those on his Ibitinga plantation did not,
and nearly all walked off. The December agreements had not yet
won the adherence of the majority of the slave owners, and the
expectation of the minority that the slaves could be gotten to work
one more year as bondsmen was both unrealistic and greedy. The
abolitionist newspaper renamed the association the Provincial
Hoodwinking Society, and the president of the province suggested
that their solution came too late. In Rio Claro the police continued to act on complaints of runaways, and even carried out
house-to-house searches.[32]

On January 6, the slaves still remaining on the plantations, or at least a considerable number of them, demanded immediate freedom and the payment of regular wages or they would leave. Some of the planters caved in during the next two weeks and more than 250 received their freedom without condition. Many others walked off and presented themselves down the road to other planters or sought work in the town. Still others returned to the same plantations, where the owners, after a few days' reflection, decided they would pay wages after all. Few of the planters made any further attempt to bring the striking slaves back.[33]

At last the townspeople began to express their sympathies openly. On January 23, a crowd of more than 1,000 persons, accompanied by a brass band, marched from the public garden to the house of the newly appointed police delegate, Cláudio da Silva Braga, to congratulate him for refusing to recapture escaped slaves. Braga was himself a planter. The next day a slave appeared in town wearing shackles and a blacksmith struck them off. On the first of February an angry crowd of townspeople forced a planter to release a runaway he had recaptured.[34]

Rio Claro was surrounded by uprisings. In Piracicaba the slaves of Luiz Gonzaga had refused term contracts and left en masse for Santos. At Jundiaí they were recaptured and brought back by rail. The train was met by hundreds of men of color, both slave and free, who liberated the captives and beat up the escort. The next day, January 12, they all roamed the streets, accosting police and provoking brawls. In Araras a landowner converted to abolition, Lourenço Dias, gave sanctuary to runaways. They came to town on Sundays, to dance the *batuque*, luring away other slaves and defying their former owners. In Passa Quatro ex-slaves who had been contracted by planters in Santos occupied the town center on January 26, and, according to the police report, raised red flags and shouted "Long live the Republic!"[35]

Underlying reports such as these was the fear of social revolution. This outcome was not really likely, but the presence of free blacks and mulattos in the streets, inciting violence and refusing to obey authority, foreshadowed a crisis graver than that of slave rebellion.

Legitimacy had to be restored, and the most effective means left in the planters' hands was to assume the cloak of abolitionism. The transformation was self-serving and generally graceless. In the provincial assembly on February 1, for example, Domingos Jaguaribe vied with all the other deputies in professing abolitionist sympathies. Accused of having been a slave owner by a disbelieving colleague, he denied it vehemently, and asserted that he had been an abolitionist since 1868. Of course, he had not *owned* any slaves, those hundreds he had managed were his wife's inheritance! In the general collapse, all raced to get clear of the falling bricks. In Jaú, São Carlos, and Tatuí the planters held public meetings to declare their counties free, thereby reestablishing credence in their generosity, public spirit, and foresight, and turning local energies to festivity.[36]

The planters in Rio Claro who had already offered their slaves term contracts decided to hold the same sort of meeting on February 5. The Largo do Teatro was decorated for the occasion, a band played patriotic airs, the church bells were tolled, and fireworks were set off. From the platform speeches were delivered by the baron of Grão-Mogol, who was president of the county council, Cláudio da Silva Braga, and Benedito Barbosa. Three thousand came to the ceremony, including many from Limeira and other towns. The president of the province sent a company of soldiers to add pomp and a dash of color. The press in São Paulo and Rio de Janeiro reported the event as the freeing of the slaves, and so it has passed down to the present as a principal element of municipal tradition. Indeed, throughout the state, local histories mention similar ceremonies, which demonstrate that abolition was bestowed.[37]

The tradition, however, is really a myth, not only because the ceremony was an afterthought preceded by a widespread slave strike and desertions, but also because it did not accomplish total emancipation in the county. The planters did not have the power to liberate the slaves of those among them who still insisted on their rights of property. They carried out an act that was merely symbolic and exemplary, and there is no evidence that it persuaded any of the recalcitrant. Indeed, there are indications that there were slaves working on some of the plantations of Rio Claro up to the day the final law of emancipation was passed.

On February 8, José Luiz Borges obliged a labor broker to sign a promise of good behavior to stop him from "seducing" his slaves. Borges had offered his slaves contracts at Christmas, according to the newspapers; perhaps they had refused and Borges had restored the *ancien régime.* In late February the baron of Grão-Mogol proposed to the council that a "Book of Gold" be opened, in which would be recorded the names of those who had freed their slaves, so that "we might arrive more quickly at the goal aimed at by hearts and souls who feel sympathy for the unfortunate portion that lies under the heaviest of yokes." The use of the present tense shows that there were still slaves in Rio Claro. On March 6 another good behavior guarantee was signed; this time the offender was a seller of "slaves" who ran off soon after they were paid for. Five planters made the complaint, again a useless exercise if slavery had been eliminated. In mid-March the county council reported to the president of the province that of the 3,304 slaves registered a year before, 33 had died, 13 had turned sixty, and 1,595 had been manumitted, leaving 1,663 still in captivity.[38]

The council, no doubt, merely subtracted declarations of manumission from the total registered (the wave of manumissions from Christmas on, incidentally, was not recorded in the notarial offices; apparently the planters did not want to go to the trouble, and the slaves did not think it worthwhile to insist). How many others had run off was a matter ignored by the council. It is probable that only a few hundred remained, and that the number continued to decline, but it did not reach zero before May 13, 1888. One of the slaves of Manuel Barbosa Guimarães kept his pecúlio on account at the Orphans Court. He appeared a few days after final abolition to withdraw the money: he had not been freed until May 13. Domingos Feltrin, a planter in Itaqueri, was awakened, a family tradition recounts, early in the morning of May 14 by his slaves, who asked permission to go to the chapel to cut weeds in the patio as an act of thanksgiving. The story has other dimensions—the religiosity of the slaves, their formal treatment of their ex-owner, and their uncanny reception of news from the court, for Feltrin was still unaware that emancipation had taken place—but it shows also that at least one gang of slaves still existed in the county on the final day.[39]

The descendants of the immigrant townspeople, by now intermarried with the less favored by fortune of the planter families, uphold a tradition that does honor to the slave owners. It is easy to see why. The credit thereby accrues ultimately to law and order, to the properties of class, to social decorum, all of which shore up their own sense of dignity. The idea that the mass of the people might claim successfully their rights does not accord with their disesteem for the working class, and such an idea would threaten them extremely. Nevertheless, the planters were not generous or enlightened—or even shrewd—bourgeois. They merely offered concessions to try to keep their control from further deteriorating. Invariably their offers were too late and too small, and invariably they were accompanied by threats. A local advocate of abolition, Lucas Ribeiro do Prado, mocked their pieties a few years afterward. "Man ought not to be enslaved," they repeatedly declaimed, "because it is a law against God," but what really converted them, said Ribeiro, was the fact that the slaves were "a very inconstant property!"[40]

He only served his owner as long as he wanted to, as long as it suited him. Then suddenly he declared he didn't want to serve his master any longer; either he was sold to another, or he ran away never to return, thus conquering his own freedom, or he committed suicide, or he malingered, or else he slit his master's throat. This having been thoroughly proved with repeated instances, liberty was proclaimed!

A postscript is necessary. At the public ceremony in the Largo do Teatro there were no freedmen present. According to one account, they had decided, after observing the arrival of troops, that the celebration was a trap to capture them en masse and impress them into the army. They went into hiding and a few days later held a commemoration of their own. It is also possible that that explanation is also a myth; perhaps they boycotted the ceremony because they felt no desire to listen to the self-congratulations of men who had been their tormentors short weeks before.[41]

Belief in the bestowed emancipation had other uses. The ex-owners employed it to extract continued gratitude and respect. Lucas Ribeiro do Prado, for example, insisted continually on his moral superiority before ex-slaves. On one occasion, having been insulted by a freedwoman, he retorted, "Shut your mouth, *negra*, I didn't snatch you from the . . . *senzala*, as an abolitionist, to have to listen to your insolence." But the black woman knew better: "God it was who freed me!"[42]

The process of liberation was not completed in Rio Claro. The planters argued that they should receive compensation for the loss of their property rights. But the slaves' right to compensation for years of unpaid labor and unnecessary suffering went unnoticed. The planters were more than quits. Had emancipation followed a course of equity and reason, the ex-slaves would have been awarded the land they had toiled on all their lives. Abolition and land reform were linked by a few among the abolitionists, and certainly the slave owners dreaded that possibility, and not merely the loss of their slaves. The departure of the freedmen from the plantations, given no other source of field labor, would shortly have effectuated land reform of a sort. Although land values were greatly increased in Rio Claro, and estates had obtained at least part of their mortgages on the value of improvements, a lack of hands would have put the plantations on the block, and even the freedmen would have bought them up, as they did in Guyana and Jamaica.[43]

The prospect of that calamity impelled the planters' insistence that freedmen be required to stay in their counties of residence and keep regular jobs or be put to hard labor. But self-interest was disguised as national interest. Senator Godoy considered the vagrancy clause a necessity because of "the lack of ambition in the national proletariat, from which results its lack of motivation for work." Civilized nations, he asserted, all had such laws, and in Brazil it would keep the freedmen from swelling the "mass of disturbers of the public order and calm." Domingos Jaguaribe, proposing the same solution in 1884, was quite clear that its purpose would be to deal with the "question of class, which is the social question." The freedmen had "elevated notions, very often erroneous," of their position, which gave rise to "a nascent hatred which is bound to influence the future." A new employment law would create a class of tenured but feudatory peasants, who would not challenge their former owners in the marketplace or at the ballot box.[44]

Although the freedmen were the preferred victims of police harassment in town and were often jailed for vagrancy, there never developed any need to coerce them to work on the plantations. The repressive clause in the 1885 Law lapsed upon final abolition, and no other laws were written. European workers came in great numbers as soon as they became convinced that they would not themselves be enslaved, and the planters easily dispensed with freedmen for tending the groves. In towns, too, they lost most of the positions they had held in craft occupations and were relegated to day labor, petty trading, factory work, and service occupations without prestige. The planters did not entirely eliminate them, however. Indeed their continued presence was essential to the viability of the plantation, because they took on the seasonal, precarious jobs that were not sufficiently well paid to be attractive to the immigrants. They became *camaradas*, general laborers, who were paid by the month. When there was a local excess of immigrants, the freedmen might be further demoted to day labor.

The social consequences of labor marginalization were disastrous for the entire population of color. Abolition had eliminated, at a stroke, the legal rights they had been granted as slaves. The elderly no longer had a legal right to remain on the plantation as pensioners. Ingênuo status was ended, and therefore that group was no longer entitled to continued support from their mothers' former owners. Privileges like these had been of slight advantage, but their disappearance left a gap. If the planters sometimes restored them, it was in exchange for the acceptance of paternalism, not as a just compensation owed an independent individual. Normally the freedman had to compete, but his disabilities were great.

Hardly any could read or write, some had not handled money, none had managed their own affairs. But no trustees were appointed for them, and those free whites who had proclaimed themselves abolitionists believed they had fully acquitted themselves of their responsibilities. The freedmen suffered the consequences. Precarious jobs led to a nearly nomadic existence for most males and the near impossibility of forming nuclear families. Women were usually trapped in domestic employment, which rooted them in the towns but left them with sole responsibility for raising the children. Extremely few landholdings in Rio Claro were owned by persons of color, and these were minifundia.[45]

Abolition released racism, latent in the slave system but obscured by it. Now all persons of color were free, but all were presumed freedmen. Those who had acquired status through free birth were thus leveled with those just liberated. They vainly sought to regain the position they had once had. Now all were anonymous *prêtos* (blacks), mentioned in the town newspaper only when they appeared before the police delegate. Thieves, drunks, whores, disturbers of the peace: "The black Lourença So-and-so [*de tal*], ex-slave of Sr. Joaquim José de Nascimento," attempted suicide; "Benedita Conceição, black, woman of loose habits, resident in the Largo da Várzea," burglary. "Major Cornélio Schmidt, energetic delegate in charge, has ordered put in the *cooler* a bunch of black tramps, to get them to go to work. Well done!" The newspaper, which had a better memory for the names of the freedmen's former owners than for those of the freedmen, did not scruple to carry personal advertisements in which racial insults were employed. Whites looked upon the freedmen with sexual fascination and fear. The customary repression of white women was threatened by the "licentiousness" of black men and by the ambitiousness of mulatto men. Violence against freedmen was daily, and when suspected of rape of a white woman, they were lynched. Persons of color were segregated residentially in the town center, and those newly freed were obliged to occupy hovels on the fringe. Persons of color were excluded from the *footing* (the evening promenade around the town square), and from other social events. Although they maintained their own lay brotherhood, band, and social clubs, their exclusion by subtle means from those of the whites took place only after abolition, and had the effect of blocking the main paths of social mobility. The disability of social class meshed with that of race. In the school, the bank, the county prefecture, it was enough to be lower class to be denied fair treatment.[46]

Although the planters had feared that the slaves would not work for wages, they did. Since most of them remained on the plantations to work for lower wages than the Europeans, it was an absurd cavil that the immigrants were needed because the freedmen had an exaggerated idea of their worth. The planters evidently thought the work of the freedmen was less satisfactory than that of the Europeans. It will be shown that that was also a false assumption, hence mere prejudice. For the freedmen the plantation represented minimal security, but they knew that their employment there was granted contemptuously. Nevertheless, the planters thought themselves free of prejudice. Domingos Jaguaribe expressed the attitude shortly after abolition: "Fortunately, there is no race prejudice in Brazil." Then he added the corollary article of faith, "and one sees men of color marrying white women, and vice-versa, so that the black population has diminished extraordinarily. In fifty years it will have become quite rare in Brazil." Probably the decline was and continues to be due mainly to higher death rates and lower acceptability as marriage partners, but in any case it cannot be said that whites had any regard for blacks if they could look upon their total disappearance through miscegenation as a happy resolution of the question of race. Both of these utterly contradictory ideas are still nearly universal in São Paulo, where the final solution is indeed close to realization.[47]

Abolition in Rio Claro was violent, but so sudden that it passed, leaving no further scores to be settled. The provincial president reported a few months later, with evident great relief, that "the violent agitation of spirits" had passed, that the free population had gotten over its fright, that the planters "with traditional prudence and good sense" had accepted their loss, and that public order and the prestige of the government were restored. Though he foresaw the breakdown of the great estates as inevitable and necessary to the future progress of Brazil, he also noticed that the province had experienced not the slightest decline in agricultural production. The planters, fresh from one close call, were at the beginning of a new stage in their evolution, the exploitation of immigrant wage labor. They were not ready to fade away; on the contrary, they were radiant with self-confidence and ambition.[48]

# CHAPTER 6

# The Wage Labor Regime

IN GENERAL, the planters of São Paulo continued irresolute to the last. The departure of their slaves meant bankruptcy for them and their displacement as an elite: "a species of anarchy," one of them mourned. For years the solution lay before them, but they did not take it up until the last possible moment. In 1870 José Vergueiro proposed that European immigrants who were apt for field labor and willing to sign labor contracts be given completely free passage, at the expense of the government. Free passage, he hoped, would represent an effective lure to divert the immigrant flow from Argentina and the United States. By tapping the public treasury the planters would be freed of risk, indentures would be obviated, and hence also coercion of the immigrant to compel him to remain on a given plantation. In 1871, during the earlier period of slave unrest in São Paulo, a small subsidy was voted by the provincial assembly to cover part of the cost of transport, but it was poorly executed and inadequate.[1]

The planters remained unconvinced. Paulista delegates at the Agricultural Congress of 1878 strongly favored the importation of coolies. Even though they thought of them as vice-ridden, disease-carrying degenerates, racially inferior to Europeans, they were willing to populate the province with them because they would accept meager wages and might be subjected to a regime of force halfway between slavery and freedom. The delegates also wanted the Employment Law tightened, so that it would apply equally to nationals and immigrants, with jail terms of a year or two for "agitators," preventive imprisonment, and summary trials en masse.

Neither scheme was carried out, but the central conception, that a free wage labor system was impractical and force was still necessary, clearly influenced the revised Employment Law of 1879, the Electoral Law of 1881, and the Sexagenarian Law.[2]

The planters resisted fully subsidized mass migration partly because they were unwilling to allow government so large a role in their labor relations. Even though the introduction of plantation workers would be wholly to their benefit, the planters assumed that the government would empower itself to protect immigrants whose transportation it had paid for. Besides, the scale of the potential enterprise was staggering. Full passage for all the laborers the planters would require appeared to be an assault on the provincial finances too vast to be practicable. Certainly the imperial government balked at the idea. Its funds had been spent only for immigrants who were to settle as freeholders on official colonies in the southern provinces.[3]

It was not until March 1884 that the provincial assembly voted a full-fare subsidy. Two years later full-fare subsidization on a large scale passed the assembly, but not until July 1887 did the assembly approve a contract that was to introduce a significant number of immigrants to the plantations. The importing agency was the Sociedade Promotora de Imigração, founded the year before on the principle of nonprofit by a group of planters, among whom were nine with properties in Rio Claro. It was not, therefore, until slavery was already in collapse in São Paulo that effective measures were taken by the planters to replace their field labor.[4]

The first full-subsidy contract brought in 33,163 immigrants by the early months of 1888. Two more contracts, signed in January and March, introduced 52,964 more by the end of the year. The planters had weathered the storm. Succeeding contracts with the provincial government maintained the flow, and in 1890 the new federal Republican junta, strongly under the influence of the Paulistas, decreed an unlimited guarantee of free passage to all able-bodied workers, which remained in effect until 1895. In the same year the Sociedade Promotora decided that it could safely turn its organizing efforts over to the state government (the provinces became states when the republic was proclaimed) and dissolve itself. The plantations were not only saved, they were energized by this massive inflow of labor. After a nearly complete halt in the planting of trees in the last four or five years of slavery, 350 million trees were planted in the decade of the 1890's, across a broad swathe of the interior as far as Ituverava, São José do Rio Preto, and Bauru.[5]

By 1904 the federal government and the state of São Paulo had paid 42 million milreis for immigrants. Any calculation of the viability of the plantation system after the breakdown of slavery must begin with this stunning fact: it did not pay for the replacement of its labor supply; instead it was paid for by the entire population, including the freedmen. Domingos Jaguaribe, who put so many inconvenient thoughts into print, though he was so well connected to the planter elite, wrote in 1892 that the system "favored the rich, and weakened the nation, whose real force lies in its working class. And at the moment the latter are witnesses and victims of the most scandalous of abuses: they labor day and night to pay the costs of travel of emigrants."[6]

Early in 1888, when the desperate experiment seemed to be succeeding, the planters thought themselves providentially delivered. Only later did they portray themselves as the bold innovators of a new model society. Their claims must, in any event, be modified, for they do not consider how largely the immigrant flow was externally caused, and how important were the decisions of the immigrants in the process. The subsidies awakened little interest except in Italy, where disastrous economic conditions were forcing hundreds of thousands of peasants off the land. The year 1887 was, not by coincidence, the first in which overseas emigration surpassed 100,000, and the first year it was larger than emigration to other European countries. Even though passage was free, those who dared to travel to the slave empire were usually relatives who had been sent favorable notice. In 1887 the news was that slavery was coming to an end and that entire plantations were being turned over to free workers. Those letters also contained

money orders. Italian postal records show a sudden surge in remittances in the years 1887 and 1888, the equivalent of 250,000
milreis. If bank checks were at least equal in amount for those
years, the already emigrated covered about 10 percent of the cost
of the replacement of the slaves during the critical years. During
the whole period the immigrants had to pay a still larger share,
about half of the total. The provincial government did not pay
the passage of the unmarried, lest the Argentine pattern of rootless
annual migrations be established. Therefore bachelor cousins,
brothers-in-law, and nephews had to be provided for. Other migrants who transferred from Argentina and Uruguay were wholly
self-financed.[7]

It was essential that slavery be abolished before mass migration
could begin. Since that was the work of the slaves, not of the
owners, again the congratulations have been misplaced. The re-
vulsion felt by the European immigrants for slavery cannot be
measured by the small extent of their active participation in the
abolitionist movement. They appeared indifferent to the institution only because of their prejudice against the blacks. The end of
the slave system, however, meant for them the collapse of a hier-
archical society that had barred their ascent and had equated their
labor with that of the Africans and their descendants. In the four
months following final abolition, 21 heads of immigrant families
came before the county council of Rio Claro to swear allegiance
to Brazil. Republicanism was not a factor, since the overthrow of
the monarchy was still a year away. These men were nearly a third
of the immigrant middle class of the town, including Swiss and
Germans who had arrived in the 1850's like João Jacob Meyer,
Matthias Pott, and Frederico Büll. João Vollet, himself a former
slave owner, was among those who came forward. The most important of the Italian residents also naturalized, including Silverio
Minervino and Domingos Cartolano.[8]

Rio Claro received a share of the immigrant flow (Table 6.1). It
can be seen that the rate of population increase in the county,
which had declined sharply after 1872, rose once again (Table 6.2).
In 1888 the Italian consulate in São Paulo estimated that there

TABLE 6.1

Immigrant Arrivals, 1883–1921

| Year | Number | Year | Number | Year | Number |
|------|--------|------|--------|------|--------|
| 1883 | 222 | 1904 | 88 | 1913 | 1,053 |
| 1893 | 2,089 | 1905 | 470 | 1914 | 770 |
| 1894 | 1,088 | 1906 | 811 | 1915 | 447 |
| 1895 | 2,523 | 1907 | 275 | 1916 | 333 |
| 1897 | 2,209 | 1908 | 319 | 1917 | 505 |
| 1898 | 488 | 1909 | 396 | 1918 | 202 |
| 1900 | 237 | 1910 | 413 | 1919 | 504 |
| 1901 | 1,013 | 1911 | 405 | 1920 | 1,072 |
| 1902 | 812 | 1912 | 581 | 1921 | 211 |
| 1903 | 161 | | | | |

SOURCES. 1883: SP(P), President of Province, *Relatorio*, 1883. 1893–1921: SP(S), Repartição de Estatística e Arquivo, *Anuario estatístico*, 1893–1927.
NOTE. Figures are for arrivals via immigrant hostel only.

TABLE 6.2

Population, 1822–1920

| Year | Total | Percent annual growth | Year | Total | Percent annual growth |
|------|-------|------------------------|------|-------|------------------------|
| 1822 | 1,514 | — | 1886 | 20,133 | 2.4% |
| 1835 | 2,906 | 6.5% | 1890 | 24,584 | 5.5 |
| 1857 | 6,564 | 6.0 | 1900 | 38,426 | 5.6 |
| 1872 | 15,035 | 8.6 | 1920 | 58,262 | 2.6 |

SOURCES. 1822, 1835: APESP, População Piracicaba. 1857: SP(P), President of Province, *Relatorio*, 1857. 1886: SP(P), Comissão Central de Estatística, *Relatorio*, 1886. 1872, 1890, 1900, 1920: Census. The year 1857 includes Brotas; all dates include Analândia.

were already 650 Italians on the plantations of Rio Claro, and another 650 resided in town. Immigrant arrivals via the hostel during the decade from 1891 to 1900 may be estimated at 12,700, while the total population increase amounted to 13,842. The net rate of natural population growth during this period was probably 1.5 percent, or about 4,725 more births than deaths. There must have been a sizable migration into the county from other counties. From 1901 to 1920 immigrant arrivals accounted for a smaller part of population growth, 10,630, compared to a natural increase of about 13,200. Evidently the first two decades after abolition were extremely agitated demographically, with in- and out-migration among nearby counties churning the population intensely.[9]

In 1886 Rio Claro was the third largest producer of coffee in the province. The clearing of virgin forest and the planting of new trees had not yet been completed. There were still 16,153 hectares of forest in 1905, more than 10 percent of its area, although part of that may have been second growth. The peak of coffee output came in 1901 (see Table 2.5, p. 39), when 14,824 tons were gathered, but by then Rio Claro was no longer among the ten largest coffee counties of São Paulo. The opening of the area of Ribeirão Preto, and the extension of planting beyond Jaú and Araraquara had overshadowed it. An irreconcilable split within the local Republican Party caused the district of Anápolis (at first called Cuscuseiro and later Analândia) to be separated in 1897. After the state decree of 1903 which taxed the planting of new trees, there were, at least officially, no new plantings except to replace abandoned groves. The county's trees, according to an expert observer in 1909, were less productive than average because many were on poor soils (Table 6.3). The coffee cycle in Rio Claro was quite protracted, and very gradual in its decline. Planting did not cease until 1929, and in 1940 the harvest was still 4,000 tons.[10]

The transformation of the labor regime on the plantations led to the diversification of the economy of the state. A much wider range of goods was needed to satisfy consumer demand, and the nature of the Brazilian commodity-exporting economy was such that imports could not keep pace with it. Some of the immigrants abandoned plantation work to apply their skills more fully in

TABLE 6.3
*Condition of Coffee Trees, 1909*

| Condition | Thousand trees |
| --- | --- |
| Mature and producing | 7,200 |
| Mature, planted in weak soil, 12–14 years maximum usefulness; should be manured every 3 years | 5,000 |
| Mature, in decadence; poor soil, or badly planted or pruned, or exhausted by corn inter-planting | 5,300 |
| Trees up to 8 years old | 1,700 |
| TOTAL | 19,200 |
| Total officially registered | 18,040 |

SOURCE. Adapted from Isidro Gomes Teixeira, *Estatística de café e cafesais*, pp. 16–17. Includes Analândia.

craft occupations. Small-scale factories multiplied all over the interior of São Paulo. Rio Claro's town center became quite remarkably industrialized. Its position, first as a railhead, then as a transfer point between the Paulista and the narrow-gauge Rio Claro Railway, made it the logical place for car barns of both lines. A hydroelectric plant began operating regularly on the Ribeirão Claro in 1900. The town was lit with arc lamps and had a telephone system. There were carriage shops, saddlery shops, sawmills, brickworks, lime works, a shoe factory, several typographers, and machine and foundry shops. Smaller firms made pasta, soap, vinegar, mattresses, straw hats, cigars, fireworks, and ice. A large brewery sold an output of 600,000 liters of stout all over the state.[11]

The plantation work force and the sizable town proletariat provided a clientele for a large service sector: government offices, hospitals, a theater, cinemas, and churches. In turn the town marketed the subsistence surplus of the smallholders. The town market and slaughterhouse sold produce, and local brokers and merchants with processing machinery dealt in small quantities of coffee, corn, rice, dairy products, and cane brandy. The accumulation of commercial and small-scale industrial undertakings engendered a relatively large urban middle class, whose ambitions and consumption patterns further diversified employment. Rio Claro possessed one of the principal institutions of this expanding group, a German-language high school, which boarded students from all over the southern states.

All of these changes were evidence of a revival of urban growth which had been inhibited by the slave system. It is quite likely that the town center grew faster than the county as a whole from abolition onward, despite the great influx of plantation workers. Nevertheless, the survival of the plantations restrained this development partially, since nearly all their business was carried out in Santos and São Paulo. The small scale of local trade can be seen in the fact that Rio Claro had no bank until 1926. This dependence on São Paulo for credit rendered the town middle class quite unable to grasp a larger share of the commercialization of coffee. Since the largest urban employers in the county, the railroads, were also absentee-owned, capital accumulation was trifling. Therefore the burghers concerned themselves with monopolizing their lower-class clientele. On many occasions the county council levied prohibitive taxes upon itinerant coffee brokers and upon shops located outside the town center. Thus the middle class collaborated in muting the developmental potentialities of wage labor.[12]

Increasingly foreign firms, or their fronts, absorbed a considerable part of the commercial sector: the Banco de Crédito Hipotecário e Agrícola (French), Schroeder Gebrüder, Theodor Wille, Hard Rand and Company, and Zerrener-Bülow, among others. Transfers of estates to new owners involved more and more persons residing in the capital and quite unconnected to local families. Absentee management of estates became more marked. As long as the labor force had to be driven, the planters were sure to spend at least the harvest season in the county, but after abolition their visits became remarkable occasions.[13]

Coffee holdings remained very concentrated (Table 6.4) until the end of the coffee cycle. In 1919 there were still only 287 coffee-raising properties, but by 1927 there were 561 and by 1932 there

TABLE 6.4
*Concentration of Coffee Production, 1892 and 1905*

| Size of harvest, in arrobas (arroba = 15 kg) | Number of producers | Percent of producers | Arrobas produced | Percent of production |
|---|---|---|---|---|
| 1892 | | | | |
| 10,000 | 15 | 9.9% | 231,000 | 45.0% |
| 4,000–9,999 | 24 | 15.8 | 133,000 | 25.9 |
| 1,000–3,999 | 68 | 44.7 | 129,000 | 25.1 |
| 999 and under | 45 | 29.6 | 20,000 | 4.0 |
| TOTAL | 152 | 100.0% | 513,000 | 100.0% |
| 1905 | | | | |
| 10,000 and over | 26 | 8.1% | 437,000 | 49.7% |
| 4,000–9,999 | 38 | 11.8 | 220,000 | 25.0 |
| 1,000–3,999 | 79 | 24.4 | 167,100 | 19.1 |
| 999 and under | 180 | 55.7 | 54,020 | 6.2 |
| TOTAL | 323 | 100.0% | 878,120 | 100.0% |

SOURCES. 1892: MHP-ABV, "Relação dos agricultores de café no município de São João de Rio Claro, no anno de 1892." This tax roll underrepresents real production, but probably reproduces concentration fairly accurately. 1905: SP(S), Secretaria de Agricultura, Comércio e Obras Públicas, *Estatística agrícola e zootechnica, 1904–1905*. Includes Analândia.

were 650. The larger plantations suffered somewhat from the crisis of 1901 to 1906, and there were bankruptcies and auctions of several of them before and after, most notably the division of the Angélica plantation, and the creation of state-sponsored smallholding colonies on the bankrupt Cascalho and São José do Corumbataí plantations. Angélica was broken up into six properties, and the Vergueiros' gigantic Ibicaba lost tracts to four other plantations and was finally sold at auction. The buyer was João Levy, one of the original *parceria* workers who had become a merchant in Limeira. He had persuaded the boss of Limeira to discourage others from bidding, in return for which Levy gave him a share. The share was later repurchased, for more than the winning bid. While some estates were dismembered, new ones were put together, until the late 1920's. Usually the divested lands were tracts unsuitable for coffee, or depleted groves. Sometimes bankrupt estates were bought up entire and run at a profit for another generation. The velocity of sales accelerated with the abolition of slavery. Martinho Prado's saying was apt: *"Se café dá casaca, tambem tira a camisa"* (Though coffee gets you a suit, it also removes your shirt).[14]

Because the smallest properties were likely to contain aging coffee trees, or trees planted on unsuitable lands, their productivity was much lower than that of the larger holdings (Table 6.5). It is apparent, however, that they specialized in food production, and disposed of a surplus in town, and perhaps to the plantations. The smallest producers in Table 6.5 grew 150 liters of rice per worker,

TABLE 6.5
*Coffee and Corn Output per Worker,*
*by Size of Producer, 1905*

| Size of coffee harvest in arrobas | Output per worker in liters | |
|---|---|---|
| | Coffee | Corn |
| 10,000 and over | 149 | 1,170 |
| 4,000–9,999 | 134 | 1,840 |
| 1,000–3,999 | 151 | 1,480 |
| 999  and under | 71 | 2,020 |

SOURCE. SP(S), Secretaria de Agricultura, Comêrcio e Obras Públicas, *Estatística agrícola e zootechnica, 1904–1905.* Includes Analândia.
NOTE. Holdings reporting no coffee output were excluded.

three times the output of the largest. They grew only 274 liters of beans per worker, however, less than half the amount grown on the largest holdings, 655 liters.[15]

Partial records of two Rio Claro plantations are available for the early post-abolition period. The two complement each other, for one of them, Santa Gertrudes, was among the largest and most successful in the state, and the other, Palmares, was medium-sized and constantly on the edge of bankruptcy. The Santa Gertrudes documentation includes the administrative correspondence and account books. The Palmares records include the owner's correspondence and his running cash account.

Santa Gertrudes can be described in considerable detail, since it was a model plantation frequently visited by foreign dignitaries accompanied by journalists. The planting of coffee was begun on Santa Gertrudes in 1854 by its second owner, Amador Rodrigues Jordão, baron of São João de Rio Claro. The estate had fallen to him by inheritance, and after his death his widow, Maria Hipólita, married Joaquim Egídio de Souza Aranha, baron, and later viscount, count, and marquis of Três Rios. He was one of the richest men in São Paulo, a developer of the Santos-Jundiaí and Paulista railroads, and a founder of the Banco de Comércio e Indústria de São Paulo. Upon his death in 1893 the plantation, by then expanded to half a million trees and valued at 2.4 million milreis, passed to his wife's sister. She in turn married Eduardo Prates, another extremely wealthy capitalist, from a family in Rio Grande do Sul. Prates, styled a count by papal bestowal, also resided in São Paulo.[16]

Prates planted another half-million trees and improved the machinery and processing installations. There were conveyors, a watercourse, and a sawmill. The plantation was electrified and had a telephone system. The peak of Santa Gertrudes' production probably came in 1906 (Table 6.6). The asphalted terraces were flanked in an unusual arrangement by the great house and a chapel, with the machine house in between. The plantation had a school, a clinic, and a pharmacy. Prates improved the pasturage and tried to raise purebred cattle, although, it appears from the administra-

TABLE 6.6

Coffee Production, Santa Gertrudes Plantation, 1857–1916

(Arrobas)

| Year | Plantation records | County tax declaration | Year | Plantation records | County tax declaration |
|---|---|---|---|---|---|
| 1857–59 ave. | 4,300 | — | 1902 | 43,000 | 38,000 |
| 1883–84 ave. | 28,400 | — | 1903 | 36,200 | 39,000[a] |
| 1892 | — | 30,000 | 1904 | 51,400 | 39,200[a] |
| 1895 | 23,400 | — | 1905 | 60,300 | 50,000 |
| 1896 | 34,000 | 20,000 | 1906 | 107,100 | — |
| 1897 | 34,200 | 20,000 | 1907 | 35,000 | — |
| 1898 | 36,000 | 20,000 | 1908 | 61,000 | — |
| 1899 | 31,800 | 25,000 | 1909 | 75,000 | — |
| 1900 | 48,000 | 25,000 | 1916 | 40,000 | — |
| 1901 | 55,000 | 30,000 | | | |

SOURCES. 1857–59: APESP, OD/RC 396. 1883–84: Van Delden Laerne, Brazil and Java, p. 327. 1892–1909: MHP-ABV, Santa Gertrudes, Copiadores and Costaneira; MHP-ABV, "Lançamento de Imposto Sobre Cafe" (title varies). 1905: Estatística agrícola e zootechnica, 1904–1905. Figures for 1907 and 1909 are estimates: harvest of berries divided by two. Tax declarations are railroad station loadings, reported by station master.
    [a] Includes declaration for another plantation.

tor's reports, with little success. He went to considerable expense to make the estate enjoyable, even luxurious, though he spent little time there. A staff of more than a hundred kept up his house and grounds. His gardeners planted several hundred fruit trees, not just orange trees, but pomegranate, cashew, lime, and lemon, and there were at least twenty kinds of vegetables in the kitchen garden. His cellar held six hundred bottles of French and Portuguese wines. The Prates table in the city was provisioned from the estate; he had the administrator frequently ship lambs, pigs, and calves from his pens. Visitors were impressed with the great house, not large in scale, but furnished expensively in art nouveau from Vienna and Paris. The stables quartered superb horses, which were mounted with silver-embellished saddles.[17]

The management of Santa Gertrudes and Palmares is not fully decipherable from the account books that remain. There is no double-entry system, but it is possible that Prates, at least, kept books in São Paulo. The administrator sent daily reports to him, and it is clear that Prates read them carefully. The letters were invariable in format. They recorded the weather, the tasks undertaken and completed by each *turma* (gang) and the contractors, the quantities and qualities of coffee shipped, requests for materials or guidance from the owner, and copies of all correspondence to others, including remittances or vouchers. There were other books in which the accounts of the workers were kept: purchases in the company store, cash advanced against work performed, and crops sold to the plantation. Although other kinds of records may have been compiled, they did not find their way to the archives. The Santa Gertrudes books do not form complete runs, and there is considerable damage from the elements. The Palmares correspondence, a continuous run from 1889 to 1907, provides some understanding of connections with coffee brokers and local merchants. The owner, Jorge Whitaker, dealt with a number of brokers in turn, but for most of the period with Penteado and Dumont, of Santos. The Três Rios broker for the period up to the war was Santos, Gomes and Company. Whitaker was constantly in debt. He drew advances on his brokers which he had to discount with local merchants. Large purchases for both plantations were made in São Paulo, even foodstuffs. Whitaker bought some of his stocks for the plantation store from merchants in Rio Claro, whom he paid off in bags of coffee.[18]

Palmares, with a quarter of the output of Santa Gertrudes, was extremely pressed for cash because outlays for many charges were seasonal and preceded the harvest, and because the workers had to be given credit at the plantation store and cash. Whitaker had no processing machines for most of the period and was forced to pay other planters for the service and wait upon their convenience. His indebtedness reached the point of having to mortgage the crop on the tree, at a high rate of interest, and then of having to write painful explanations to his broker for delays in delivery. Once the railroad reported to the broker that Whitaker's weight was short, prompting an impassioned denial of responsibility from Whitaker. In 1893 Penteado and Dumont refused to honor his notes, and Whitaker had to beg for restoration of his credit. In 1899 he seems to have drawn advances so heavily that there was almost nothing left in his favor when delivery of the harvest was complete.

His cash recording is inexpressive of the kinds of payments that were made, since he rarely notes the purpose of a disbursement. In general his files give an impression of loose control and wasted funds.

The work force at Santa Gertrudes was entirely slave as late as 1884. By 1888 there were about 60 free workers, all of them with Portuguese, German, or Swiss-French names. Italians were hired only in the year of abolition. Eventually eight separate "colonies" were established, each containing several dozen houses. These hamlets, like any factory town, were located for convenience of administration amid the groves, and everywhere had the same dreary regularity of appearance: two rows of duplex buildings with a dirt road between.

The labor regime on the plantations of Rio Claro was quite uniform. Newly arrived immigrant families were given contracts to sign while still in the Immigrant Hostel in the capital. The conditions of the contracts were printed in booklets called *cadernetas* provided to the workers. They were largely standardized, partly through government encouragement. The term was yearly, from harvest to harvest. The family received a grove of trees, usually 2,000 per adult. A fixed amount was paid for the hoeing of each 1,000 trees, and for the harvesting of each alqueire of berries (Table 6.7). Both rates were stated in the caderneta. A house was provided rent-free. If the groves were new, the interplanting of subsistence crops might be allowed. In that case a lower wage might be specified for hoeing, since it was much easier to tend both at once. A few contracts in Rio Claro show wages 25 or 30 percent lower for hoeing with interplanting. In mature groves extra land was made available for subsistence, and sometimes a cow or a goat was loaned along with pasture to graze it. The family had to hoe the grove five or six times, and at the last hoeing the debris from the trees was piled around them. The workers had to replace dead trees, and had to contribute their labor to repair roads, fences, wagons, and drainage ditches. The contracts specified that the workers were responsible for bringing the berries to the terraces after the harvest. At Santa Gertrudes there was no constant supervision over these

TABLE 6.7

*Wages in Coffee Culture, Santa Gertrudes Plantation, 1886–1915*

(Milreis)

| Year | Day labor (10–12 hours) | Hoework, per 1,000 trees | Harvest, per 50 liters |
|------|------|------|------|
| 1886 | 1.40 | 11.00 | .30 |
| 1887 | — | 11.00 | .30 |
| 1889 | 1.40 | 11.00 | .30 |
| 1892 | — | 10.00 | .50 |
| 1894 | 2.50 | 11.13 | .50 |
| 1895 | — | 13.33 | .60–1.00 |
| 1896 | 2.17 | 21.50 | .60 |
| 1897 | — | 20.00 | .60 |
| 1899 | 2.50 | 20.00 | .60 |
| 1900 | 2.17 | 18.50 | .60 |
| 1902 | 2.00 | 13.50 | .50 |
| 1905 | 2.00 | 15.00 | .50 |
| 1907 | 2.00 | 17.50 | .50 |
| 1911 | 2.00 | 17.50 | .50 |
| 1915 | — | 20.00 | .55 |

SOURCES. 1886–1902, 1907: MHP-ABV, Santa Gertrudes, Deve-Haver, Correntes. 1905: *Estatística agrícola e zootechnica, 1904–1905*. 1911: Brazil, Ministério de Agricultura, Indústria e Commércio, *Questionario . . . 1913*. 1915: *Boletim do Departamento Estadual de Trabalho* (1915).

tasks, but their completion was looked after by the administrator and his assistants. The workers, said one observer, "have no illusion of independence." They were "no more than a rural proletariat."[19]

The wage labor regime did not extinguish the jurisdiction of the planters. It still survived in contractual clauses concerning good behavior and the owner's right to maintain order and decorum. Neither party was to insult the honor of the other. The Employment Law of 1879 was canceled in 1890, and later efforts to restore it were unsuccessful. Equity of contract was at last a legal principle in Brazil. The Civil Code of 1916 prohibited debt peonage, which was not in Rio Claro a weapon needed by the planters once the Europeans arrived en masse.[20]

The yearly contracted workers were called *colonos*, like those who had been subject to the parceria contracts, and equally inappropriately. They were, after all, wage-paid tenants, not pioneering smallholders. There were other forms of employment on the plantations. Workers, called *camaradas*, who were paid by the month, tended trees in a gang, which no longer was called an *eito*, recalling slave labor, but a *turma*. The groves in their care were usually those too decadent to be attractive to contracted families. On Santa Gertrudes plantation in the 1890's there were two turmas, one composed of unmarried Italians and one of nationals, for the most part freedmen. Palmares plantation depended heavily on turmas supplied by independent labor contractors. The workers of the turmas were not given subsistence plots, but were boarded by the plantation. They were also housed by the plantation, in the *quadrados*, if they were still standing. The camaradas were not as secure as the colonos, not only because their tenure was merely by the month, but also because the contracts were less generous or specific. There were, below the level of the gang worker, camaradas paid by the day for casual labor, harvesting, and the drying of the berries on the terraces. Palmares also employed many day workers, mainly during harvest. The agregados had nearly disappeared as a class, and the camaradas who succeeded them clearly were not a favored or privileged group. The constitution of a family repre-sented a distinct advance in employability. In one of the adminis-trator's letters to Eduardo Prates, he tells of turning away "six single young men without family who presented themselves saying they came to be *camaradas de turmas*, which was absolutely not needed, since there are a lot of these people around here, and they aren't hired anywhere."[21]

On the larger estates there was generally another small group of skilled workers whose wages were higher than those of the colonos. These were the gang foremen, carpenters, stonemasons, teamsters, tree pruners, operators of the processing machinery, plowmen, and ant exterminators. On Santa Gertrudes in 1905 there were about 90 skilled workers out of a force of about 700. Certain tasks irreg-ularly undertaken were let out to *empreteiros*, or contractors. For-est clearing, tree planting, and the construction of housing for colonos were the most important sorts of contracted work. At Santa Gertrudes the laying out of artificial pasture and the building of barbed wire fences were the work of empreteiros. Machinery was

TABLE 6.8

*Payrolls, Santa Gertrudes Plantation, 1896–99*

| Category | Milreis | Percent |
|---|---|---|
| *Colonos* | 53,048 | 41.4% |
| *Camaradas*, masons, and carpenters | 46,298 | 36.2 |
| *Empreteiros* | 18,335 | 14.3 |
| Skilled workers | 10,368 | 8.1 |
| TOTAL | 128,049 | 100.0% |

SOURCE. MHP-ABV, Santa Gertrudes, Daybook, Copiador, 1896–99.
NOTE. Figures represent sum of five months: May 1896, June 1896, Oct. 1897, Sept. 1899, and Nov. 1899. These were the only months with complete records of expenditures for labor.

repaired by the importer who had sold and installed it. The distribution of payroll among the workers and contractors is estimated for Santa Gertrudes in Table 6.8.

The labor force was extremely mobile. Generally the immigrants preferred a plantation where they had relatives, and the planters encouraged these connections. At Santa Gertrudes the administrator sought free tickets for relatives of workers already resident on the plantation. New arrivals without family had to choose among the offers of agents who were given access to the Immigrant Hostel. Once in the county there were other ways of finding employment. Old workers recall that their parents changed plantations several times in the first few years, but that they moved seldom thereafter. On Santa Gertrudes two-thirds of the colonos stayed more than three years. Evidently it was easy to make comparisons, through comments passed in the town center on Sundays, through the operation of relative-networks, or even through advertisements in local newspapers. The market seems to have been competitive. One planter in Araras is said to have made no representations to prospective workers, but sent them into the groves to learn about conditions of employment from those already hired. The planters, at least during the 1890's, were so little concerned about replacing workers that they willingly provided wagons for families who wanted to transfer to other plantations. The administrator of Santa Gertrudes also exchanged information on indebtedness, and was often willing to assume debts that workers had incurred elsewhere.

A few of the workers, in Rio Claro perhaps 5 percent, took on sharecropping or cash tenancy contracts on small properties, *sítios*, owned by members of the town middle class.[22]

Prospective colonos sought plantations with the most fertile soils and newest trees, since they could offer the highest wages at the least effort. A variable of nearly as much importance was the amount and fertility of land made available for subsistence and pasture, and the intensiveness of supervision to which workers were subjected. In areas just opened to coffee, such as Jaú, workers were not permitted to interplant in the groves, since they could expect a high return from coffee. In Rio Claro it was necessary to permit colonos to divert some of their effort to subsistence, and even to crops that could be sold for cash. On Santo Antônio plantation, for example, an area of two hectares was allotted per family. For this reason the near doubling of the population in the county between 1886 and 1900 resulted in a coffee output only 20 percent greater.[23]

Immigrants were generally preferred for colono contracts, undoubtedly the best positions on the plantation. In Rio Claro there were nationals employed on nearly every plantation; however, of the 326 coffee-growing holdings counted in 1905, only six employed nationals exclusively, and of these only one had a work force of more than 100. Brazilian-born workers were in a minority on all the other plantations save seven. The census shows that smaller and larger estates were somewhat more likely to employ nationals (Table 6.9). The size of the foreign-born group on the plantations, in relation to the number of trees tended, suggests that at least

TABLE 6.9
*Employment of Nationals on Plantations, 1905*

| Size of work force | National workers | Total workers | Percent nationals |
|---|---|---|---|
| 20–50 | 500 | 1,598 | 31% |
| 51–99 | 377 | 1,883 | 20 |
| 100 and over | 463 | 1,757 | 26 |
| TOTAL | 1,340 | 5,238 | 26% |

SOURCE. *Estatística agrícola e zootechnica, 1904–1905.* Analândia included.

some of the nationals, either as colonos or in turmas, were employed to tend the groves on about half the estates. Since the nationals were mostly people of color, including the caboclos, and many of them were freedmen, their marginal position on the plantations appears likely to have been the result of discrimination. On Santa Gertrudes by 1900 the turma of national camaradas had been abolished, and was replaced by a second Italian turma. The remaining nationals were relegated to day work.[24]

Once the planters had a chance to hire Europeans, whom they considered racially superior, perhaps even to themselves, they were bound to make operative their prejudices against mulattos, blacks, and mestizos. In particular, it was generally accepted that Italians were better farmers—more careful and hardworking, and therefore more productive. This lamentable theory has been received quite pacifically by historians, up to the present.[25]

The 1905 agricultural census contains data to refute the idea of the supposed inefficiency of the Brazilian-born worker. Output per worker correlates strongly with output per tree. Plantations in Rio Claro with above-average productivity by both measures had a slightly higher percentage of nationals in their work force (Table 6.10). On plantations with above-average productivity per tree but below-average productivity per worker, nationals formed a still higher percentage, but this figure is skewed by a single plantation with an entirely national work force of 162; otherwise their proportion in that category would be 22 percent. The four planta-

TABLE 6.10
*Productivity of Nationals on Plantations, 1905*
(Percent of work force Brazilian-born)

|  | Productivity per worker | |
|---|---|---|
|  | Above average | Below average |
| Productivity per tree |  |  |
| Above average | 24% (n=1,314) | 30% (n=739) |
| Below average | 49% (n=165) | 21% (n=1,621) |

SOURCE. *Estatística agrícola e zootechnica, 1904–1905*. Plantations with average output per tree have not been included. Analândia included.

tions with a higher-than-average productivity per worker in spite of a lower-than-average productivity per tree had the highest percentage of Brazilian-born workers. Clearly, in Rio Claro the Italians did not improve coffee productivity on the plantation sector.

Therefore the relative prosperity of the immigrants was partly founded upon discrimination against the national workers, especially the blacks. Had they been paid equally on the basis of productivity without making distinctions of whiteness, the Italians might not have come at all. Discrimination was a precondition of mass migration; it was an even heavier cost to the freedmen than the taxes paid and the government services forgone in order to subsidize passage from Europe.

It is possible to estimate the family incomes of colonos from the Santa Gertrudes accounts (Table 6.11). For a four-year period the final balances of a small number of families were found. The average wage payment for the whole period was 334 milreis. In addition, a colono family might sell a wagonload of corn for each 1,000 trees tended, or the equivalent in effort and price of some other product like cheese or pigs. The sales were generally made to itinerant merchants who had their own wagons, or to the plantation owner, to feed his newly contracted families and camaradas. In the late 1880's a wagonload of corn sold for 15 milreis, less 3 for cartage, so that the average cash income of these workers would have been 380 milreis. According to one work contract, a family's monthly ration of cornmeal, beans, and rice might be estimated at one alqueire (13.8 liters), a half, and a half respectively. The total value of these amounts of foodstuffs in 1886–89 would come to 5 milreis

TABLE 6.11

*Colonos' Balances, Santa Gertrudes Plantation, 1885–89*

| Year | Number of families | Average yearly family wages in milreis | Balance after deduction of advances | Number of families with negative balance |
|---|---|---|---|---|
| 1885–86 | 12 | 260 | 19 | 5 |
| 1886–87 | 12 | 230 | −41 | 10 |
| 1887–88 | 12 | 452 | 171 | 3 |
| 1888–89 | 10 | 396 | 78 | 0 |

SOURCE. MHP-ABV, Santa Gertrudes, Deve-Haver, 1885–89. Cf. Table 4.5, p. 119.

a month. In addition, it would not be difficult to raise for slaughter a few pigs a year, or their equivalent in value of another 4 milreis a month. Coffee, a half arroba a month, valued at 2 more milreis, could be filched easily enough if it was not provided by the owner. If the colono family produced no more than this, they would add another 122 milreis a year to their income, for a total of about 500 milreis.[26]

Since conditions of production and sale remained fairly constant in the period up to World War I, it is possible to estimate the total incomes of colonos for several of these years in Rio Claro (Table 6.12). The rise in incomes between 1885 and 1896 was rapid, partly on account of a general inflation, and also because of the buoyancy of the local coffee economy. By 1911 incomes had declined to 67 percent of the 1896 average, but in real terms they declined somewhat less, since the cost of living had decreased by 10 percent. The decline in colono incomes in Rio Claro was to some degree the result of lower productivity of the trees. Workers would tend to move on to newer areas to offset potential losses; thus the individual experience might not be the same as the general apparent condition of the colonos. The wage rates of the colonos ought not to be confused with those of the work force as a whole. As productivity per tree declined, colonos were partly replaced with lower-paid camaradas. Thus real wages suffered a more extreme cycle than can be observed in the table.[27]

During the first year on the plantation the colono family was

TABLE 6.12

*Estimated Yearly Income of Colonos, 1885–1911*

| Year | Yearly family wages | Sale of corn, etc. | Value of subsistence | Estimated yearly family income |
|------|------|------|------|------|
| 1885–87 | 245 | 48 | 128 | 421 |
| 1887–89 | 426 | 48 | 122 | 596 |
| 1896 | 600 | 110 | 280 | 990 |
| 1900 | 570 | 65 | 175 | 810 |
| 1905 | 500 | 100 | 240 | 840 |
| 1911 | 520 | 42 | 105 | 667 |

SOURCES. Derived from sources listed in Tables 6.7 and 6.11, and MHP-ABV, Santa Gertrudes, Copiador 2, Daybook 1899, Correntes, 1899–1902; APESP, Secretaria de Agricultura, 44, "Regulamento . . . Fazenda Angelica."

obliged to spend most of its earnings in advances to feed itself and to buy tools, household equipment, and perhaps some animals. Company store records show purchases mainly of cornmeal, beans, and rice. Wheat flour was a luxury, and beef was purchased no more than once or twice during the year. Lard took the place of olive oil. Once the subsistence plantings were harvested, however, purchases at the company store became more varied. The store stocked cottonseed oil, salt, bacon, sugar, vinegar, and salt cod. It also carried soap, matches, kerosene, and cloth, including sheeting. Undoubtedly there were other purchases made in town, since nearly half the advances were in cash. Besides staple foods, pigs, goats, and chickens, the colonos often planted watermelon, pumpkins, and peanuts. Probably they are responsible for the introduction of tomatoes, carrots, and mushrooms, but the range of plant domesticates remained limited compared to Italy. Immigrants who became smallholders attempted to produce wine, though other areas of São Paulo were more favorable. They planted orange trees, with considerable success. Aged second-generation immigrants recollect that their parents were quite satisfied with their lot in Rio Claro, mainly because they ate better. One remarked that his father had never accumulated savings because then he would have had to continue living *na miséria*, as he had in Veneto, and that he could not endure any more.[28]

The women made clothing from store-bought fabric. Sometimes there was a sewing machine that could be borrowed, or a neighbor who was willing to sew in exchange for some other favor or cash payment. The work costume consisted of an unbleached cotton smock and trousers, and a broad-brimmed straw hat. Women covered their hair with a bandanna. Every family could afford bleached and printed cloth, and even woolens, for dress clothing, and the men usually owned felt hats and leather shoes. The greatest luxury was a horse, which turned a young camarada into a gallant, or a husband into a squire. The possession of a horse must have seemed an extraordinary contrast with the European living standard, but it also demonstrates the degree of exploitation of family labor by the male, since he was the sole beneficiary of it. Since women and children were as able to hoe and harvest as the male adult, and plowing was done by skilled workers along with pruning and fumigating, he was without any special function. All domestic labor was performed by the women, except for shopping, which would have put money in their hands, and in any case served as an excuse to ride to town.[29]

The plantation workers' contacts with the town middle class were expensive, although probably less humiliating than in Italy. The county government offices charged fees for their services, and so did the church. A civil or church marriage cost 30 milreis around 1900, that is, two weeks' wages. By law, the plantations had to provide a school building for the workers' children, but a fee was collected to pay the teacher. At Angélica plantation it amounted to a 2 percent deduction from wages. Often the children were withdrawn from school by the father, who sought to exploit them as soon as possible. Italian children, like the children of slaves, had to begin to work in the groves at age eight. Physicians and pharmacists charged heavily for their services, and a prolonged illness was generally disastrous for a family, even when the ill member recovered completely. A visit by a physician might cost a staggering 50 milreis, if he was called out of his office.[30]

The death rate of the county in the early years of the century was quite low, about 21 per thousand, mainly because the population was young and well-fed. Infants were carried off by enteritis, which was the disease of poor sanitation, dirt floors, and flies. The water supply was commonly simply a nearby stream, so that the colonos were exposed to water-borne infections, including the dreadful schistosomiasis. Chagas disease, spread by insects that live in thatch, was also endemic; indeed, this disease was first isolated in the district of Analândia. Smallpox had finally been reduced to small outbreaks by the increasing use of vaccination. In 1910 there were 109 cases, but only 15 deaths; in 1874 several hundred had died. In spite of public health measures of considerable intensity, yellow fever was not eliminated, and there were periodic outbreaks. There was also at least one epidemic of trachoma. The leading causes of death, however, when the causes were reported, were tuberculosis, pneumonia and other bronchial infections, and arteriovascular diseases.[31]

Labor conflicts were not regularly recorded in the press (none of those that occurred on Santa Gertrudes, for example, were mentioned). Rarely was the cause explained or the outcome noted. The incidents, in fact, were not considered worthy of note unless someone was injured or the police were called in. In October 1888, only a few months after the slave crisis, an intriguing report appeared in the local newspaper that the administrator of Santo Antônio plantation petitioned to have his fine removed for galloping in town. He had come to call the police because his colonos were "in revolt." In September 1893, when two Brazilians who were "promoting disorders" on Morro Pelado plantation were arrested by the police, twelve or more Italians came to their aid. The *capangas* sided with the police, and there was a melee in which several persons were wounded. Evidently the planters had lost their terror of worker unrest, but this time there was no Davatz to publicize the workers' complaints.[32]

At least three murders occurred in the county on account of labor disputes, one an Italian killed by a capanga in the presence of the administrator on Santa Ana plantation, which was at the time in the hands of the Zerrener-Bülow importing house. Another victim was an administrator of Walther Reitmann's plantation in Analândia. The killer, an agregado, may have been hired to carry out the murder, since he was protected afterward by capangas of the baron of Araraquara. The third victim was a planter, killed by one of his workers, a case that will be discussed below. There are more reports of beatings administered by capangas and sometimes by the police. A Rio Claro newspaper reported in 1901 that a local lawyer, hired by a group of colonos in Araraquara, was assaulted by two planters and their gunmen when he stepped off the train, while police stood by and watched. Other violent events lurk half-remembered, perhaps distorted, under the surface: an aged former field worker says her husband always believed that his father, sick with yellow fever, had been poisoned by a capanga, so that he would not spread the disease. Immigrant workers must have been constantly wary, and disposed to meet force with force, for the capangas were still the planters' principal means of dealing with militant workers.[33]

On Santa Gertrudes there were at least three strikes during the five years for which the letter copybooks are available. On the first occasion, during the harvest of 1895, incoming workers were encouraged by those already on the plantation to ask for 1.00 milreis, instead of the going .60 milreis for collecting 50 liters of berries, in the expectation that this raise would be applied generally. Because the administrator was desperate for help, he requested that Prates concede the raise, for a total added expense of 1,600 to 2,000 milreis. Sometime in May 1896, there was a strike on Santa Gertrudes that may have involved other plantations in the county. There is no indication of the causes. Three colonos were ejected from the estate as agitators. Twenty-nine more families quit, which represented nearly a quarter of the colono work force. In October 1899, there was another dispute in which 27 families quit. In this case Prates was not informed until the administrator had already found replacements. Evidently he would have been displeased, and a strike reflected on the management. Interestingly, not only were those who quit paid their wages promptly, but the wagons of the estate were made available to move their belongings, and the administrator even bought the corn remaining in their cribs.[34]

More common than strikes, probably, was simple flight. When workers found themselves too heavily in debt, the temptation arose to disappear in the night and take up a contract in some other county. The parallel with slavery, or at least its final years, is clear. The capangas were still useful, therefore, to inhibit flight, by force if necessary, and planters were obliged to send intimidating letters to their competitors, demanding payment of back debts owed by their former employees.

Strike movements, extending over several plantations, occurred in Rio Claro in 1902 and 1905, and there was a widespread wave of strikes all over the Paulista West in August 1911. The general cause was the slump in coffee prices, but the specific provocations were varied. These actions left no organizations, and gained no sympathy in town among factory workers. The town proletariat engaged in numerous strikes. The first recorded was in 1892, and there were important general strikes, initiated by railroad employees, in 1901 and 1906. There were several unions in town, but they did not extend their organizing into the countryside. The planters forbade any kind of association among the colonos for fear that they might become vehicles for labor protest. The town workers were heavily politicized and were drawn into the power struggles of the middle class. It is not clear why they displayed no solidarity with the workers of the plantations.[35]

Immigration was in itself a cause of labor conflict. The initial engagement was nearly always disappointing, not only because false expectations were often raised by reports of relatives, consular propaganda, and claims of labor brokers in the hostel, but because emigration was itself traumatic, and led to self-doubt that turned into hostility. The forms assumed by that sense of malaise were, nevertheless, realistic. The wage system was exploitive, in a particular as well as a general sense. The provision of subsistence plots, essential to attracting contract workers, contained the same element of opposing interests that had been present in the *parceria* regime. The worker would tend to carry out the hoeing of the trees quickly and superficially, in order to devote as much time as possible to his food and cash crops. In the short run no decline in coffee yield would be noticed, and in the long run the worker could move to some newer, more fertile plantation. Thus wage labor was only relatively more productive, in terms of coffee output, than slave labor had been, and the effort to maximize the estate's share necessarily led to conflict. The resolution was characteristically in the worker's favor, because the planter was as speculatively oriented as he. Supervision was slight—one contract shows a single administrator for 450 workers, and others show that the administrator was allowed to tend his own grove, or to reside on another property or even in town. On Santa Gertrudes the daybooks record far more supervision of the turmas than of the colonos.[36]

Another source of disputes was nonpayment of workers. Poor management, a heavy mortgage, or a bad run of crops made nonpayment always a last resort of failing planters. There was no defense, since the financial condition of the estate was usually unknown to the employees, and in case of bankruptcy, they did not have prior claim to its assets. The owner might try to find pretexts for lowering their claims by fining them unjustly for alleged derelictions of contract, or he might goad them into leaving the estate or fire them without cause. One former colono remembers that his father quit the plantation of Rafael de Barros in disgust when he came home one evening to discover another worker had been moved into his house and was tending his garden plot. The worker killed on Santa Ana plantation had been fired and was demanding money owed him.[37]

Finally, the workers endured a considerable amount of the malevolent "paternalism" once displayed toward the slaves. The plantation was still quite often an enclave of private jurisdiction, where the planter sat as judge and enforced his decisions with hired gunmen. Sometimes he even sought to revive the *droit du seigneur*. The contracts perpetuated this situation, since they provided for fines, not only for failing to carry out the work assigned, but also for disrespectful or indecorous behavior, such as drunkenness or offensive language. The administrator of Santa Gertrudes applied this sort of summary punishment as though he were a justice of the peace: 40 milreis for disrespect of the administrator, 50 milreis for wifebeating (both imposed in 1902, when the estate might have had need of cutting back salaries by means of fines; hence the attitude might not have been in any sense paternalistic). Although, from the distance of the great house, the Italians seemed to be more satisfactory villeins than the emancipated Africans, that was an illusion. The immigrants made use of the law and the courts, complained in the consuls' offices, and even took out personal advertisements in the local newspaper to abuse their employers.[38]

The most startling and scandalous incident of all the conflicts in the Paulista West occurred in Analândia on October 3, 1900. Diogo Salles, political boss of the dismembered district and brother of the president of Brazil, was killed in a quarrel with one of his

colonos on his Nova América plantation. The murderer was Angelo Lungaretti, 22 years old, still living under his parents' roof.
The Lungarettis had resided on the estate for three years. Diogo
seems to have been more his son's victim than his employee's. The
son, Raul, had given Angelo a gun, possibly because he saw in him
the stuff of which capangas are made, or possibly just to get on his
good side. Raul was attracted by one, two, or possibly all three of
Angelo's sisters, aged fifteen, seventeen, and nineteen. He tried
to seduce the youngest, Isabel, who refused him, and then, accompanied by a capanga, he tried one night to carry her off, but failed.
Angelo went to another planter to try to move the household.
When Raul heard of it, he went to the planter and dissuaded him
from taking on the family. Then he had Angelo jailed. The other
colonos, having some knowledge of Raul's motive, struck the plantation, and Raul had to bring the police delegate to make the
excuse that Angelo was jailed for drunkenness.[39]

Raul then seems to have decided that he would have to evict the
family after all, in order to conceal his peccadillos. Angelo, finally
set free, provided him with a pretext. Angelo had been living his
own drama. He wanted to marry the daughter of another colono,
but her father was unwilling. On October 3, the two families engaged in noisy argument that was overheard by other workers.
Raul announced to the Lungarettis that they were a source of dissension on the plantation, and would have to leave forthwith. He
went to fetch his father, who probably knew nothing of these
events, since he resided in Rio Claro, and had just arrived on his
plantation that morning.[40]

Angelo was already armed because he had considered using his
gun against his prospective father-in-law, but when his father
refused to leave the plantation, the focus of his resentment shifted.
The whole family went out into the grove to pick coffee, to show
the Salleses ostentatiously that they had no intention of leaving.
Diogo and his son appeared, and Diogo repeated the demand that
they depart the property. Francisco, Angelo's father, insisted that
they had the right to stay until the end of the year, or at least that
they should be paid off immediately. Their credit amounted to

2,000 milreis. Diogo refused and grabbed Francisco, shaking him so roughly that he fell to the ground. Out came Angelo's gun, and Diogo was shot square in the chest. Raul ran away, and so did Angelo, lest he be caught *in flagrante*.[41]

It was as though a pebble dropped in a pool had become a tidal wave. In Analândia the police beat up neighbors in order to extract depositions favoring the Salles clan. In Rio Claro, where the Salles faction was in opposition and where the trial had to be held, the sympathy for Angelo was strong. The Italian immigrant middle class engaged one of Brazil's most distinguished lawyers to defend him. In Rio de Janeiro the bereaved president faced the prospect of a reaction from the Italian government. Angelo underwent two trials, during which it was revealed that the Lungarettis would not have been the first to lose their crops, improvements, and their balances on the Salles plantation. Angelo was declared guilty and sentenced to twelve years imprisonment, but in 1908, after a change of government in Rio de Janeiro, he was pardoned. If Angelo had not fired at Salles, the Supreme Court reasoned, one of Salles's capangas would have killed Angelo. The Lungarettis were given passage back to Italy.[42]

The Lungaretti affair demonstrated to the Brazilian government that the resident Italian immigrant middle class was sufficiently ill at ease to behave ambiguously in relation to its class position. The court had found it almost impossible to impanel a jury. Naturalized immigrants would not sit, out of a conviction that Angelo was justified. It may be that the resident Italians were as antagonistic toward the landowners as were the plantation workers; thus rural labor disputes provided a convenient means of goading them. The Italian-language *Fanfulla*, whose readers were quite certainly urban lower middle class, mentioned those disputes incessantly, never forgetting to notice if a capanga was mulatto or black. Its lavish commemorative volume, *Il Brasile e gli italiani*, printed for immigrants with considerable discretionary income, was halfhearted concerning the fate of the colonos, and even quoted the most anti-planter of the consuls, Alfredo Rossi, on the subject, although the purpose of the volume was ostensibly to demonstrate the successful integration of the Italians and the estimableness of their Brazilian hosts.[43]

The Italian government was already disturbed by the ending in 1899 of the contract system of introducing immigrants. The method thereafter employed, head bounties paid to all shipping companies on a first-come, first-served basis, seemed to the Italian foreign office an evasion of responsibility by the state of São Paulo. Consular reports of hard times on the plantations, capped by the spectacular scandal of the Lungaretti case, decided the Italian government to forbid, in March 1902, the acceptance by its nationals of offers of free transportation to Brazil. In response the embarrassed Brazilian government passed a few measures to improve the contractual position of the workers. In 1906 it made debts owed to workers privileged in cases of bankruptcy, and the state of São Paulo granted free legal assistance to immigrants during the first two years of residence. In 1911, after the Spanish government followed the example of the Italian in banning subsidized emigration, a state Patronato Agrícola was created to arbitrate labor disputes. The actions of the Italian and Spanish governments were not entirely effective. Immigrants continued to arrive, but at a slower rate. Combined with the depression on the plantations, however, they resulted in several years of net migration outflow.[44]

The drain of workers was a serious loss, but no effort was made to retain them, except for a certain minority. Those colonos who had saved enough to buy land in Italy would remove from São Paulo not only themselves but a sizable capital stock. Since they were lost to the plantation labor market in any case, they might as well be encouraged to purchase a smallholding in São Paulo. The principle of "fixing the immigrants to the soil" was observed superficially from the beginning of subsidized mass migration. The provincial law that offered the first full-fare subsidy, in 1884, also provided funds to buy up five plantations, to be subdivided in lots, so that immigrants who had "made their economies" might achieve the status of smallholders. This modest project accommodated no more than 750 families, but it was displayed in all the tracts published by the state to show immigrants how easily their ascent might be guaranteed by emigrating to São Paulo.[45]

These first *núcleos coloniais* had other serious purposes, principally that of providing "points of support and secure auxiliaries of the great estates themselves," as one of the first Republican state presidents put it in 1895—in other words, a reserve labor pool. To this end the government was frequently enjoined to place the núcleos in the coffee-growing areas. One of the núcleos provided for in 1884 was located in Rio Claro. This was Cascalho, originally one of the estates of the baron of Porto Feliz. The choice of this plantation illustrates the other important purpose of the scheme, the bailing out of influential but bankrupt members of the elite. Its owner was Domingos Jaguaribe, the baron's son-in-law, by then desperately in need of cash to keep his other inherited estates from the auctioneer's block. The committee that recommended the transfer was composed of the count of Três Rios and two other local planters. Cascalho was not salable as coffee land, because it was too low-lying and therefore subject to frost.[46]

The province bought it for 60,000 milreis, including land valued at 40 milreis per hectare. It was divided into 249 lots, of which 73 were "rural," each ten hectares in size, each with a brick house. The lots cost 500 milreis each in cash, or 600 milreis on a four-year mortgage. There were also smaller "suburban" and "urban" lots, since it was supposed that the núcleo would generate its own town center. The province provided a large shed for receiving new families, a school, a corn mill, a circular saw, and a few other pieces of equipment. A doctor was hired on retainer to treat the colonists. The lots were not attractive at the set price, and so they were lowered, first to 400, then to 300, and by 1887 to 200. The urban center proved unrealizable; the smaller plots were sold off in lots of two to five. One tract of nine unfarmable plots was sold for 100 milreis. Meanwhile the administrator appointed by the state had diligently removed all the timber worth the effort, including trees on land already bought but not yet occupied, and had sold it for his own account.[47]

At the lower prices sales were rapid. The pretenders were local, at first all with German surnames. By 1890 the buyers, however, were overwhelmingly Italian. A change of administrators had effected a policy of selling to recent immigrants so as to achieve a maximum propaganda effect abroad. In support of the petitions for lots, the administrator always mentioned need (although most sales were for cash) and diligence. There is no question that the colonists resided on their lots and farmed them, at least until the lots were all bought up and the núcleo was "emancipated." Until that event, in 1895, the smallholders were subjected to a paternalistic regime. They were selected personally by the provincial inspectors of immigration, and they were directed in their tasks by the administrator, who assigned lots, collected installments, oversaw common tasks like road repair, and made sure that the residents complied with the regulations, which even included a ban on hunting and fishing on work days. He also collected their votes on election day. The government supported the núcleo inadequately and fitfully, so that the administrator was often in arrears in his accounts.[48]

By 1893 there were 520 persons on Cascalho, roughly 120 families. The núcleo was a model success at first. The smallholders were moderately prosperous. Their average income in 1893 was 1,170 milreis, perhaps a third more than that earned by colono families in that year. Evidently the difference more than justified the capital they invested, which amounted to 1,200 milreis each in improvements and animals, beyond the average 300 milreis in land.[49]

Only seven more núcleos were added to the original five. Altogether they accommodated no more than 1,800 families. Another núcleo was founded in Rio Claro in 1905, during the second coffee crisis. It was also a bankrupt plantation, São José do Corumbataí, owned by the heirs of Antônio da Costa Alves Ferreira, descendant of one of the original *sesmaria* grantees. The estate had never been fully developed—only 185 of its 4,262 hectares were in coffee—and there remained in 1894 more than 2,600 hectares of virgin forest. In 1903 it was sold for 80,000 milreis by the bank into whose hands it had fallen, although the auctioneer had tried to start bidding a few years before at 250,000 milreis. The buyer was Fernando da Rocha Paranhos, a speculator from outside the county. He began subdividing the property, selling ten-hectare lots for 1,500 milreis, but ran out of cash. Somehow he persuaded the state government in 1905 to go shares with him. The state paid 100,000 milreis for half and agreed to build a road to the railway station. Paranhos was to get a commission of 200 milreis for every lot he sold.[50]

The núcleo was renamed Jorge Tibiriçá, in honor of the state president who had proposed reopening funds for núcleos in 1900. Clearly this was a private speculation in which the state's participation was a subsidy. The state built houses on each lot and provided a school. Paranhos, who retained a sawmill on the property, removed the timber on unclaimed lots. The lots were consolidated in 20- and 30-hectare plots. Nearly all the lots were sold on time payments, principally to newly arrived immigrants, who were given the special privilege of taking residence without making a down payment. Of the total 156 lots subdivided, 121 were sold to new immigrants—Latvians, Germans, Italians, Poles, and others. About 40 percent of the heads of these households were literate. In 1911 the population was 1,017. By then the colonists had paid off almost half their mortgages and owned about 1,000 milreis each in improvements and animals. In that year fifteen families left the núcleo, eleven entered, and four lots were consolidated. Sales of cereals and animals in 1911–12 averaged 1,270 milreis per family. The cost of state administration, at least in part a form of subsidy, amounted to 160 milreis per family. Clearly the colonists were earning considerably more than the average colono family.[51]

Although Rio Claro was far better endowed with sponsored colonies than any other county in São Paulo, they did not contribute much to the development of smallholding. The generally highly optimistic judgment concerning the ability of the immigrants to realize their ambition to own land is based mainly on individual purchases. The agricultural census of 1905 provides an opportunity to gauge their real chances (Table 6.13). Notice that many of the Germans and Swiss would be completing a second generation in Rio Claro by 1905. There were thirteen additional holdings by German-surnamed Brazilians, totaling 534 alqueires. The arrival of the Portuguese would have ranged over a long period of time, and most of the Italians and Spaniards would have come after 1885. A close inspection of the names of the landowners reveals

TABLE 6.13

*Nationality of Landowners, 1905*

| Nationality | Number of properties | Number of coffee trees | Value in milreis |
|---|---|---|---|
| Brazilians | 285 | 12,839,910 | 18,729,000 |
| Italians | 70 | 901,000 | 929,000 |
| Germans | 43 | 572,600 | 1,092,000 |
| Portuguese | 19 | 1,152,000 | 1,103,000 |
| Spaniards | 15 | 138,000 | 127,000 |
| Austrians | 4 | — | 20,000 |
| Swiss | 1 | 200,000 | 350,000 |
| TOTAL | 437 | 15,803,510 | 22,350,000 |

SOURCE. *Estatística agrícola e zootechnica, 1904–1905.* Includes Analândia.

clearly that the modest success implied by the census belonged not to colonos but to immigrants who were town merchants and professionals from the beginning, or who were absentee members of the *haut-bourgeoisie* of Santos and São Paulo. Six of the Portuguese holdings can be so identified, and they accounted for 77 percent of the value of Portuguese holdings. The German landowners were nearly all a generation removed from field labor, or had never performed it. The single Swiss holding belonged to a nonresident merchant. At least seven of the Italian owners had never been plantation workers, and their holdings were 54 percent of the value of Italian properties.[52]

The relative success of immigrant colonos is not, in any case, a measure of social mobility on the plantations, since they formed merely a sector of the rural proletariat, and the most favored sector at that. The 1905 census provides another, better indication of the attainability of land by all agricultural workers. There were, on the 437 properties surveyed, 9,239 workers. It appears that only colonos or resident camaradas were included; the county's rural work force was closer to 13,000. The census lists 285 farms with six or fewer workers, which may be taken as an upper limit for family-sized farms. This number ought to be doubled since there were surviving, unregistered minifundia in Itaqueri and other rural neighborhoods. The census counted 921 workers on the 285 farms; the minifundia, with insufficient land for a full family's subsistence, probably occupied another 600 persons. It would appear, then, that less than 12 percent of farm workers labored on their own land. It cannot be assumed, however, that all these smallholdings were owner-operated. A number were owned by townspeople and leased, as the nationality analysis suggests. The census provides another clue to this sector. Frequently the nationality of the owner and of the workers is different, implying that the workers were tenants. There were 127 workers in this group, which must be taken as a minimum figure, since it is very likely that nationals leased to nationals and immigrants to immigrants. The census suggests the reason why smallholding was so unlikely an outcome of a farm laboring career. The average size of those holdings worked by no more than six persons was 41.3 hectares, and their average value was 6,090 milreis, twelve years' cash wages for the average colono family.

The year 1905 was rather early in the era of Italian migration, and the second coffee crisis since their arrival had not yet run its course. Fourteen years later more smallholders had appeared. The census of 1919 listed 868 owners in Rio Claro, double the number of 1905. Meanwhile, however, the population had increased by about 15,000, or more than a third. The lots on the núcleo Jorge Tibiriçá represented more than half of the increase. There were indications, however, that the núcleos had already begun to concentrate. At Jorge Tibiriçá 33 fewer properties were listed than in 1912, and at Cascalho there were no more than 75 left, only half the number when the núcleo was emancipated. Only two rural neighborhoods, Assistência and Lopes, which were squatter settlements before the first sesmarias were granted, showed as many as 40 small properties each. Not until the 1930's did the number of holdings increase greatly, when the coffee regime was considerably reduced and the general collapse of the export sector led to the fractioning of many plantations. By 1939, there were 1,414 holdings registered in Rio Claro (Table 6.14). By then first-generation immigrants were owners of 39 percent of the area of all holdings and their average property was somewhat larger in size than those owned by nationals. It is likely that this growth in the number of

TABLE 6.14

Number of Rural Properties, 1822–1964

| Year | Number of properties | Year | Number of properties | Year | Number of properties |
|------|------|------|------|------|------|
| 1822 | 151 | 1897 | 2,577 [!] | 1933 | 2,039 |
| 1835 | 258 | 1905 | 437 | 1939 | 1,414 |
| 1857 | 448 | 1919 | 868 | 1964 | 1,661ᵃ |

SOURCES. 1822, 1835: APESP, População Piracicaba. 1857: Paulo Pestana, O café em São Paulo. 1897: SP(S), Repartição de Estatística, Relatorio, 1897. 1905: Estatística agrícola e zootechnica, 1904–1905. 1919: Census. 1933, 1939: SP(S), Secretaria de Agricultura, Lavoura cafeeira paulista, 1932–1933 and 1939–1940. 1964: Enoch Borges de Oliveira, "Agricultura, pecuaria, indústria, comércio," in Rio Claro 1964, pp. 48–49.
ᵃ Does not include the dismembered counties.

properties was somewhat illusory, and more gradual in any case than appears from the table. During the 1930's many squatters of long residence registered their properties at last, under the pressure of claim-jumping by town dwellers.[53]

It cannot be claimed, as some historians have, that the "average" immigrant, or "many" immigrants, achieved landownership. In Rio Claro few managed that feat. The 300 or so milreis needed to repatriate an immigrant family was much more commonly scraped up than the average 6,000 milreis for a family-sized farm. In any case, the purchasers were usually middle-class town immigrants, not plantation workers. Luiz Piccoli, who arrived in the county as a colono, soon moved to town and set up in the milling business. As he explained to his grandson, plantation work was "no way to get rich." Piccoli did indeed rise in town; he dealt in coffee and at one time owned seven plantations. The purchase of a few dozen hectares, as difficult as that was to accomplish, was not necessarily the path to security or the middle class. When Angélica was dismembered for the last time, in 1924, Pedro Rossi, whose father had been a colono, then the owner of a sítio in the neighborhood of Lopes, sold his inheritance and bought 90 hectares. His section included the anachronistic great house built by the baron of Grão-Mogol, and so he lived in it, and still does with his wife and generations of Rossis. The mansion is almost unchanged; Rossi shows visitors the iron rings in the cellar to which slaves were shackled, and the huge trough, filled with empty Coca-Cola bottles, from which the slaves were slopped. Rossi's grandchildren raise a variety of cash and subsistence crops and some coffee. Surely they live better and more independently than the workers on nearby sugar plantations; they even own a jeep. Yet there is nothing on the farm but meager essentials—a few pieces of wooden furniture, pots and pans, and tools. The children run barefoot, ragged, and rheumy-eyed through the empty, dusty halls. A hard life, not an easy one.[54]

As coffee declined, most of the bourgeoisie abandoned Rio Claro. Most of the Oliveira family withdrew to the capital. Only one of the viscount's sons played a political role in the county, and he was overshadowed by another, João Baptista, who joined the Republican Party and was appointed to the revolutionary junta that took control of the capital upon the fall of the emperor, and later became vice-president of the state. The family town house was sold and became a hotel. Of the third generation, 79 grandsons and granddaughters, only 23 were planters or the wives of planters; the rest fell into the middle class. The São José plantation remained undivided because one of the daughters had consolidated the property in her hands, and had passed it on to her only child, also a female. Her husband made a success of raising thoroughbreds there. Another of the viscount's granddaughters married Washington Luiz, who became the last president of the Old Republic, deposed in 1930. Another married Marcelo Schmidt, a shrewd second-generation immigrant, who was Rio Claro's boss during much of the Old Republic. Other enterprising petty bourgeois who married into the family included Hoffman, Farano, Castellano, Cartolano, and Klingelhoffer—merchants, professionals, and plantation administrators. In São Paulo there were marriages with the rising industrial bourgeoisie: Morganti, Puglisi, Gasparian. The founding family had scattered; its best energies were spent attempting to gain power and influence in the capital. Those who remained behind or returned were absorbed by the caretakers.[55]

In São Paulo the mass of immigrants found a new class structure, in which they luckily were placed above the native population of

African and aboriginal descent, and set upon twenty meters of *terra roxa*. They did, therefore, generally achieve a standard of living higher than they had experienced in Europe. But there was little surplus beyond subsistence, as long as they remained on the plantations. Remittances from Brazil to Italy in the years before World War I, in the form of money orders, amounted to no more than 2 milreis per immigrant — one-fiftieth the rate from the United States, although the two groups of Italians were roughly equal in number by 1910.[56]

The abolition of slavery made possible mass immigration of plantation workers, and the immigrants preserved the great estates. In Rio Claro the two decades following abolition were the zenith of coffee. The county's town center grew and its production became to a considerable degree industrialized. As the coffee trees aged, however, the plantations were divided. In Rio Claro the cycle had taken more than a century; yet its experience cannot be taken as a microcosm of the plantation system as a whole. Rio Claro was a fixed point, at first on the edge, then in the middle, and finally behind a moving frontier. There was no interest in practicing sustained-yield agriculture in a country where land appeared inexhaustible. The coffee trees, therefore, were not (until very recently, and then in small number) replanted. The groves had lasted longer, at least, than they had in the valley of the Paraíba River, where steep slopes led to erosion that left moonscapes, or at best poor pasturage. The planter families moved on. Reinvestment was made further inland, or better yet in São Paulo, in banking, trade, and real estate. Rio Claro was just a square on a vast checkerboard. The immigrants who did not get land or repatriate accompanied the advance, and spawned a second generation of colonos. The rest joined the proletariat of the towns.

The inheritors of the county were the town middle class, a few of them former colonos, but most of them immigrants who had been town residents in Europe, and who had come with a trade, a stock of capital, and family connections. By World War I the Italians among them were ready to demand parity in town affairs from the German, Swiss, and Portuguese middle class. The process was not entirely free of rancor, but it was completed by the second war. The daughters of fallen plantation families married among them, and finally they married among themselves. As they prospered and bought urban lots and houses, suburban sítios, and finally the dismembered plantations, at the same time the economic and political power of the state capital penetrated further into the county. The new factories were absentee-owned, as the plantations once were, and the new middle class learned to deal in small quantities, to await developments, and to cadge contracts from the Secretariat of Public Works. The heroic age was over.

# Conclusions

THE PLANTATION system of Rio Claro originated in the usurpation of the land and the elimination or marginalization of the existing swidden farmers by a group of persons who had accumulated capital in a colonial agricultural export trade. By this act they expropriated as well the value invested in the land by the squatters through their clearing of a considerable part of it. The new owners immediately began to buy and sell parcels, as a speculation, but with the intention of setting up large-scale agricultural exploitation. They were unable to establish a system of wage labor. Their plantations were less attractive to the rural propertyless population than the alternative of squatting on still unclaimed land, because the plantations were no more productive than swidden farming and hence could not offer greater rewards to offset the rent or other form of tax on labor that their owners would seek to impose.

Slavery was therefore an indispensable solution, for without slaves the planters would have to renounce their ambitions. The slave regime in Rio Claro was exploitative in the most extreme sense, in that it brought about a decline in the stock of slaves. Only when circumstances external to their system obliged it, did the planters, circa 1850, begin to experiment with wage workers. They imported Europeans, whose inexperience with local agricultural technique and wages and prices might contain them upon the plantations for at least a few years. The cost of bringing them to São Paulo was financed by the government, and was payable by the immigrants out of earnings. This was a truly semiservile regime, not only on that account but also because nonfulfillment of contract subjected the worker to imprisonment at hard labor. The burdensomeness and inequality of this system led the immigrants to reject it. Rather than improve upon the terms, the planters returned to higher-cost slave labor.

It cannot be maintained that this relapse was a sign of precapitalist mentality. The planters quite evidently accumulated capital and applied it to all sorts of enterprises, mainly to improved processing equipment and to railroads. They were unwilling to distribute the gains from improved productivity among their laborers, however. By the 1870's it is conceivable that the native rural population had increased sufficiently in size that it might have provided a plantation labor force, in addition to the Europeans, who were emigrating in ever greater numbers, but not to Brazil. The slave population, not the planters, at last brought ruin to the system of forced labor by refusing to participate in it, to the degree that repression became unendurably expensive.

The plantations would not have survived this crisis if another source of labor had not appeared. Italian rural proletarians, driven by extreme necessity at exactly this moment, were attracted to São Paulo by the extraordinary policy of full government subsidies. The planters then fixed them on the plantations by installing them in better paid and more secure positions than those allotted the freedmen, who were thus cut off, not only from the possibility of acquiring ownership of the estates but even from individual social mobility within the wage labor regime.

This reconstruction of the transition to wage labor is derived mainly from the records of a single county. No doubt the process left different traces in other places. Rio Claro was at the leading edge of the coffee frontier from 1850, when the African slave traffic was abolished, through the wave of Italian immigration in the 1890's. Thus it experienced with great intensity all of the elements of the crisis. Higher coffee yields generated there the highest level of slave prices and of wages in Brazil. Undoubtedly these conditions made possible the desultory experiments with bonded labor, accelerated the inflow of slaves and free laborers from other provinces, discouraged manumission, and finally enabled local planters to attract the essential immigrant substitutes. In the Paraíba Valley, where the coffee groves were long in decadence, the planters were ruined when their slaves departed. The runaways were lured to places like Bauru, Ibitinga, and Ribeirão Preto, two hundred kilometers and more beyond Rio Claro, where plantations were being formed whose soils were more fertile still, but whose owners had despaired of finding slaves at any price.

The case of Rio Claro exhibits the futility of confusing private profitability with the advancement of a society. Granted that the operations of the planters were profitable, they necessarily and inherently limited the intensive use of land resources. Their applications of technique were limited and were designed to enhance their monopoly. Income therefore remained low and highly concentrated, in spite of fertile and accessible soil resources. Was this the optimal outcome? Were total production and productivity maximized through land monopoly, forced labor, and diversion of government revenues to a fraction of the population? The planters generally thought so, and their opinion has not entirely lacked a sympathetic hearing by historians. "The great estate was the basis of the economic life of São Paulo and it brought about all the important and grandiose achievements realized in the province, such as railroads and river navigation." Thus wrote Eugenio Egas, who approved of the limited scope of the government-sponsored smallholding núcleos, a "utopia of the reformers," because the "smallholder, as a general rule, has neither the resources nor the cultivation of spirit sufficient for undertakings and improvements."[1]

Since a strong case can be made for the proposition that there was almost no growth in the Brazilian economy, per capita, until after abolition, these claims must be taken to mean that output would have declined absolutely had the planters not been allowed to aggrandize the land. Plantation farming in any case did not add to the value of the land. It would be difficult to envision devastation more complete than that effected in the hilly Paraíba Valley. In the Paulista West the surviving benefit of planter control was the railroad, an investment that might conceivably have been accomplished under other, more benign auspices.[2]

It might be more validly asserted that Rio Claro's economic development derived from concessions that the planters had to make to other social classes in order to avoid the loss of their estates. Italian immigrants had to be lent subsistence land in quantity. Hence they were able to take up cash farming that multiplied the economic functions of the town. Throughout the early post-abolition years, the continued domination by the plantations limited and distorted these developments. Yearly contracts encouraged extractive farming methods, and administration was speculative and less than rational. The town middle class, relegated to small dealings, sought to monopolize the trade of the smallholders and plantation workers. In retrospect, the planters and those who have mingled their interests with them may cause their concessions to appear heroic. Such historiography is not only self-serving; it also suggests that current decisions might best be left to them. To see things another way is not only to see them more clearly, therefore, but also to restore self-respect and the desire for self-actuation to those most in need.

# Notes

# Notes

The spelling of authors' names conforms to modern orthography. Titles remain as published.

CHAPTER ONE

1. Fernando Altenfelder Silva, "Arqueologia prehistórica da região de Rio Claro," in *Pré-história brasileira* (São Paulo: Instituto de Pré-História, Universidade de São Paulo, 1968); José Joaquim Machado de Oliveira, "Notícia raciocinada sobre as aldeas de indios da provincia de S. Paulo, desde o seu começo até a actualidade," *Revista do Instituto Histórico e Geográfico Brasileiro*, 1 (April–June, 1846): 204–54. The author also received information from Prof. Tom Miller of the Faculdade de Filosofia de Rio Claro.

2. Antônio Augusto de Fonseca, "Algumas palavras sobre a fundação da cidade de Rio Claro," in *Almanaque de S. João de Rio Claro para 1873* (Campinas: Typ. da Gazeta de Campinas, 1872), pp. 47–48; Roberto Simonsen, *História econômica do Brasil (1500/1820)* (4th ed.; São Paulo: Companhia Editôra Nacional, 1962), p. 243; Manuel Eufrásio de Azevedo Marques, *Apontamentos historicos, geograficos, biograficos, estatisticos e noticiosos da provincia de São Paulo...* (2 vols.; 2d ed.; São Paulo: Livraria Martins Editôra, n.d.), 1: 198–99; Augusto Emílio Zaluar, *Peregrinação pela provincia de S. Paulo, 1860–1861* (2d ed.; São Paulo: Edições Cultura, 1943), pp. 167–68.

3. Oscar de Arruda Penteado, "Onde começou Rio Claro," in *Rio Claro, 1964* (Rio Claro: Conselho Municipal de Turismo e Cultura, 1964), pp. 3–4; Júnio Soares Caiuby, *1827–1927, Centenario de Rio Claro* (Rio Claro: Typ. Conrado, 1927), pp. 4–5; Elza Coelho de Souza Keller, "Notícia geográfica de Rio Claro," in *Rio Claro, 1964*, p. 57. A useful study on the early settlement of the adjoining county of Limeira is Reynaldo Kuntz Busch, *História de Limeira* (Limeira: Prefeitura Municipal de Limeira, 1967), pp. 11–16.

4. Luiz dos Santos Vilhena, *Recopilação de noticias da capitania de S. Paulo* (2d ed.; Salvador: Imprensa Oficial do Estado, 1935), pp. 39–43; Auguste de Saint-Hilaire, *Viagem à província de São Paulo*, trans. by Rubens Borba de Moraes (2d ed.; São Paulo: Livraria Martins Editôra, 1945), pp. 142–43, 148–51; Louis d'Alincourt, *Memória sobre a viagem do pôrto de Santos à cidade de Cuiabá* (São Paulo: Livraria Martins Editôra, 1953), pp. 51, 68–71, 75–76.

5. Two censuses of population were taken in 1822 and 1835-36 for purposes of civil administration. The original protocols, including names, ages, race, civil status, provenance, occupation, property, output, and family income, are to be found in the Arquivo Público do Estado de São Paulo (hereafter APESP), in tins marked "População Piracicaba." For an analysis of the censuses taken in São Paulo between 1765 and 1850, see Maria Luiza Marcílio, *La ville de São Paulo, peuplement et population, 1750–1850* (Rouen: l'Université de Rouen, 1968). For a general account of settlement in the Paulista West, see Ernani Silva Bruno, *Viagem ao pais dos paulistas* (Rio de Janeiro: José Olympio, 1966), pp. 105-31.

6. Similar family structure is noted by Lucila Herrmann, "Evolução da estrutura social de Guaratinguetá num período de trezentos anos," *Revista de Administração*, 2 (March–June, 1948): 22-32. See also Maria Luiza Marcílio, "Tendências e estruturas dos domicílios na capitania de São Paulo (1765–1828)," *Estudos Econômicos*, 2 (1972): 131-43.

7. Saint-Hilaire, p. 213. On interracial marriage in Rio de Janeiro, see Herbert Klein, "Colored Freedmen in Colonial Slave Society," *Journal of Social History*, 3 (Fall 1969): 45.

8. Thomas Davatz, *Memórias de um colono no Brasil*, trans. by Sérgio Buarque de Holanda (2d ed.; São Paulo: Livraria Martins Editôra, 1951), pp. 42-44.

9. Luis Lisanti, "Sur la nourriture des 'Paulistes' entre XVIIIe et XIXe siècles," *Annales*, 18 (1963): 540.

10. On interdependence and trade in caboclo society, see Maria Isaura Pereira de Queiroz, *O campesinato brasileiro* (São Paulo: Editôra Vozes, 1973), pp. 43-44.

11. On sesmarias, see Ruy Cirne Lima, *Pequena história territorial no Brasil* (2d ed.; Porto Alegre: Edição Sulina, 1954); Brasil Bandecchi, *Origem do latifúndio no Brasil* (São Paulo: Fulgor, 1963); José da Costa Porto, *Estudo sobre o sistema sesmarial* (Recife: Imprensa Universitária, 1965); Alberto Passos Guimarães, *Quatro séculos de latifúndio* (São Paulo: Fulgor, 1964). Diana Maria de Faro Leal Diniz has carefully mapped the sesmarias of Rio Claro, "Rio Claro e o café: desenvolvimento, apogeu e crise, 1850–1900" (Ph.D. dissertation, Dept. of Social Sciences, Faculdade de Filosofia, Ciências e Letras de Rio Claro, 1973), pp. 7-9. Local tradition records somewhat different ownership of several sesmarias, suggesting that front men were involved. João Baptista de Campos Aguirra, "Sesmeiros e posseiros," *Revista do Instituto Histórico e Geográfico de São Paulo*, 34 (1938): 259-339; Zulmiro Ferraz de Campos, *Centenario de Rio Claro* (Rio Claro: Typ. Conrado, 1929), pp. 26-28; J. Romeo Ferraz, *Historia de Rio Claro* (São Paulo: Typographia Hennies Irmãos, 1922). A discussion of settlement which relates population density to agricultural exploitation is Maria Luiza Marcílio, "Crescimento demográfico e evolução agrária paulista, 1700–1836" (Livre-Docência thesis, Dept. of History, Faculdade de Filosofia, Ciências e Letras de Assis, 1974), pp. 205-68. See also Mario Neme, "Apossamento do solo e evolução da proprie-

dade rural na zona de Piracicaba," *Coleção Museu Paulista, Série de História*, 1 (1974).

12. On the nature of the elite in São Paulo at the time of independence, see Sérgio Buarque de Holanda, "São Paulo," *História geral da civilização brasileira*, ed. Sérgio Buarque de Holanda (São Paulo: Difusão Européia do Livro, 1963–      ), 2, 2: 450–58. Concentration of landownership may be seen in the land registry of 1818; see Alice P. Canabrava, "A repartição da terra na capitania de São Paulo, 1818," *Estudos Econômicos*, 2 (Dec. 1972): 77–129. The author was unable to gain access to that registry. It is also used effectively by Maria Thereza Schorer Petrone, *A lavoura canavieira em São Paulo* (São Paulo: Difusão Européia do Livro, 1968).

13. Antônio Rodrigues Veloso de Oliveira, "Memoria sobre o melhoramento da provincia de São Paulo," *Revista do Instituto Histórico e Geográfico Brasileiro*, 22 (1868): 84–87. See also speeches of José Bonifácio in the Constituent Assembly in 1823, collected in José Bonifácio de Andrada e Silva, *Escritos políticos* (São Paulo: Editora Obelisco, 1964), p. 73.

14. Passos Guimarães, p. 49.

15. Governor to Viceroy, Dec. 3, 1766, *Documentos interessantes para a história e costumes de São Paulo*, 73 [*sic*], cited in Petrone, p. 16; José Arouche de Toledo Rendon, "Reflexões sobre o estado em que se acha a agricultura na capitania de S. Paulo," *Documentos interessantes . . .*, 44 (1915): 196.

16. "Ordem circular, Capitão-Geral às Camaras Municipais," dated April 29, 1772, *Documentos interessantes . . .*, 33 (1901): 57–58; Alfredo Ellis, Jr., *O café e a paulistânea* (São Paulo: Universidade de São Paulo, Faculdade de Filosofia, Ciências e Letras, 1951), p. 386.

17. APESP, Registro de Terras, Rio Claro and Itaqueri, 1855–57. This registry was collected by the parish priest in accordance with the Land Law of 1850 and its regulation of 1854 (Law 601, Sept. 18, 1850).

18. Petrone reports a similar proportion of sales in land transfers in Itu, p. 57.

19. On land titles after 1822, see the author's "Latifundia and Land Policy in Nineteenth-Century Brazil," *Hispanic American Historical Review*, 51 (Nov. 1971): 606–25. Public lands are reported on by Daniel Pedro Müller, *Ensaio d'um quadro estatistico da provincia de S. Paulo* (São Paulo: Typographia de Costa Silveira, 1838), p. 47.

20. Passos Guimarães, p. 84. For an account of land alienation in the province of Rio de Janeiro, see Stanley Stein, *Vassouras* (Cambridge, Mass.: Harvard University Press, 1957), pp. 10–17. On forced sales, see Maria Sylvia de Carvalho Franco, *Homens livres na ordem escravocrata* (São Paulo: Instituto de Estudos Brasileiros, 1969), p. 92.

21. The conflicts inherent in the acquisition of title, in effect the beginning of capital accumulation, are discussed in José de Souza Martins, "Frente pioneira: contribuição para uma caracterização sociológica," *Estudos Históricos*, 10 (1971): 33–42.

22. Paula Beiguelman, *Pequenos estudos de ciência política* (2 vols.; São Paulo: Livraria Pioneira, 1968), 2: 81–82; Carvalho Franco, pp. 82–89. Emilio Willems hypothesizes a stratified peasant class, "Social Differentiation in Colonial Brazil," *Comparative Studies in Society and History*, 12 (Jan. 1970): 31–49. See also Pereira de Queiroz, *O campesinato brasileiro*, pp. 33–41.

23. Antônio Augusto da Costa Aguiar, *O Brasil e os brasileiros* (Santos: Typ. Commercial, 1862), pp. 33–34, 55–56; and Domingos Jaguaribe, *Algumas palavras sobre a emigração* (São Paulo: Typ. do "Diario," 1877), p. 15. João Menezes e Souza, *Theses sobre a colonização do Brazil* (Rio de Janeiro: Typographia Nacional, 1875), pp. 172–76, was one of the official reports that favored smallholding. See analysis of the caboclos' position in Emília Viotti da Costa, *Da senzala à colônia* (São Paulo: Difusão Européia do Livro, 1966), pp. 126–28; and same author, "O escravo na grande lavoura," *História geral da civilização brasileira*, 2, 3: 164–65.

24. Carvalho Franco, pp. 82–89; Müller, pp. 104–6.

25. Souza Martins notes the significance of the term *frente pioneira*. For a similar remark, see Michael Craton, "Searching for the Invisible Man," *Historical Reflections*, 1 (June 1974): 43.

CHAPTER TWO

1. Maria Thereza Schorer Petrone, *A lavoura canavieira em São Paulo* (São Paulo: Difusão Européia do Livro, 1968), pp. 92–94; APESP, População Piracicaba, 1822, 1835.

2. APESP, População Piracicaba, 1822, 1835.

3. Petrone, pp. 56–61, 97; APESP, População Piracicaba, 1835.

4. Petrone, pp. 43–44, 49, 58–59.

5. Auguste de Saint-Hilaire, *Viagem à província de São Paulo*, trans. by Rubens Borba de Moraes (2d ed.; São Paulo: Livraria Martins Editôra, 1945), p. 150; Petrone, p. 114.

6. Museu Histórico Paulista, "Amador Bueno da Veiga" (cited hereafter as MHP-ABV), report dated Oct. 14, 1862.

7. Petrone, pp. 163–65. On the introduction of coffee to the province of Rio de Janeiro, see Stanley Stein, *Vassouras* (Cambridge, Mass.: Harvard University Press, 1957), pp. 3–54.

8. Afonso d'Escragnolle Taunay, "Os primeiros cafesais do Oeste de S. Paulo," *Revista do Instituto de Café*, March 1935, pp. 626–31; same author, *Historia do café no Brasil* (15 vols.; Rio de Janeiro: Departamento Nacional do Café, 1943), 15: 321–22; Sérgio Buarque de Holanda, "São Paulo," *História geral da civilização brasileira*, ed. Sérgio Buarque de Holanda (São Paulo: Difusão Européia do Livro, 1963– ), 2, 2: 420–21; *Almanach de Campinas para 1908* (Campinas: Typ. e Stereotyp. da "Casa Mascotta," 1908), pp. 35–36. Treatises in Stein, pp. 302–10. Widely read was Francisco Peixoto de Lacerda Werneck, *Memoria sobre a fundação e custeio de uma fazenda na provincia do Rio de Janeiro* (Rio de Janeiro, 1847).

9. A. Lalière, *Le café dans l'état de Saint Paul (Brésil)* (Paris: Augustin Challamel, 1909), pp. 82–86; C. F. van Delden Laerne, *Brazil and Java* (London: W. H. Allen, 1885), pp. 256–60.

10. José Vergueiro, *Memorial acerca de colonização e cultivo de café* (Campinas: Typographia do Constitucional, 1874), pp. 17–18; José Alexandre Diniz, "Organização agrícola do município de Araras" (thesis, Dept. of Geography, Faculdade de Filosofia, Ciências e Letras de Rio Claro, 1968), pp. 34–37; Isidro Gomes Teixeira, *Estatistica de café e cafesais* (São Paulo: Typ. Selecta, 1909), pp. 16–17.

11. Van Delden Laerne, pp. 280–87; Lalière, pp. 100–108.

12. João Pedro Carvalho de Moraes, *Relatorio apresentado ao Ministerio de Agricultura, Commercio e Obras Publicas . . . em execução das instrucções de 17 de março ultimo* (Rio de Janeiro: Typographia Nacional, 1870), p. 75; André Rebouças, *Agricultura nacional* (Rio de Janeiro: Lamoureux, 1883), p. 134. See also Walter Gay McCreery and Mary L. Bynum, *The Coffee Trade in Brazil*, U.S. Bureau of Foreign and Domestic Commerce Trade Promotion Series, no. 92 (Washington, D.C.: Government Printing Office, 1930).

13. Petrone, pp. 176–78.

14. Rio Claro, Cartório do Primeiro Ofício, and Cartório do Segundo Ofício (First and Second Notarial Offices; cited hereafter as RC/C-1 and RC/C-2), Livros de Notas (Contract Ledgers), 1864–78.

15. RC/C-2, Livros de Notas, Feb. 14, 1864.

16. Fábio Ramos, *O café no Brasil e no estrangeiro* (Rio de Janeiro: Papelaria Santa Helena, 1923), pp. 113–15, 142–53, 167; Van Delden Laerne, pp. 312–16.

17. Taunay, *Historia do café no Brasil*, 8: 222.

18. *Ibid.*; Rebouças, p. 134; José Maria Lisboa, *Almanak de Campinas, seguido do almanak do Rio-Claro, 1873* (Campinas: Typographia da Gazeta de Campinas, 1873), p. 30.

19. Production was not significant until after 1865. APESP, Ofícios Diversos, Rio Claro (cited hereafter as OD/RC), José Luis Borges to President of Province, Dec. 8, 1864, and County Council to President of Province, Sept. 26, 1865. See Alice P. Canabrava, *O desenvolvimento da cultura do algodão na provincia de São Paulo (1861–1875)* (São Paulo: Indústria Gráfica Siqueira, 1951), pp. 95–96; Lisboa, pp. 27–30.

20. APESP, OD/RC, County Council to President of Province, Dec. 7, 1857; County Council to President of Province, May 27, 1878. RC/C-2, Livros de Notas, Aug. 26, 1877. Christopher Columbus Andrews, *Brazil, Its Conditions and Prospects* (New York: Appleton, 1887), p. 153. On diversification of the plantations, see Diana Maria de Faro Leal Diniz, "Rio Claro e o café: desenvolvimento, apogeu e crise, 1850–1900" (Ph.D. dissertation, Dept. of Social Sciences, Faculdade de Filosofia, Ciências e Letras de Rio Claro, 1973), pp. 106–13.

21. MHP-ABV, "Mappa demonstrativo dos productos de exportação d'este municipio de S. João do Rio Claro no anno de 1861 a 1862."

22. Johan Jacob von Tschudi, *Viagem às províncias do Rio de Janeiro e São Paulo*, trans. by Eduardo de Luna Castro São Paulo: Livraria Martins Editôra, [1953]), pp. 189–91; Taunay, *Historia do café* ..., 4, 2: 362–65. On the state of roads, see Daniel Pedro Müller, *Ensaio d'um quadro estatistico da provincia de S. Paulo* (São Paulo: Typographia de Costa Silveira, 1838), pp. 105–13.

23. MHP-ABV, letter without date, probably 1857, unsigned, to County Council; RC/C-1 and C-2, Livros de Notas, various contracts, 1858–72; São Paulo (Province), Assembléia Legislativa Provincial, *Annaes*, 1857, speech by Amador Lacerda Rodrigues Jordão, March 23, 1857. Description of roads in U.S. Department of State, Consular Despatches, Santos, William T. Wright to Secretary of State, Nov. 14, 1860; Tschudi, pp. 178, 190.

24. Description of roads and costs of maintenance in Assembléia Legislativa Provincial, *Annaes*, 1864, April 2, 1864.

25. History of road construction in Richard P. Momsen, *Routes over the Serra do Mar* (Rio de Janeiro: By the author, 1964), pp. 38–60; Holanda, p. 418; debates on Vergueiro's road in *Annaes*, 1864, Feb. 15 and April 6, 1864.

26. Robert H. Mattoon, Jr., "The Companhia Paulista de Estradas de Ferro, 1868–1900: A Local Railway Enterprise in São Paulo, Brazil" (Ph.D. dissertation, Dept. of History, Yale University, 1971), pp. 119–23. Much information on the transportation systems of Rio Claro is contained in Leal Diniz, pp. 133–79.

27. Mattoon, pp. 162–63; Cândido Neves, *Almanak do Rio Claro, 1895* (Rio Claro, Officina Typographica da Gazeta, 1895), p. 41; APESP, OD/RC, May 8, 1873, County Council to President of Province.

28. William Scully, *Brazil: Its Provinces and Chief Cities* (London: Trübner, 1868), p. 311; Mattoon, p. 167.

29. Maria Paes de Barros, *No tempo de dantes* (São Paulo: Brasiliense, 1946); RC/C-1, Inventories, 1880, accounts of the estate of the baron of Porto Feliz.

30. Accounts of the estate of the baron of Porto Feliz; RC/C-1 and C-2, Livros de Notas, sales contracts, mortgages, and power-of-attorney agreements, 1870–90.

31. Paes de Barros, p. 60.

32. RC/C-2, Livros de Notas, building contract, May 16, 1874; RC/C-1, Inventories, 1855–90, list household goods.

33. Van Delden Laerne, *Brazil and Java*, p. 277; Andrews, *Brazil, Its Conditions and Prospects*, pp. 152–54.

34. Manuel Eufrásio de Azevedo Marques, *Apontamentos históricos, geográficos, biográficos, estatisticos, e noticiosos da provincia de São Paulo, seguidos da cronologia dos acontecimentos mais notaveis desde a fundação da capitania de São Vicente até o anno de 1876* (2 vols., 2d ed.; São Paulo: Livraria Martins Editôra, n.d.), pp. 58, 72–73; Paes de Barros; Museu Paulista, Arquivo Aguirra (hereafter cited as MP-AA), Rio

Claro, Aug. 22, 1823, transcribed from contract registered in São Paulo, Cartório do Primeiro Ofício, 1899.

35. Francisco de Barros Brotero, *Oliveiras: descendentes de Estanislau José de Oliveira, Professor de Rhetorica* (São Paulo: Graphica Paulista, 1942); "O centenário da fazenda São José," *O Estado de São Paulo* (Dec. 24, 1939). RC/C-2, Livros de Notas, contains many mortgage contracts signed by Oliveira, the first on April 23, 1853. Landholdings in APESP, Registra de Terras, Rio Claro, 1855–57, and Rio Claro, Registro de Imóveis (Registry of Real Property), 1884–86. Scattered details on the Oliveira family can be found in the writings of Alfredo Ellis, Jr., especially *Um parlamentar paulista da Republica* ("Boletim CII, História da Civilização Brasileira, No. 9"; São Paulo: Universidade de São Paulo, Faculdade de Filosofia, Ciências e Letras, 1949).

36. Djalma Forjaz, *O Senador Vergueiro* (São Paulo: Officinas do "Diario Official," 1924); Thomas Davatz, *Memórias de um colono no Brasil*, trans. by Sérgio Buarque de Holanda (2d ed.; São Paulo: Livraria Martins Editôra, 1951), p. 150. Vergueiro's slave dealing is remarked by the Provincial President in a report to the Minister of Justice, March 23, 1850. In Arquivo Nacional, IJ/507, Africanos. Noted by Leal Diniz, "Rio Claro e o café: desenvolvimento, apogeu e crise, 1850–1900," p. 71.

37. Alfredo Ellis, Jr., *Tenente-Coronel Francisco da Cunha Bueno* (São Paulo: By the author, 1960), p. 189, notes that Oliveira arranged the marriages of all his children.

CHAPTER THREE

1. On the slave trade, see Leslie Bethell, *The Abolition of the Brazilian Slave Trade* (Cambridge, Eng.: Cambridge University Press, 1970); Mircea Buescu, "Novas notas sobre a importação de escravos," *Estudos Históricos*, 7 (1968): 79–88. For a recent discussion of writings on Brazilian slavery, see Richard Graham, "Brazilian Slavery Re-Examined: A Review Article," *Journal of Social History*, 3 (Summer, 1970): 431–53; a comparison with the United States is Carl Degler, *Neither Black nor White* (New York: Macmillan, 1972), especially chap. 1.

2. Brazil, Comissão Central de Estatistica, *Recenseamento geral da população . . . em 1 de setembro de 1872*, 19; APESP, População Piracicaba, 1835.

3. Recent attempts at calculating the profitability of slavery in Brazil are H. O. Portocarrero de Castro, "Viabilidade econômica da escravidão no Brasil: 1880–1888," *Revista Brasileira de Economia*, 27 (Jan.–March, 1973): 43–68; and Nathaniel Leff, "Long-Term Viability of Slavery in a Backward Closed Economy," *Journal of Interdisciplinary History*, 5 (Summer, 1974): 103–8.

4. São Paulo (Province), Assembléia Legislativa Provincial, *Annaes*, 1857, March 23, 1857; APESP, Colonos, 2, Joaquim Franco de Camargo to President of Province, Dec. 8, 1856. On slave labor in the Paraíba Valley, see Stanley Stein, *Vassouras* (Cambridge, Mass.: Harvard University

Press, 1957), pp. 62–80; in Pernambuco, see Peter Eisenberg, *The Sugar Industry in Pernambuco, 1840–1910* (Berkeley: University of California Press, 1974), pp. 146–79. A general study of the coffee areas, based on many manuscript sources, is Emília Viotti da Costa, *Da senzala à colónia* (São Paulo: Difusão Européia do Livro, 1966). See also another local study, Beatriz Westin de Cerqueira, "Um estudo de escravidão em Ubatuba," *Estudos Históricos*, 5 (1966): 7–58; 6 (1967): 9–66.

5. RC/C-2, Livros de Notas, May 17, 1861; Alfredo Ellis, Jr.,*Tenente-Coronel Francisco da Cunha Bueno* (São Paulo: By the author, 1960), pp. 111–15.

6. RC/C-2, Livros de Vendas de Escravos, Doria transaction listed March 18, 1877.

7. RC/C-2, Livros de Vendas de Escravos.

8. See male/female immigrant ratio in Pietro Ubaldi, *L'espansione coloniale e commerciale dell'Italia nel Brasile* (Rome: Ermanno Loescher & Co., 1911), p. 58.

9. São Paulo (Province), Comissão Central de Estatística, *Relatorio*, 1888.

10. São Paulo (Province), President of Province, *Relatorio*, 1888, p. 28. Infant mortality in the city of São Paulo was 239 per thousand in the period 1796–1809. Maria Luiza Marcílio, *La ville de São Paulo, peuplement et population, 1750–1850* (Rouen: l'Université de Rouen, 1968), pp. 200–201. Another mortality figure for slaves is shown in Eisenberg, p. 151.

11. Maria Paes de Barros, *No tempo de dantes* (São Paulo: Brasiliense, 1946), p. 70.

12. Eyewitness accounts of slavery in Rio Claro and Limeira were provided by Johan Jacob von Tschudi, *Viagem às províncias do Rio de Janeiro e São Paulo*, trans. by Eduardo de Luna Castro (São Paulo: Livraria Martins Editôra, [1953]), pp. 156–83; Christopher Columbus Andrews, *Brazil, Its Conditions and Prospects* (New York: Appleton, 1887), pp. 144–67; and Mauricio Lamberg, *O Brasil*, trans. by Luiz de Castro (Rio de Janeiro: Lombaerts, 1896), pp. 326–29. A vivid account of sugar plantation slavery is in Adolphe d'Assier, *Le Brésil contemporain* (Paris: Durand et Lauriel, 1867), pp. 88–93. Subsistence production of plantations was reported in APESP, População Piracicaba, 1822 and 1835, and in replies to government inquiries in APESP, OD/RC, Jan. 26, 1854, and MHP-ABV, "Mappa demonstrativo dos productos de exportação d'este municipio de Cidade de S. João do Rio Claro no anno de 1861 a 1862." See also Luis Lisanti, "Sur la nourriture des 'Paulistes' entre XVIIIe et XIXe siècles," *Annales*, 18 (1963): 531–41.

13. Accounts of the estate of the baron of Porto Feliz, RC/C-1, Inventories, 1880.

14. Paes de Barros, p. 81; Andrews, pp. 154–56.

15. Tschudi, pp. 169–70; APESP, Polícia, Dec. 23, 1876.

16. RC/Registro de Imóveis, Processos, July 8, 1862, Nov. 28, 1866.

17. Transcription from *Correio do Oeste* (Rio Claro) in *Correio Paulistano*, Sept. 8, 1880.

18. RC/Registro de Imóveis, Processos, May 10, 1884.

19. APESP, Polícia, May 20, 1886.

20. On paternalistic control, see Octavio Ianni, *As metamorfoses do escravo* (São Paulo: Difusão Européia do Livro, 1962), pp. 157–69.

21. RC/C-1, Livros de Notas, March 27, 1857; Westin de Cerqueira, "Um estudo de escravidão em Ubatuba" (1967), p. 37. An important study of manumissions in Bahia is being carried out by Stuart Schwartz, Arnold Kessler, and Katia de Queiroz Mattoso. See Katia de Queiroz Mattoso, "A propósito de cartas de alforria, Bahia, 1779–1850," *Anais de Historia*, 4 (1972): 50. Another more detailed study of manumissions in Paraty, province of Rio de Janeiro, has been carried out by James Kiernan, "Slavery and Manumission in Paraty, Brazil, 1789–1822" (paper presented at Columbia University Brazilian Seminar, May 1, 1975, mimeo.).

22. RC/C-2, Livros de Notas, April 27, 1857.

23. *Ibid.*, Aug. 4, 1857.

24. *Ibid.*, Nov. 22, 1848.

25. *Ibid.*, Feb. 9, 1860; March 20, 1864; March 6, 1866.

26. RC/C-1, Inventories, 1879; "A policia de São Paulo em 1874," *Arquivos da Policia Civil de São Paulo*, 14 (Second semester, 1947): 505.

27. Estimates of slave life expectancy in Roberto Simonsen, *História econômica do Brasil* (4th ed.; São Paulo: Companhia Editôra Nacional, 1962), p. 135; Viotti da Costa, *Da senzala à colônia*, p. 256; and a contemporary estimate in Brazil, Câmara de Deputados, *Annaes*, 2, 2 (Sept. 2, 1850).

28. Eduardo Arriaga, *New Life Tables for Latin American Populations in the Nineteenth and Twentieth Centuries* (Berkeley: University of California Press, 1968), p. 29.

29. RC/Registro de Imóveis, Processos, Nov. 11, 1876. On slave families, see Viotti da Costa, pp. 270–71, and Lucila Herrmann, "Evolução da estrutura social de Guaratinguetá num período de trezentos anos," *Revista de Administração*, 2 (March–June, 1948): 158–59.

30. RC/C-2, Livros de Vendas de Escravos, Aug. 12, 1878. The buyer in the 1878 sale was Escolástica de Godoy Almeida. Note that this sale was prohibited by the Law of 1871.

31. *Thabor* (São Paulo), Feb. 28, 1884.

32. *Diario Popular*, July 15, 1885.

33. Paes de Barros, *No tempo de dantes*, p. 81; Andrews, *Brazil, Its Conditions and Prospects*, p. 158.

34. APESP, Polícia, 228, Annual Report, 1885, Delegate to Chief of Police; São Paulo (Province), *Leis*, Law 33, July 7, 1869.

35. *O Alpha*, Jan. 30, 1902; Augusto Emílio Zaluar, *Peregrinação pela provincia de S. Paulo* (2d ed.; São Paulo: Edições Cultura, 1943), p. 166; RC/C-1, Livros de Notas, Oct. 23, 1890. On *quilombos* in another prov-

ince, see Oilam José, *A abolição em Minas* (Belo Horizonte: Editôra Itatiaia, 1963), pp. 39–61.

36. RC/C-2, Livros de Notas, Sept. 26, 1870; Thomas Davatz, *Memórias de um colono no Brasil*, trans. by Sérgio Buarque de Holanda (2d ed.; São Paulo: Livraria Martins Editôra, 1951), pp. 89, 91; d'Assier, *Le Brésil contemporain*, p. 141.

37. APESP, OD/RC, July 14, 1860, and Aug. 6, 1860; APESP, Juiz de Direito, Rio Claro, May 25, 1877; RC/C-2, Processos, June 4, 1877; President of Province, *Relatorio*, 1879, pp. 14, 39.

38. Ellis, *Tenente-Coronel Francisco da Cunha Bueno*, pp. 162–63, 164, 246–47; Instituto Hans Staden, GIVh, Nr. 1, "Jubilaeumsfest," typewritten transcript of speech by Theodor Koelle, Dec. 1, 1933; Maria Stella de Novaes, *A escravidão e a abolição no Espirito Santo* (Vitória: Departamento da Imprensa Oficial, 1963), p. 46.

39. Andrews, p. 156.

40. RC/C-2, Livros de Notas, March 5, 1856; Paes de Barros, p. 119.

41. *Diario Popular*, July 21, 1885; RC/Registro de Imóveis, Processos, Oct. 14, 1877.

CHAPTER FOUR

1. APESP, Colônias, 2, Nicolau Vergueiro to President of Province, Jan. 6, 1853; Emília Viotti da Costa, "Colônias de parceria na lavoura de café: primeiras experiências," in II Simpósio dos Professores Universitários de História, *Anais* (Curitiba: Faculdade de Filosofia do Paraná, 1962); Johan Jacob von Tschudi, *Viagem às províncias do Rio de Janeiro e São Paulo*, trans. by Eduardo de Luna Castro (São Paulo: Livraria Martins Editôra, [1953]), pp. 134–35; Djalma Forjaz, *O Senador Vergueiro* (São Paulo: Officinas do "Diario Official," 1924), pp. 34–51.

2. Jean Roche, *A colonização alemã e o Rio Grande do Sul*, trans. by Emery Ruas (2 vols.; Pôrto Alegre: Editôra Globo, 1969), 1: 100. On official colonies in São Paulo, see Vicenzo Grossi, *Storia della colonizzazione europea al Brasile e della emigrazione italiana nello stato di S. Paulo* (2d ed.; Milan: Società Editrice Dante Alighiere di Alberghi, Segati & C., 1914), pp. 340–50; Emília Viotti da Costa, *Da senzala à colônia* (São Paulo: Difusão Européia do Livro, 1966), pp. 65–70, 78. On racial attitudes, see A. A. da Costa Aguiar, *O Brasil e os brasileiros* (Santos: Typ. Commercial, 1862), pp. 22–23; and Afonso d'Escragnolle Taunay, *Historia do café no Brasil* (15 vols.; Rio de Janeiro: Departamento Nacional do Café, 1943), 8: 137. Another source on early immigration policies is Eduardo da Silva Prado, "l'Immigration," in M. F.-J. da Santa Ana Nery, ed., *Le Brésil en 1889* (Paris: Librairie Charles Delagrave, 1889), pp. 478–81. On *parceria* as the preservative of latifundia, see João Pedro Carvalho de Moraes, *Relatorio apresentado ao Ministerio de Agricultura, Commercio e Obras Publicas ... em execução das instrucções de 17 de março ultimo* (Rio de Janeiro: Typographia Nacional, 1870), pp. 61–162.

3. Charles Expilly, *La traite, l'émigration et la colonisation au Brésil* (Paris: Guillaumin et Cie., 1865); Tschudi, pp. 129–33.

4. Daniel D. Kidder and J. C. Fletcher, *Brazil and the Brazilians* (Philadelphia: Childs and Paterson, 1857), pp. 405–10; Arquivo do Museu Imperial, Petrópolis (hereafter AMI-P), Nicolau Vergueiro to Nabuco de Araujo, June 6, 1852.

5. Pierre Denis notes the peculiarity of calling the bonded workers *colonos*, in *Le Brésil au XXe siècle* (Paris: Librairie Armand Colin, 1909), p. 121. *Parceria* in this sense did not originate with Vergueiro; it was suggested in a provincial report published in 1822, modeled on the labor system of Madeira and on the British experiment with Greek workers in Florida. Antônio Rodrigues Veloso de Oliveira, "Memoria sobre o melhoramento da provincia de São Paulo," *Revista do Instituto Histórico e Geográfico Brasileiro*, 22 (1868): 76–77, 84–85. Copies of contracts are shown in Robert Christian Berthold Avé-Lallement, *Viagem pelo sul do Brasil no ano de 1858*, trans. by Teodoro Cabral (2 vols.; Rio de Janeiro: Instituto Nacional do Livro, 1953), 2: 342–45; Thomas Davatz, *Memórias de um colono no Brasil*, trans. by Sérgio Buarque de Holanda (2d ed.; São Paulo: Livraria Martins Editôra, 1951), pp. 234–35; an original copy in APESP, Colônias, 2, signed by Souza Queiroz, Feb. 29, 1852.

6. Davatz, pp. 76–77.

7. J. Christian Heusser, *Die Schweitzer auf den Kolonien in St. Paulo in Brasilien* (Zürich: Friedrich Schulthess, 1857), p. 4.

8. APESP, OD/RC, Dec. 7, 1857; Jean Louis Moré, *Le Bresil en 1852, et sa colonisation future* (Geneva: Julian Frères, 1852), p. 158; Kidder and Fletcher, p. 405. Early accounts, unfortunately, were biased: Moré was paid by Vergueiro, and Kidder was an abolitionist who sought to prove free labor would work.

9. AMI-P, Nicolau Vergueiro to Nabuco de Araujo, June 6, 1852.

10. *Ibid.*; APESP, Colônias, 2, João Alfredo Jonas to President of Province, Dec. 31, 1853, Jan. 2, 1854, Dec. 31, 1855.

11. Kidder and Fletcher, p. 413; São Paulo (Province), President of Province, *Relatorio*, 1855; Viotti da Costa, *Da senzala*, pp. 78–83; Brazil, *Colecção das leis*, Law 601, Sept. 18, 1850; São Paulo (Province), *Leis*, Law 14, July 19, 1852, Law 31, April 25, 1855, Law 31, May 7, 1856, authorize expenditures for immigrants. Another law lent funds to another group of Paulista planters, Law 7, March 30, 1854.

12. APESP, Colônias, 2, José Vergueiro to President of Province, "Mappa da Colonia Angelica e Colonia Senador Vergueiro," Jan. 6, 1858, and "Mappa das colonias visitadas e examinadas," [Jan. 1857?], probably by Machado de Oliveira. AMI-P, Nicolau Vergueiro to Nabuco de Araujo. Vergueiro proposed a much grander scheme in Jan. 1855. He asked the imperial government for a loan of 200,000 milreis at no interest so that he could import 10,000 immigrants. AMI-P, José Vergueiro to Luis Pedreira do Couto Ferraz, Jan. 19, 1855.

13. *Ibid.*

14. Brazil, Congresso Agrícola, *Colecção de documentos* (Rio de Janeiro: Typographia Nacional, 1878), p. 240. MHP-ABV, Santa Gertrudes, Copiador 4, Oct. 19, 1897, Sept. 5, 11, 1899.

15. Davatz, *Memórias*, pp. 80–82; Heusser, p. 84.

16. Brazil, *Colecção das leis*, Law 108, Sept. 11, 1837.

17. Davatz, pp. 105–10.

18. APESP, Colônias, 2, Domingos José da Costa Alves, Oct. 21, 1856; Benedito Antônio Camargo, Oct. 26, 1856; Francisco Gomes Botão, Dec. 14, 1856; Joaquim Franco de Camargo, Dec. [no date], 1856.

19. APESP, OD/RC, Ensign of the Detachment to President of Province, April 7, 1858; Tschudi, *Viagem às provincias do Rio de Janeiro e São Paulo*, p. 185. Later imprisonments noted in OD/RC, Nov. 29, 1858; Oct. 1, 1859; April 3, 1860.

20. Davatz, *Die Behandlung der Kolonisten in der Provinz St. Paulo in Brasilien und deren Erhebung gegen ihre Bedrücker* (Chur: Druck von L. Hitz, 1858). The Portuguese translation, footnoted above and below, contains a valuable preface by Sérgio Buarque de Holanda, and appended documents. Davatz, *Memórias*, pp. 146–55.

21. Davatz, *Memórias*, pp. 110–11.

22. *Ibid.*, pp. 158–63.

23. *Ibid.*, pp. 165–72.

24. *Ibid.*, pp. 172–73.

25. *Ibid.*, pp. 180–84.

26. São Paulo (Province), Assembléia Legislativa Provincial, *Annaes*, 1857, speech by Queiroz Telles, Feb. 27, 1857. Another hint of distaste for Vergueiro's success is to be found in the refusal of his request for the loan of 200,000 milreis (see note 12), written in the hand of the marquis of Paraná.

27. Nicolau Vergueiro to President of Province, and José Vergueiro to Nabuco de Araujo, both dated Feb. 10, 1857, in Davatz, *Memórias de um colono no Brasil*, pp. 261–69; APESP, OD/RC, County Council to President, Feb. 23, 1857.

28. Heusser, *Die Schweitzer auf den Kolonien in St. Paulo in Brasilien*, pp. 84, 92–93; J. Tavares Bastos, report in Davatz, pp. 269–73; APESP, OD/RC, County Council to President, Dec. 7, 1857.

29. Manuel de Jesús Valdetaro, "Colonias de S. Paulo," annex to Brazil, Repartição Geral das Terras Públicas (hereafter RGTP), *Relatorio*, 1858; Sebastião Machado Nunes, report transcribed in Carvalho de Moraes, *Relatorio apresentado ao Ministerio de Agricultura, Commercio e Obras Publicas ... em exeçucão das instrucções de 17 de março ultimo*, pp. 16–25. Tschudi, *Viagem às provincias do Rio de Janeiro e São Paulo*, pp. 156, 177–82. Brazil, RGTP, *Relatorio*, 1859, pp. 82–83.

30. Tschudi, pp. 136, 180, 184–86.

31. Taunay, *Historia do café no Brasil*, 8: 102, 162–63; da Silva Prado, "l'Immigration," pp. 493–94. Hostility of the Austrian government in

Ezequiel Stanley Ramires, *As relações entre a Austria e o Brasil* (São Paulo: Companhia Editôra Nacional, 1968), pp. 182–211. Avé-Lallement, *Viagem pelo sul do Brasil no ano de 1858*, 2: 347–50; Expilly, *La traite, l'émigration et la colonisation au Brésil*, pp. 90–91, 92n, 118, 123–25; Jacaré-Assu, *Brazilian Colonization from a European Point of View* (London: Edward Stanford, 1873), pp. 22–26.

32. Machado Nunes in Carvalho de Moraes, pp. 16–17; President of Province, *Relatorio*, 1859, reference to *colônias* agrees with Machado Nunes. Viotti da Costa, *Da senzala à colônia*, pp. 100–105. It is not suggested of course that Viotti da Costa exonerates them.

33. Heusser, pp. 33–41; Carvalho de Moraes, pp. 70–73; Viotti da Costa, *Da senzala*, pp. 100–105.

34. APESP, RC/OD, Subdelegate to President of Province, January [date illegible], 1856.

35. Heusser, pp. 35–41; Friedrich Sommer, "Die Deutschen in São Paulo" (6 vols., typewritten; in the collection of the Instituto Hans Staden), 3: 119; Brazil, RGTP, *Relatorio*, 1855; Expilly, pp. 156–59. For a calculation that slaves were less profitable, see Assembléia Legislativa Provincial, *Annaes*, 1878, speech by Queiroz Telles, who had kept a *colônia*, March 27, 1878.

36. APESP, RC/OD, Benedito Antônio Camargo to President of Province, Nov. 23, 1859; RC/C-1, Inventories, Feb. 9, 1861; Valdetaro, p. 67. The slave quarters were valued, per head, somewhat higher than the free workers' housing.

37. For claims that slavery was more profitable, see Louis Couty, *Le Brésil en 1884* (Rio de Janeiro: Faro & Lino, 1884), p. 145; Paula Beiguelman, *Pequenos estudos de ciência política* (2 vols.; São Paulo: Livraria Pioneira, 1968), 2: 41; President of Province, *Relatorio*, 1859.

38. Assembléia Legislativa Provincial, *Annaes*, 1857, speech by João da Silva Cairão, Feb. 13, 1857; Viotti da Costa, *Da senzala*, pp. 87–88.

39. Taunay, 8: 84; Viotti da Costa, *Da senzala*, pp. 85–90, following J. Tavares Bastos, in Davatz, *Memórias de um colono no Brasil*, p. 272. Beiguelman seems to agree, 2: 41–42. Domingos Jaguaribe's epithet was "the scum of Europe." *Algumas palavras sobre e emigração* (São Paulo: Typ. do "Diario," 1877), p. 10.

40. Mack Walker, *Germany and the Emigration* (Cambridge, Mass.: Harvard University Press, 1964), pp. 44, 57, 63–76, 170, 178. Theoretical discussions in Clifford Jansen, ed., *Readings in the Sociology of Migration* (Oxford: Pergamon, 1970), p. 14; and Marc Fried, "Deprivation and Migration: Dilemmas of Causal Interpretation," in Eugene Brody, ed., *Behavior in New Environments* (Beverley Hills, Calif.: Sage Publications, 1969), pp. 31–34.

41. Davatz, pp. 136–39; Heusser, *Die Schweitzer auf den Kolonien in St. Paulo in Brasilien*, pp. 35–41. Carvalho de Moraes copied a contract displaying this remarkable attitude: "The plow will be furnished by the proprietors, but since its employment is in the interest of the *colonos*, they

will pay a rent of 5 milreis per 1,000 trees." *Relatorio apresentado ao Ministerio de Agricultura, Commercio e Obras Publicas . . . em execução das instrucções de 17 de março ultimo,* Annex 2.

42. Paul Chair, "Summary of the Last Census of Switzerland," *Journal of the Royal Geographical Society,* 24 (1854): 316–17. Population density was 13/km². Taunay, *Historia do café no Brasil,* 8: 141; Sérgio Buarque de Holanda, introduction in Davatz, pp. 9, 18, 21; Kidder and Fletcher, *Brazil and the Brazilians,* p. 407; APESP, Colônias, 2, João Alfredo Jonas to President of Province, Dec. 31, 1855.

43. Tschudi, *Viagem às provincias do Rio de Janeiro e São Paulo,* p. 185; APESP, OD/RC, Ensign of Detachment to President of Province, July 1, 1858 (records arrest of Benedito Antônio Camargo for drunkenness); RC/C-1 and C-2, Livros de Notas, 1855–60 ($n = 120$).

44. Buarque de Holanda in Davatz, p. 31; da Silva Prado, "l'Immigration," p. 489; C. F. van Delden Laerne, *Brazil and Java* (London: W. H. Allen, 1885), p. 362.

45. Davatz, p. 124; Heusser, p. 5; RC/C-2, Livros de Notas, June 13, 1858, Nov. 13, 1881. Antônio da Costa Alves Ferreira was the tenant.

46. Carvalho de Moraes, p. 12; Davatz, p. 219. Davatz's remarks were hardly comparable to the racism of upper-class European travelers like Agassiz and Gobineau.

47. Brazil, RGTP, *Relatorio,* 1859, pp. 86–87; Brazil, *Colecção das leis,* Regulamento, Nov. 18, 1858, and Law 2,827, March 15, 1879. Many county councils, solicited by the government, would have preferred a harsher law; Brazil, Ministério da Fazenda, *Informações sobre o estado da lavoura* (Rio de Janeiro: Typographia Nacional, 1874), p. 148. The council of Rio Claro also leaned toward longer sentences, but was uneasy about preventive arrest. It never sent an opinion to the ministry; Rio Claro, Câmara Municipal, "Atas," July 16, 1874.

48. APESP, OD/RC, County Council to President of Province, Dec. 7, 1857.

49. V. L. Baril, *L'Empire du Brésil* (Paris: F. Sartorius, 1862), p. 245. APESP, Colônias, 1, Nov. 23, 1863; 3, Oct. 26, 1876. RC/C-2, Livros de Notas, Feb. 11, 1877; Feb. 13, 1877; April 8, 1877.

50. On later *colônias* see Carvalho de Moraes, and Visconde de Indaiatuba, "Memorandum sobre o início de colonização da fazenda 'Sete Quedas' no município de Campinas em 1852," in Campinas, Câmara Municipal, *Monografia histórica do município de Campinas* (Rio de Janeiro: Instituto Brasileiro de Geografia e Estatística, 1952), pp. 243–56. The viscount's colony also ended in a labor dispute. A late contract in APESP, Colônias, 3, F. A. Souza Queiroz, Oct. 26, 1876.

51. APESP, OD/RC, Chief of Police to President of Province, Dec. 20, 1867. These children had been imported by the Associação Central de Imigração, an organization described by Michael Hall, in "The Origins of Mass Immigration to Brazil, 1871–1914" (Ph.D. dissertation, Dept. of History, Columbia University, 1969).

52. Carvalho de Moraes, *Relatorio apresentado ao Ministerio de Agricultura, Commercio e Obras Publicas . . . em execução das instrucções de 17 de março ultimo*, p. 97; Jaguaribe, *Algumas palavras sobre a emigração*, pp. 29–40; President of Province, *Relatorio*, 1871. São Paulo (Province), *Leis*, Law 42, March 30, 1871; Law 73, April 26, 1872. The latter authorized larger loans to planters who had no slaves. Maria Paes de Barros, *No tempo de dantes* (São Paulo: Brasiliense, 1946), pp. 88–89; G. B. Marchesini, *Il Brasile e le sue colonie agricole* (Rome: Typografia Barbera, 1877), pp. 127–28; Oscar de Arruda Penteado, "Arquivo do município," *Diario de Rio Claro* [no date, in Mr. Arruda's clipping file]; *O Futuro*, Jan. 1, 1876, death of Angélica's administrator at the hands of a worker. APESP, OD/RC, President of Province to County Council, July 8, 1874.

53. APESP, OD/RC, County Council to President of Province, Oct. 7, 1878, asking for assistance in feeding large numbers of refugees from Ceará. Roger Cunniff, "The Great Drought: Northeastern Brazil, 1877–1880" (Ph.D. dissertation, Dept. of History, University of Texas, 1970), pp. 31–32; APESP, Juiz de Direito, Rio Claro, June 28, 1878. Also, Anna Maria Martínez Corrêa reports large numbers of free migrants in Araraquara, "História de Araraquara" (M.A. thesis, Dept. of History, Faculdade de Filosofia, Ciências e Letras de Araraquara, 1967), pp. 137–38.

54. President's remarks in Eugênio Egas, *Galeria dos presidentes de São Paulo* (3 vols.; São Paulo: O Estado de São Paulo, 1926), 1: 274–75.

55. The data presented by Kuntz Busch vary extremely from those given by José Sebastião Witter, *Um estabelecimento agrícola da província de São Paulo nos meados do século XIX* (São Paulo: Revista de História, 1974), pp. 37, 43. Witter, also employing Livro Mestre V, finds 67 families in debt in 1863 and 23 with credits; in 1864, 71 and 18; in 1865, 65 and 20. Unfortunately the ledger in question seems to have disappeared. Both samples may be unrepresentative.

56. RC/C-1 and C-2, Livros de Notas, 1853–73. APESP, Registro de Terras, Rio Claro and Itaqueri, 1855–57. On smallholding, see Henrique de Beaurepair-Rohan, "O futuro da grande lavoura e da grande propriedade no Brasil," in Brazil, Congresso Agrícola, *Colecção de documentos*; José Vergueiro, *Memorial acerca de colonização e cultivo de café* (Campinas: Typographia do Constitucional, 1874); there is much on local German population in Sommer, "Die Deutschen in São Paulo," 3. The estimate on land costs is for land unsuitable for coffee; coffee land would cost about twice as much.

57. Vergueiro, p. 10; Carvalho de Moraes, p. 101; Moré, *Le Bresil en 1852, et sa colonisation future*, pp. 136–37; Taunay, *Historia do café no Brasil*, 3: 121, 351, 354; President of Province, *Relatorio*, 1855; M. F.-J. de Santa Ana Nery, *Guide de l'émigrant au Brésil* (Paris: Librairie Charles Delagrave, 1889), p. 7; Antônio Prado in Couty, pp. 162–64, 390–91. An official view favoring smallholders in Brazil, Ministério da Fazenda, *Informações sobre o estado da lavoura*, p. 151.

58. *A Provincia de São Paulo,* Aug. 27, 1876, provides a listing of planters; Brazil, Comissão Central de Estatistica, *Recenseamento geral de população . . . em 1 de setembro de 1872,* 19.

59. Federico Barros Brotero, *Oliveiras descendentes de Estanislau José de Oliveira, Professor de Rhetorica* (São Paulo: Graphica Paulista, 1942); *A Provincia de São Paulo,* Sept. 10, 1884; RC/C-1, Inventories, Oct. 31, 1884.

CHAPTER FIVE

1. APESP, OD/RC, 57, Rioclarenses to President of Province, May 1, 1871. Among the signers were the baron of Porto Feliz, Cândido Vale, Francisco de Assis Negreiros, the baron of Araraquara, Rafael Tobias de Barros, and José Luiz Borges. Also APESP, Polícia, 101, Subdelegate Rio Claro to Chief of Police, May 14, 1871, escaped slaves.

2. APESP, Escravos, 1, 275, Campineiros to President of Province, April 11, 1871. Emília Viotti da Costa noted this document and quoted its last line, *Da senzala à colónia* (São Paulo: Difusão Européia do Livro, 1966), pp. 306, 307–8. São Paulo (Province), President of Province, *Relatorio,* 1872, p. 4. The troops, it appears, were not removed thereafter, although the high cost of maintaining them was complained of by the president.

3. For a discussion of explanations of abolition, see Richard Graham, "Causes for the Abolition of Negro Slavery in Brazil: An Interpretive Essay," *Hispanic American Historical Review,* 46 (May 1966): 123–37; see also the same author's "Brazilian Slavery Re-Examined: A Review Article," *Journal of Social History,* 3 (Summer, 1970): 431–53; and Paula Beiguelman, *A formação do povo no complexo cafeeiro: aspectos políticos* (São Paulo: Livraria Pioneira Editôra, 1968), pp. 37–50.

4. RC/Registro de Imóveis, Processos, Tribunal do Jury, Nov. 28, 1866. On the self-determination of the slaves, see Clovis Moura, *Rebeliões da senzala* (São Paulo: Edições Zumbi, 1959). On the psychological dimensions of race relations, see Eugene Brody, ed., *The Lost Ones* (New York: International Universities Press, 1973).

5. Brazil, *Colecção das leis,* Law 2,040, Sept. 28, 1871; Decree 5,135, Nov. 13, 1872. Sérgio Buarque de Holanda, "Do Império à República," *História geral da civilização brasileira* (São Paulo: Difusão Européia do Livro, 1963–     ), 2, 5: 113–15, 128, 132.

6. APESP, OD/RC, baron of Araraquara, A. A. da Fonseca, J. Teixeira das Neves, to County Council, forwarded to President of Province, Nov. 15, 1871; Viotti da Costa, pp. 369–99; Robert Conrad, *The Destruction of Brazilian Slavery, 1850–1888* (Berkeley: University of California Press, 1972), pp. 106–12. RC/C-2, Processos, reports of Tax Collector to Juiz de Orfãos, 1884, 1886; President of Province, *Relatorio,* 1877–87; APESP, Escravos, 1, classification lists and reports of the Tax Collector, 1881, 1882, 1884; Brazil, Ministério de Agricultura, Comércio e Obras Públicas, *Relatorio,* 1880, 1886.

7. João Pedro Carvalho de Moraes, *Relatorio apresentado ao Mini-*

*sterio de Agricultura, Commercio e Obras Publicas . . . em execução das instrucções de 17 de março ultimo* (Rio de Janeiro: Typographia Nacional, 1870), p. 101.

8. Brazil, Congresso Agrícola, *Colecção de documentos* (Rio de Janeiro: Typographia Nacional, 1878), p. 135; [Antônio Coelho Rodrigues,] *Manual do subdito fiel, ou cartas de um lavrador a sua majestade o imperador sobre a questão do elemento servil* (Rio de Janeiro: Typ. e Lith. de Moreira Maximo e Cia., 1884), p. 8; APESP, OD/RC, Subdelegate to President of Province, Sept. 25, 1877; RC/C-2, Livros de Notas, Dec. 23, 1881. Another declaration, Aug. 27, 1881, records purchase of Angélica. APESP, OD/RC, Baron of Grão-Mogol to President of Province, Oct. 3, 1881. Statement of Mr. and Mrs. Pedro Rossi, Rio Claro, Dec. 13, 1968.

9. São Paulo (Province), Assembléia Legislativa Provincial, *Annaes*, 1887, speech by Rangel Pestana, Jan. 26, 1887; Brazil, Congresso Agrícola, *Colecção de documentos*, speech by Manuel Furtado da Silva Leite, pp. 47, 53.

10. RC/C-2, Livros de Notas, Feb. 24, 1872, June 26, 1872. Viotti da Costa, pp. 402–3. RC/C-2, Livros de Notas, Aug. 27, 1872.

11. RC/C-2, Livros de Notas, Oct. 11, 1876. Other examples of term transfers, among many: Oct. 19, 1885, April 12, 1886, Jan. 17, 1887, Jan. 22, 1887.

12. RC/C-2, Processos, Jan. 3, 1878, March 12, 1878; Livros de Notas, Feb. 28, 1879.

13. APESP, Juiz de Direito, Rio Claro, Juiz de Direito to President of Province, Sept. 20, 1877; RC/C-2, Livros de Vendas de Escravos; RC/C-1, Inventories, July 13, 1876; APESP, OD/RC, Tax Collector to President of Province, various letters, dated 1875–79.

14. *Diario Popular*, July 24, 1885, July 31, 1885; Brazil, Congresso Agrícola, *Colecção de documentos*, p. 108; a delegate claimed that the *ingênuos* were "dying like flies." On the other hand, Louis Couty suggested that they were better treated than slave children, *Le Brésil en 1884* (Rio de Janeiro: Faro & Lino, 1884), pp. 296–97.

15. Assembléia Legislativa Provincial, *Annaes*, 1878, speech by Queiroz Telles, March 27, 1878. Robert Brent Toplin, *The Abolition of Slavery in Brazil* (New York: Atheneum, 1972), p. 48; Roger Bastide, "A criminalidade negra no estado de São Paulo," in Abdias do Nascimento, ed., *O negro revoltado* (Rio de Janeiro: Edições GRD, 1968), pp. 164–66.

16. Assembléia Legislativa Provincial, *Annaes*, 1878, committee report, Feb. 23, 1878, and debate, March 27, 1878.

17. *Ibid.*, A. A. da Fonseca remarks, March 27, 1878; *Correio Paulistano*, Dec. 17, 1880; São Paulo (Province), *Leis*, Law 1, Jan. 23, 1881. On enforcement see petitions, APESP, OD/RC, baron of Grão-Mogol to President of Province, Oct. 3, 1881. The Republican Party sought in 1883 to repeal the tax; see Domingos Jaguaribe, *Organização do trabalho; questões sociaes* (São Paulo: Typographia do King, Leroy King Bookwalter, 1884), pp. 38–39.

18. President of Province, *Relatorio*, 1883, p. 6; Coelho Rodrigues, *Manual do subdito fiel, ou cartas de um lavrador a sua majestade o imperador sobre a questão do elemento servil*, p. 13; Toplin, p. 6, quoting *Rio News*, Nov. 11, 1882, and pp. 30–31; Vice-President of Province, *Relatorio*, 1884, p. 8; APESP, Polícia, 228, Annual Report, 1885, Delegate to Chief of Police. Louis Couty, generally an apologist of the planters, noted the increased violence and work slowdowns in 1883, *Pequena propriedade e imigração europeia* (Rio de Janeiro: Laemmert, 1884).

19. RC/Registro de Imóveis, Processos, Sept. 27, 1884, Feb. 28, March 1, 1885; *O Tempo*, March 5, 1885.

20. Joaquim Floriano Godoy, *O elemento servil e as camaras municipais da provincia de S. Paulo* (Rio de Janeiro: Imprensa Nacional, 1887), p. 116. On dependency, see Toplin, pp. 35–37. He finds no significant abolitionist activity as late as 1883, p. 202.

21. Godoy, pp. 116–18; Conrad, *The Destruction of Brazilian Slavery, 1850–1888*, p. 128; Domingos Jaguaribe, *Organização*, pp. 1–7, and same author's *Homens e ideas no Brasil* (Rio de Janeiro: Typ. de G. Leuzinger, 1889), pp. 37–47. Martinho Prado in Paula Beiguelman, *Pequenos estudos de ciência política* (2 vols.; São Paulo: Livraria Pioneira, 1968), 2: 48.

22. Brazil, *Colecção das leis*, Law 3,270, Sept. 28, 1885.

23. *Diario de Rio Claro*, Sept. 19, 1886, contains a public notice published by the Juiz de Orfãos. RC/C-2, Processos, Feb. 6, 1886, March 7, 1887, Jan. 31, 1887. RC/C-2, Livros de Notas, Jan. 28, 1886.

24. Partido Conservador (São Paulo Province), *Bolletim*, Jan. 5, 1888. RC/C-2, Livros de Notas, Dec. 12, 1886. On slaves as collateral, see Flag Junior, *Considerações sobre a crise financeira e o elemento servil* (Rio de Janeiro: Typ. União de A. M. Coelho da Rocha, & C., 1884), pp. 29–35.

25. Toplin, *The Abolition of Slavery in Brazil*, pp. 207–8; Partido Conservador, *Bolletim*, Jan. 7, 1888, mentioned that some planters were beginning to go to Santos to hire runaways.

26. RC/C-2, Processos, Feb. 8, 1888, March 6, 1888, March 7, 1888.

27. Brazil, *Colecção das leis*, Law 3,310, Oct. 15, 1886; *A Redempção*, Dec. 11, 1887, Jan. 1, 1888.

28. RC/C-2, Livros de Notas, March 4, 1887; APESP, Escravos, 2, "Resumo geral dos libertos ... 30 de março de 1886 até ... 30 de março de 1887 [Rio Claro]."

29. These events in President of Province, *Relatorio*, 1888, pp. 6–10, 23–24; Conrad, pp. 246–48, 252; Toplin, pp. 208–15. On fears of fraternization and instances, see Diana Maria de Faro Leal Diniz, "Rio Claro e o café: desenvolvimento, apogeu e crise, 1850–1900" (Ph.D. dissertation, Dept. of Social Sciences, Faculdade de Filosofia, Ciências e Letras de Rio Claro, 1973), pp. 90–91; Cleveland Donald, "Slavery and Abolition in Campos, Brazil, 1830–1888" (Ph.D. dissertation, Dept. of History, Cornell University, 1973), pp. 127–66. The raised consciousness of the officers is

mentioned in Thomas Skidmore, *Black into White* (New York: Oxford University Press, 1974), p. 8.

30. Conrad, pp. 248–50, 252, 254; *Correio Paulistano*, Dec. 17, 1888.

31. *Diario Popular*, Nov. 26, Dec. 12, 20, 24, 28, 29, 1887; *Correio Paulistano*, Dec. 13, 14, 17, 23, 28, 29, 31, 1887; quotation in Suely Barsotti, "Estudo de comunidade" (paper presented in Pedagogy, Faculdade de Filosofia, Ciências e Letras de Rio Claro, 1968), p. 41; João Pedro da Veiga Filho, *Estudo economico e financeiro do estado de S. Paulo* (São Paulo: Typ. do "Diario Official," 1896), p. 63n.

32. APESP, Polícia, Subdelegate to Chief of Police, Jan. 15, 1888; *A Redempção*, Dec. 18, 1887, Jan. 1, 1888.

33. *Diario Popular*, Jan. 7, 9, 11, 14, 1888.

34. *A Redempção*, Jan. 29, 1888; *Diario Popular*, Jan. 26, Feb. 1, 3, 1888.

35. José Alexandre Diniz, "Organização agrícola do município de Araras" (thesis, Dept. of Geography, Faculdade de Filosofia, Ciências e Letras de Rio Claro, 1968), p. 40; President of Province, *Relatorio*, 1888, pp. 6–10; *Diario Popular*, Feb. 6, 1888.

36. Assembléia Legislativa Provincial, *Annaes*, 1888, speech by Domingos Jaguaribe, Feb. 1, 1888. On March 8 the provincial assembly sent a petition to the Chamber of Deputies for immediate abolition.

37. *Diario Popular*, Jan. 18, Feb. 6, 1888; P. Nardy Filho, "Em Rio Claro Livre," *O Estado de São Paulo*, March 7, 1951; J. Romeo Ferraz, *Historia de Rio Claro* (São Paulo: Typographia Hennies Irmaos, 1922).

38. RC/C-2, Processos, Feb. 8, 1888, March 6, 1888. On March 7, Paschoal Afonso Rinaldi complained that an ex-slave had not carried out his work contract to completion, RC/C-2, Processos, March 7, 1888.

39. RC/C-2, Processos, March 23, 1885; Maria Ines Rauter Mancuso, "Município de Itirapina" (paper presented in Primeiro Ano, Ciências Sociais, Faculdade de Filosofia, Ciências e Letras de Rio Claro, 1967). Reynaldo Kuntz Busch implies that there were slaves in Limeira *after* May 13! *História de Limeira* (Limeira: Edição da Prefeitura Municipal, 1967), p. 280.

40. Lucas Ribeiro Prado, *Os crimes do Barão* (São Paulo: By the author, 1895), p. 178.

41. Nardy Filho.

42. Ribeiro Prado, p. 32.

43. Conrad, *The Destruction of Brazilian Slavery, 1850–1888*, p. 255; President of Province, *Relatorio*, 1888, p. 23. On abolitionist advocacy of land reform, see Nilo Odalia, "A abolição da escravatura," *Anais do Museu Paulista*, 19 (1964): 126–28; and Richard Graham, "Landowners and the Overthrow of the Empire," *Luso-Brazilian Review*, 7 (Dec. 1970): 44–56.

44. Godoy, *O elemento servil e as camaras municipais da provincia de S. Paulo*, p. 118. Domingos Jaguaribe, *Organização do trabalho; questões*

*sociaes*, pp. 6–7, 69–73. See also his *Algumas palavras sobre e emigração* (São Paulo: Typ. do "Diario," 1877), p. 23. The President of the Province expected that the ex-slaves would turn to idleness and vagrancy, *Relatorio*, 1888, p. 22.

45. President of Province, *Relatorio*, 1889, Annex, p. 18. Interview with Mr. José do Nascimento, Rio Claro, Dec. 2, 1968; RC/C-1, Livros de Notas, Oct. 23, 1890. On the freedmen, see Florestan Fernandes, *The Negro in Brazilian Society*, trans. by Jacqueline Skiles, A. Brunel, and Arthur Rothwell (New York: Columbia University Press, 1969), pp. 1–54. On the failure of the legislature to provide social welfare for the ex-slaves, see Odalia, pp. 138–39.

46. *Diario de Rio Claro*, Sept. 21, 1893; *O Alpha*, Jan. 15, 1902, Jan. 29, 1904. Newspapers withheld the distinctive "Senhor" when referring to persons of color; they were merely "o prêto." The nonderogatory formula was "a man of color, but of irreproachable conduct." *O Alpha*, Jan. 27, 1902. Pio Lourenço Correa, "A abolição em Araraquara," in Nelson Martins de Almeida, *Album de Araraquara* (Araraquara: Empreza "O Papel," 1948), p. 27. Barsotti, "Estudo de comunidade," pp. 33–36; *Diario de Rio Claro*, May 13, 16, 1888.

47. Domingos Jaguaribe, *Influence de l'esclavage et de la liberté* (Brussels: Gustave Fischlin, 1892), p. 146; Michael Hall, "The Origins of Mass Migration to Brazil, 1871–1914" (Ph.D. dissertation, Dept. of History, Columbia University, 1969), pp. 162–63.

48. President of Province, *Relatorio*, 1889, pp. 144–45.

CHAPTER SIX

1. *Correio Paulistano*, Oct. 11, 1870; São Paulo (Province), *Leis*, Law 42, March 3, 1871. Robert Conrad has pointed out slave owners' determination to keep slaves to the very end, *The Destruction of Brazilian Slavery, 1850–1888* (Berkeley: University of California Press, 1972), pp. 128–30; and Michael Hall's major thesis is that the collapse of slavery led to immigration, and not the other way round, "The Origins of Mass Migration to Brazil, 1871–1914" (Ph.D. dissertation, Dept. of History, Columbia University, 1969), p. 88.

2. Brazil, Congresso Agrícola, *Colecção de documentos* (Rio de Janeiro: Typographia Nacional, 1870), pp. 77–78, 156–59, 184, 193. The county council of São José do Rio Pardo was still advocating the introduction of coolies in 1893! MHP-ABV, Ofícios, circular from County Council of São José do Rio Pardo, April 10, 1893.

3. Vicenzo Grossi, *Storia della colonizazzione europea al Brasile e della emigrazione italiana nello stato di S. Paulo* (2d ed.; Milan: Società Editrice Dante Alighieri, Segati & C., 1914), p. 372; Partido Conservador (São Paulo), *Bolletim*, Jan. 7, 1888, also Jan. 14, 17.

4. São Paulo (Province), *Leis*, Law 25, March 28, 1884; Hall, pp. 88–96; Lucy Maffei Hutter, *Imigração italiana em São Paulo (1880–1889)* (São Paulo: Instituto de Estudos Brasileiros, 1972), pp. 28, 33; Paula Beiguel-

man, *Pequenos estudos de ciência política* (2 vols.; São Paulo: Livraria Pioneira, 1968), 2: 54–58.

5. Maffei Hutter, p. 159; Brazil, *Colecção das leis*, Decree 528, June 28, 1890; Pierre Denis, *Le Brésil au XXe siècle* (Paris: Librairie Armand Colin, 1909), p. 129.

6. Robert F. Foerster, *The Italian Migration of Our Times* (Cambridge, Mass.: Harvard University Press, 1919), p. 290; Domingos Jaguaribe, *Influence de l'esclavage et de la liberté* (Brussels: Gustave Fischlin, 1892), pp. 158–61.

7. Interview with Mr. and Mrs. Pedro Rossi, Rio Claro, Dec. 13, 1968. Pietro Ubaldi, *L'espansione coloniale e economica dell'Italia nel Brasile* (Rome: Ermanno Loescher, 1911), pp. 50–51; Warren Dean, "Remittances of Italian Immigrants: From Brazil, Argentina, Uruguay and U.S.A., 1884–1914" (New York University, Ibero-American Language and Area Center, Occasional Papers, no. 14, 1974), p. 3; MHP-ABV, Santa Gertrudes (hereafter SG), Copiador, Sept. 5, 11, 1896, and Deve-Haver, 1885–89.

8. Roger Bastide, "Relações raciais entre negros e brancos em São Paulo," *Anhembi* (July 1953), pp. 242–50; Florestan Fernandes, "Immigration and Race Relations," in Magnus Mörner, ed., *Race and Class in Latin America* (New York: Columbia University Press, 1970), pp. 127–42. Oscar de Arruda Penteado, "Arquivo do município," *Diario de Rio Claro* [no date, in Mr. Arruda's clipping file], Secretario do Governo to County Council; APESP, OD/RC, County Council to President of Province, Oct. 10, 1888. Province-wide, 265 naturalized in 1888, while 122 and 89 had naturalized in 1886 and 1887. Eugenio Egas, *Galeria dos presidentes da provincia de S. Paulo* (3 vols.; São Paulo: O Estado de São Paulo, 1926), 1: 722.

9. Enrico Perrod, *La provincia di San Paolo (Brasile)* (Rome: Tipografia de Ministerio degli Affari Esteri, 1888), p. 52; *Il Brasile e gli italiani* (Florence: R. Bemporad & Filho), p. 396.

10. Sérgio Milliet, *Roteiro de café e outros ensaios* (São Paulo: Coleção Departamento de Cultura, 1939), pp. 53–66; Afonso d'Escragnolle Taunay, *Historia do café no Brasil* (15 vols.; Rio de Janeiro: Departamento Nacional do Café, 1943), 6: 365; Rio Claro, Câmara Municipal, "Atas," March 14, 1897.

11. Konrado Krettlis, ed., *Almanak de Rio Claro, 1906* (Rio Claro: Typ. Conrado, 1906); *Diario de Rio Claro*, Sept. 19, 1886; Júlia Maria Leonor Scarano, "Considerações preliminares sobre uma cidade de imigração teuto-italiana, e os efeitos do segundo conflito mundial," in IV Simpósio Nacional dos Professores Universitários de História, *Anais* (São Paulo: Universidade de São Paulo, 1969), pp. 510–13.

12. Interview with Mr. João Meira, Banco Comercial do Estado de São Paulo, Rio Claro, July 20, 1968; *O Alpha*, Feb. 23, 1912.

13. MP-AA, Fichário, Rio Claro, mortgages made out in São Paulo on Rio Claro estates, 1895–1905; RC/C-1, Livros de Notas, Aug. 19, 1890. Acts

222                              NOTES TO PAGES 164–72

of the county council contain petitions by planters to be relieved of town affairs because of changed address and orders for demolition of town houses. *Diario de Rio Claro* noted arrivals of planters in town.

14. Prado in Oscar de Arruda Penteado, "O café em Rio Claro," *Diario de Rio Claro*, Jan. 19, 1957; MP-AA, Rio Claro, sale of Angélica, Nov. 28, 1879; interview with Mr. Flamínio Levy, Cordeirópolis, Oct. 5, 1968.

15. Cf. Table 1.1 (p. 8), which provides family output of basic food-stuffs.

16. View of Santa Gertrudes and production figures in C. F. van Delden Laerne, *Brazil and Java* (London: W. H. Allen, 1885), pp. 327, 334–35, 362; São Paulo (State), Secretaria de Agricultura, Comércio e Obras Públicas, *O café, estatistica de producção e commercio*, 1914. Much of the following data is from Maria Silvia C. Beozzo Bassanezi, "Fazenda de Santa Gertrudes" (Ph.D. dissertation, Dept. of Social Sciences, Faculdade de Filosofia, Ciências e Letras de Rio Claro, 1973). See pp. 40–46.

17. MHP-ABV, SG, Copiador, Sept. 30, 1895, Oct. 11, 1895; Paul Adam, *Les visages du Brésil* (Paris: Aillaud, Alves & Cie., 1912), pp. 112–14; MP-AA, Rio Claro, inventory of marquis of Três Rios, July 25, 1893; Bassanezi, p. 63. Santa Gertrudes contained nearly 3,000 hectares by 1905.

18. MHP-ABV, SG, Diarios, 1885–89; Copiador, 1885–89; Deve-Haver and Correntes, 1886–1900; Costaneira, 1895–99; Livro do Ponto, 1900–1919. Preservation is due to the Prates family and to Prof. Jeanne Berrance de Castro, director of the museum. See her "Inventário analítico de uma fazenda paulista, Santa Gertrudes (1885–1961)," in Eurípedes Simões de Paula, ed., *Colonização e imigração* (São Paulo: Universidade de São Paulo, 1967). More detailed analysis of the books in Bassanezi. Palmares records are located in the University of São Paulo, Dept. of History, Setor de Documentação, hereafter USP/DH-SD.

19. "Condições de trabalho," *Boletim do Departamento Estadual de Trabalho* (4th quarter, 1911), pp. 19–33; APESP, Secretaria de Agricultura, 44, 1895, enclosure in file dated Nov. 7, 1895, "Regulamento para as colonias Angelica e Matto Negro." Candido F. de Lacerda, *Estudo de meação, parceria, etc., e das suas vantagens* (São Paulo: Typographia Brazil de Carlos Gerke, 1903), pp. 14–21; Denis, *Le Brésil au XXe siècle*, p. 139.

20. Ranulfo Bocayuva Cunha, "Organização do trabalho livre," in Brazil, Câmara de Deputados, *Livro do Centenario* (3 vols.; Rio de Janeiro: Empresa Brasil Editora, 1926), 3: 374–81; Brazil, *Colecção das leis*, Decree 213, Feb. 22, 1890; Brazil, *Código Civil*, 1916, Articles 1216–36.

21. MHP-ABV, SG, Copiador, Feb. 18, 19, 1896. USP/DH-SD, Palmares.

22. São Paulo (State), Secretaria de Agricultura, Comércio e Obras Públicas, *Estatistica agricola e zootechnica, 1904–1905*; MHP-ABV, SG, Copiador, Sept. 27, Dec. 28, 1895, July 6, Oct. 4, Dec. 16, 1896; Bassanezi, p. 149. A. Lalière, *Le café dans l'état de Saint Paul (Brésil)* (Paris: Augustin Challamel, 1909), p. 269; *O Alpha*, Oct. 25, 1904.

23. Thomas Holloway, "Condições do mercado de trabalho e or-

ganização do trabalho nas plantações na economia cafeeira de São Paulo, 1888–1915," *Estudos Econômicos*, 2 (Dec. 1972): 166–67; Angélica and Mato Negro, "Regulamento," 1895; MHP-ABV, SG, Copiador, Nov. 24, 28, 1896.

24. *Estatística agrícola e zootechnica, 1904–1905*; Fábio Ramos, *O café no Brasil e no estrangeiro* (Rio de Janeiro: Papelaria Santa Helena, 1923), pp. 203–6; MHP-ABV, SG, Daybooks. There was at least one freedman on Santa Gertrudes, Antônio Novo, employed as a colono in 1896, Copiador, Nov. 30, 1896. Bassanezi, pp. 149, 210.

25. Holloway believes ex-slaves were demoted to turmas because they were easier for Portuguese-speaking foremen to direct, pp. 163–64. See also Douglas Graham, "Migração estrangeira e a questão da oferta de mão-de-obra no crescimento econômico brasileiro," *Estudos Econômicos*, 3 (April 1973): 49–50. Apparently the immigrants thought themselves superior, too, Eunice Ribeiro Durham, *Assimilição e mobilidade* (São Paulo: Instituto de Estudos Brasileiros, 1966), p. 23.

26. MHP-ABV, SG, Copiador, 1896; Daybook, 1899; Correntes, 1901–2. USP/DH-SD, Palmares, May 13–21, 1901.

27. RC/C-1, Livros de Notas, July 15, 1871; *Estatística agrícola e zootechnica, 1904–1905*; compare contracts in Denis, pp. 140–52. Oscar Onody, *A inflação brasileira* (Rio de Janeiro: By the author, 1960), p. 23. Decline in incomes is a central theme of Michael Hall in "The Origins of Mass Migration to Brazil, 1871–1914." Maria Silvia C. Beozzo Bassanezi, "Fazenda de Santa Gertrudes," pp. 205–9.

28. *O Rio Claro*, Jan. 15, 1895; MHP-ABV, SG, Deve-Haver, 1885–89; interview with Mr. Antônio Guerra, Rio Claro, Dec. 3, 1968.

29. Guido Maistrello, "Fazendas de café—costumes," in Ramos, pp. 553–74; interview with Mrs. Dominga Silvana, Rio Claro, Dec. 2, 1968.

30. Alfredo Rossi, "Attraverso le 'Fazendas' dello stato di San Paolo (Brasile)," *Rivista d'Italia* (Oct. 1902), pp. 647–87; Ramos, p. 206. Hall bases himself strongly upon Rossi's outraged description, but there are opposing views in Denis, *Le Brésil au XXe siècle*, and F. Canella, "Le condizioni degli italiani nello stato di San Paolo," *L'Italia Coloniale* (Jan. 1903), pp. 43–62.

31. MHP-ABV, Circular, Secretaria dos Negócios do Interior, March 12, 1894; Rio Claro, Câmara Municipal, *Relatorio*, 1910; Luigi Mazzotti, "Una grave malattia che colpisce al Brasile gli imigranti italiani," *Revista della Beneficenza Pubblica*, 30 (1902): 469–76; Ramos, p. 208.

32. Penteado, "Arquivo do município"; *Diario de Rio Claro*, Sept. 5, 1893.

33. *Fanfulla*, Oct. 19, 1897, Aug. 1, 21, 1901; *O Estado de São Paulo*, May 7, 1902; *O Alpha*, July 30, Oct. 21, 1901, May 5, 8, 13, 18, 1902; Silvana interview.

34. MHP-ABV, SG, Copiador, Aug. 22, 1895, Jan. 12, 13, June 2, 3, 1896, Sept. 29, Oct. 9, 1899.

35. Câmara Municipal, "Atas," March 10, 1896; José Constante Bar-

reto Archive, flyer titled "Liga Operaria," dated May 25, 1906; *O Estado de São Paulo*, May 7, 1906; *O Alpha*, Sept. 17, 1901, May 5–30, 1905; *Fanfulla*, Aug. 2–11, 1911; Neusa da Costa Davids, "Poder local: aparência e realidade" (Ph.D. dissertation, Dept. of Political Science, Faculdade de Filosofia, Ciências e Letras de Rio Claro, 1968).

36. Other conflicts with newly arrived immigrants in MHP-ABV, SG, Copiador, Jan. 12, Feb. 18, 1896; and on Boa Vista, *La Libertà*, Oct. 25, 1891; Isidro Gomes Teixeira, *Estatistica de café e cafesais* (São Paulo: volver a pequena agricultura," *Boletim da Agricultura* (Jan. 1903), pp. Typ. Selecta, 1909), p. 159; Julio Brandão Sobrinho, "Os meios de desen-273–76.

37. Rossi interview; *Fanfulla*, Oct. 19, 1897.

38. *O Alpha*, July 1, 1905, report of an administrator seducing a colono woman; see also following note, the Lungaretti affair and Whitaker correspondence; *O Alpha*, July 23, 29, 1905.

39. RC/Registro de Imóveis, Processos, 1901, Angelo Lungaretti file. Contains depositions and interrogations, jury selection, testimony, and sentencing, first and second trials and record of appeals and pardon. Raul's preoccupations were not unique among planters; see letter of Jorge Whitaker to unidentified friend in Ribeirão Preto, Sept. 12, 1890: "I'm still with the *Italianinha*, who gets prettier all the time. Haven't you arranged one for yourself over there?" USP/DH-SD, Palmares.

40. RC/Registro de Imóveis, Processos, 1901, Lungaretti file.

41. *Ibid.*

42. *Ibid.*; *O Estado de São Paulo*, Oct. 4, 5, 1900; *O Alpha*, Sept. 29, Oct. 17, 1901, March 20, June 12, 1902; *Diario de Rio Claro*, June 24, 1902; José Constante Barreto Archive, flyer dated Dec. 10, 1908; *Última Hora*, Oct. 11, 1960.

43. Grossi, *Storia della colonizazzione europea al Brasile e della emigrazione italiana nello stato di S. Paulo*, pp. 399–409; Rossi, "Attraverso le 'Fazendas' dello stato di San Paolo," p. 648.

44. There was an earlier suspension of subsidized emigration from Italy, March 1889–Aug. 1891, Foerster, *The Italian Migration of Our Times*, p. 294. Brazil, *Colecção das leis*, Law 1,150, Jan. 5, 1904; Law 1,607, Dec. 29, 1906. São Paulo (State), *Leis*, Law 1,045C, Dec. 27, 1906; Law 1,299A, Dec. 27, 1911. Antonio Piccarolo, *L'emigrazione italiana nello stato di S. Paulo* (São Paulo: Magalhães, 1911), pp. 30–32, 56–57, 136. An earlier Patronato was organized by the Italian Consulate in 1902, to assist in locating employment and gaining repatriation, *Il Brasile e gli italiani*, p. 947.

45. Miyoko Makino, "Contribuição ao estudo de legislação sobre núcleos coloniais no período imperial," *Anais do Museu Paulista*, 25 (1971–75): 83–130. Denis, *Le Brésil au XXe siècle*, pp. 163–65; "Colonização das terras particulares," *Boletim da Agricultura* (June 1904), pp. 435–37. São Paulo (Province), *Leis*, Law 28, March 28, 1884; Law 101, Aug. 8, 1889. São Paulo (Province), President of Province, *Relatorio*,

1888 (April 27), pp. 64, 68, (Jan. 10), p. 32. Sociedade Promotora da Imigração, *A provincia de São Paulo no Brasil; emigrante lede este folheto antes de partir* (São Paulo: Lombaerts & C., 1886), p. 52.

46. São Paulo (State), *Mensagens apresentadas ao Congresso Legislativo de S. Paulo pelos Presidentes do estado e Vice-Presidentes em exercicio* (São Paulo: "Diario Official," 1916), pp. 46, 71, 75; Grossi, pp. 391–94, 404; *Diario Popular*, Jan. 29, 1885. For a study of núcleos in the suburbs of the state capital, see José de Souza Martins, *A migração e a crise do Brasil agrário* (São Paulo: Livraria Pioneira Editôra, 1973), esp. pp. 103–31. APESP, Núcleo Colonial de Cascalho (hereafter NCC), 2, Inspection Committee to President of Province, Dec. 31, 1884.

47. Sociedade Promotora de Imigração, p. 52. APESP, NCC, 2, State Treasury Inspector to Vice-President of Province, Sept. 12, 1884; letters from pretendents to lots, Sept. 12, 1891, Oct. 17, 1892, Feb. 8, 1895; Administrator to Secretary of Agriculture, Aug. 9, 1886.

48. Piccarolo, p. 100; São Paulo (State), *Leis*, Reglamento 4, Aug. 14, 1886; Maffei Hutter, *Imigração italiana em São Paulo*, pp. 106–7. APESP, OD/RC, Administrator of Cascalho to President of Province, March 4, 1886; Superintendent of Núcleos to President, May 12, 1886. Complaint on votes in São Paulo (Province), Assembléia Legislativa Provincial, *Anais*, March 14, 1887.

49. APESP, OD/RC, Carlos Bolle to President of Province, March 22, 1887; São Paulo (State), Secretaria de Agricultura, Comêrcio e Obras Públicas, *Relatorio*, 1893, Annex 2, pp. 49–50; APESP, NCC, 1, petition from 164 residents, Aug. 10, 1893. Souza Martins believes that the núcleos surrounding São Paulo did not earn enough to repay capital invested, pp. 113–14.

50. *Mensagens apresentadas . . .* , p. 40; Brazil, Sexto Congresso Agrícola, 1912, *Relatorio* (Piracicaba: n.p., 1912), pp. 4, 17; *Diario de Rio Claro*, June 16, 1894, Jan. 3, 1899.

51. Paul Perrin, *Les colonies agricoles au Brésil* (Paris: Société Générale d'Impression, 1912), p. 66. APESP, Secretaria de Agricultura, Requerimentos Diversos 1, 1904; Núcleo Colonial de Jorge Tibiriçá, 2. Grossi, p. 368.

52. Maffei Hutter, p. 102; Holloway, "Condições do mercado de trabalho e organização do trabalho nas plantações na economia cafeeira de São Paulo," pp. 163–64, 175; Durham, *Assimilição e mobilidade*, p. 25. Krettlis's *Almanak de Rio Claro, 1906*, identifies merchants.

53. Brazil, Ministério de Agricultura, Indústria e Comércio, Directoria Geral de Estatística, *Recenseamento geral . . . 1920*, 3: 31–45. Robert Shirley, *The End of a Tradition* (New York: Columbia University Press, 1971), p. 118.

54. Interview with Mr. Luiz Fernando Höfling, São Paulo, Dec. 12, 1968; Rossi interview.

55. Federico Barros Brotero, *Oliveiras descendentes de Estanislau José de Oliveira, Professor de Rhetorica* (São Paulo: Graphica Paulista, 1942),

pp. 24–28; "Centenario da Fazenda São José," *O Estado de São Paulo*, Dec. 24, 1939.

56. Dean, "Remittances of Italian Immigrants," p. 7.

CONCLUSIONS

1. Eugenio Egas, *Galeria dos presidentes de São Paulo* (3 vols.; São Paulo, 1926), 1: 668.

2. Nathaniel Leff, "Economic Retardation in Nineteenth-Century Brazil," *Economic History Review*, series 2, 25 (Aug. 1972): 489–507.

# Index

# Index

Abolitionism, 126, 131, 137, 139–40,
    142–43, 148–49f, 159; of slaves, 82,
    126, 151; of freedmen, 144–45; final
    crisis, 149, 153f
Abolitionist press, 143, 146
Aboriginal inhabitants, 2, 17–18, 52n
Absenteeism, 15, 44, 163, 188, 191ff
African cultural elements, 82
African slave traffic prohibited, 50, 54,
    93. *See also* Slave, internal traffic
African slaves, 58
*Agregados*, 6, 20, 71, 71n, 73, 84, 118,
    170
Agricultural census of 1905, 187–88
Agricultural Club of Campinas, 138
Agricultural Congress of 1878, 156
Alincourt, Louis d', 4
Alves, Francisco da Costa, 12
American Southern emigrants, 112–13
Analândia, 47, 161, 177, 181–82
Anápolis, *see* Analândia
Andrade, Joaquim José de, 15, 30
Angélica plantation, 48, 67–68, 117–
    18, 131, 164, 190
Anhaia, Ana Veloso de, 72
Animal husbandry, 8–10
Araraquara, baron of, 117, 178
Archives, xii–xv
Army, 66, 101, 124f, 144–45
Arruda, Manuel Paes de, 16
Assistência, rural neighborhood, 189
Associação Libertadora, 145
Atrocities, 66–67
Avé-Lallement, Robert C. B., 104

Banks, 162
Bankruptcies, 164, 181, 185
Barbosa, Antônio José Vieira, 36

Barbosa, Benedito, 148
Barros, Antônio Paes de (elder), 30,
    41, 46–47
Barros, Antônio Paes de (younger),
    117, 145
Barros, Maria Paes de, 45, 64, 86
Barros, Rafael de, 181
Belgian immigrants, 93
Birth control by slaves, 62
Blacks in Brazilian society, xiv
Boa Vista de Passa Cinco plantation,
    33–34
Bohn, Eduardo, 146
"Book of Gold," 149
Borges, José Luis, 143, 146, 149
Botão, Francisco Gomes, 79
Braga, Claudio da Silva, 147f
Brasil, João Joaquim Lopes de
    Figueiredo, 73
Brazilian-born free workers, 93, 118f,
    172–73
Brazilian-born slaves, 125, 127
Brickworks, 39
Brotas, 22
Bueno, Francisco da Cunha, 54–55,
    84–85
Büll, Frederico, 159

*Caboclos*, 7, 13–14
Cabral, José de Souza Leite, 56
Cabral and Negrão, slave dealers, 56
*Cadernetas*, 168
*Camaradas*, 20, 152, 169–70, 173
Camargo, Benedito Antônio de, 103,
    108
Campos, José Ferraz de, 84
Cane brandy, 27
*Capangas*, 21, 69, 71, 178, 182f

Capital accumulation, 24f, 34, 38, 195. *See also* Eviction
Capitalism and slavery, 195
Capitão-do-mato, *see* Slaves, catchers
Cardoso, Felisberto José, 145
Caribbean coffee production, 49
Cartolano, Domingos, 159
Carvalho, Leôncio de, 145
Carvalho, Manuel José de, 27, 30
Cascalho: plantation, 117, 185; Núcleo Colonial of, 164, 185–86, 189
Cash-cropping, 9, 11
Castro, Jeanne Berrance de, 222n18
Catholic church and slaves, 66, 80–82
Catholic religion, 86
Censorship of mail, 96, 99, 102
Census records, 1822–35, 202n5
Chagas disease, 177
Child labor, 79, 106, 116–17, 176–77
Chinese indentured workers, 156
Civil rights, 96
Climate, 1, 30
Civil Code of 1916, 169
*Coffea arabica*, 31–33
Coffee: cultivation, 30–33, 35–38, 64, 158; plant, 31–33; groves, 32–33, 36–37, 168; processing, 33, 37–38, 95; production, 33–35, 38, 45–46, 106, 108–9, 161; harvesting, 36; beans, 37, 95; brokers, 44, 167–68; tending, 116, 119–20, 168–69, 172, 179; cycle, 175, 189, 192–93
Coffee plantations, 32, 38–39, 49. *See also by name*
Colonial government, 12–13, 25
*Colonos*, *see* Free plantation workers; Indentured plantation workers; *Núcleos coloniais*
*Comissários*, 44, 167–68
"Communism" suspected, 102
Companhia Paulista de Estradas de Ferro, 41–42
Compensation to ex-slaves, 151
Conceição, Benedita, 153
Congress, on blacks in Brazil, xiv
Conrad, Robert, 129, 140
Conspiracies of slaves, 85–86
Consuls, 100, 104, 181, 183–84, 224n44
Contraception, 62
Contract, equality of, 115, 169
Contractors, labor, 170–71
Corn production, 8, 19, 107, 174

Correa, Joaquim da Costa, 146
Correa, José Fermino, 133
Cotton cultivation, 38
Council of State, 128
County Council, xii, 22, 102, 140
County seat, *see* Town center
Craft occupations, 51–52, 118
Credit, 56, 57, 131f, 167
Creole slaves, 125, 127
Crisis, 1901–6, 164
Cuscuseiro, *see* Analândia

Davatz, Thomas, 98–104 *passim*, 111, 114
Deforestation, 1, 11, 32, 161, 185, 186f
Depreciation of slaves, 53
Descalvado, 22
Dias, Lourenço, 147
Donations of slave children, 74
Dourados, baron of, *see* Borges, José Luis

Economic development, 162, 196–97
Egas, Eugenio, 196
Elections, 19–20
Electrification, 162
Ellis, Alfredo, 146
Ellis, Alfredo, Jr., 55, 84–85
Emancipation, 12–13, 148–50, 151, 153, 157, 159, 162f; funds, 128–29, 131, 133–34, 138–39, 141; ceremony in Rio Claro, 148–49, 150–51. *See also* Abolitionism
Emigration, 190
*Empreteiros*, 170–71
*Engenhos*, 15, 25–26
Entrepreneurs, 35–36, 55–56
Equality of contract, 115, 169
Escaped slaves, 3, 53, 82–84, 139, 141–44, 146f, 149, 196
Eviction, 10, 16–17, 23
Expilly, Charles, 104
Exploitation, *see* Planter exploitation
Export orientation, 24, 30, 35
Expropriation, 10, 16–17, 23

Family, and production, 6, 106, 170, 176–77
*Fanfulla*, 183
Farming, swidden, 7–8

*Feitores, see* Slave, drivers
Feltrin, Domingos, 149–50
Ferraz, Antonio Leite, 143
Ferraz, Maria Luiza, 132
Ferreira, Antônio da Costa Alves, 146, 186
Ferreira, José Ignácio Ribeiro, 12
Fertilizers, 37
Fines, 181
Flight to avoid debts, 179
Fonseca, Antônio Augusto da, 138
Foreign capital, 35, 41–42, 42n, 163
Forest, virgin, 1–2, 11, 32
Fraternization, freedmen and slaves, 144–45, 147–48
Free frontier householders, 4, 6–10, 14, 16–19, 194
Free plantation workers, 20, 45, 50, 53, 93, 116, 140, 143, 168ff, 171, 174–80, 187–88
Freedmen, 72, 129, 141f, 144–45, 149–54, 173–74, 191–92, 195f
Freedwoman named Lourença, 153
Free women, 62–63
Frontier, 2–3, 12–13, 17–18, 25, 192, 195
Frost, 30, 31–32

Gama, Luiz, abolitionist, 67
General assembly, 125, 128, 140, 143
General Department of Public Lands, 103
German-Swiss immigrant workers, 88–105 *passim,* 110–14, 121, 188
Godoy, Senator Joaquim Floriano de, 140, 151
Government, provincial (state), 88, 101, 117, 124–25, 184
Government intervention, 101–2, 107, 114–15, 130
Grão-Mogol, baron of, 67–68, 68n, 75, 130, 144, 148, 190
Graubünden, Swiss canton of, 98, 110, 112
Guerra, João Cordeiro da Silva, 146
Guilherme, Negrão and Co., 56

Health conditions, 177
Heusser, J. Christian, 102
Hiring and firing, 45, 98, 171–72
Historiography, xiii–xiv, 52, 110, 125–26, 197

Hog raising, 9–10, 19
Holanda, Sérgio Buarque de, 112–13
Horse ownership, 176–77

Ibicaba plantation, 15, 30, 46, 65, 71, 85, 93, 143, 164; "colony," 88ff, 91–93, 98–101, 109, 120
Ideology and history, xiii–xv
Immigrants, 95f, 119, 157–60, 168, 172–73, 176–77, 183–92 *passim,* 195; and Brazilian workers, 93, 119, 159, 172–74, 185–86; remittances, 122, 159, 192. *See also* German-Swiss immigrant workers; Italian immigrants
Immigration, 61, 91, 111, 152, 157, 159–60, 180, 184, 192; subsidies, 88, 117, 156–58, 159, 174, 176, 184; policy, 88–89, 110, 114–15, 121–23, 137, 156–59, 174, 184, 186, 194–95
Imported goods, 40
Incomes, family, 9–10, 22, 105, 176, 186
Indenture contracts, 89–91, 93–109 *passim,* 113–17 *passim,* 194–95, 211n5
Indentured plantation workers, 90–91, 93, 96–109 *passim,* 120–21
Industry, 162
Infant mortality, 62ff, 177
Inflation, 97, 175
*Ingênuos,* 58, 63, 128, 131, 134–36, 152, 217n14
Italian government, 184
Italian immigrants, 158–60, 168, 173f, 176–84 *passim,* 188
Itaqueri, 22, 149–50, 188
Interprovincial slave traffic, *see* Slave, internal traffic
Investment in coffee, 33–34

"Jacaré-Assu," 104
Jaguaribe Filho, Domingos, 148, 151, 154, 158, 185
Jordão, Amador Lacerda Rodrigues, 54, 165
Jordão, José Elias Pacheco, 116–17
Jordão, Manuel Rodrigues, 44
Jordão, Silvério Rodrigues, 117
Jorge Tibiriçá, Núcleo Colonial of, 164, 186–87, 189

Koch, Carlos, 121

Krug, G. H., Prussian consular agent, 104

Labor: shortage, 54; conflicts, 97–104 passim, 109–10, 178–83
Labor relations, see Planter exploitation
Laerne, C. F. van Delden, 113
Lamberg, Mauricio, 85
Land: titles, 10–12, 16, 189–90; sales, 11, 14–15, 120–21, 164, 189; policy, 12–13, 16, 184–85; concentration, 12–13, 24, 189–90; reform, 151, 155
Lashing prohibited, 143
Law of Emancipation, 149–50
Law of Employment, 96, 115, 152, 156–57, 169
Law of Free Birth, 57, 63, 125, 128–29, 131, 135
Law of Sexagenarians, 140–41, 152
Lebeis, Guilherme, 121
Levy, João, 164
Limeworks, 39
Liberal Party, 42, 46, 48, 102
Liberal rebellion of 1842, 90
London and Brazilian Bank, 118, 131, 144
Lopes, João, 69
Lopes, rural neighborhood, 189
Lungaretti, Angelo, 181–83
Lungaretti family, 182–83

Machinery, coffee-processing, 37ff, 165–66, 170–71
Mail service, 44
Male domination of family, 176–77
Mandinga, 82
Manumission, 60, 72–75, 83, 127–34 passim, 139, 145–46
Masonic Lodge "Fraternidade," 131
Meyer, João (Johan) Jacob, 113, 159
Middle class, 22, 126, 139–40, 163, 177, 183, 191–93
Migration, internal, 118–19
Minervino, Silverio, 159
Minifundia, 18–19, 188–89
Miscegenation, 2, 6–7, 62, 79, 125, 154
Moral contradictions of slavery, 86
Morro Pelado plantation, 178
Mortality, 63, 77, 177, 217n14
Mortgages, 34, 56, 109, 142
Mulattos, 7, 60, 125, 127

Mule trains, 3–4, 19, 40, 43, 46
Município, 22
Murders, 21, 67, 69, 79, 84–85, 178–79, 181–83
Mutirão, 14

Naturalization, 159
Negrão, José Duarte da Costa, 56
Negrão, José Guilherme da Costa, 56
Negreiros, Estevão Cardoso de, 15, 52n
Negreiros, Estevão Xavier de, 146
Negreiros, Francisco de Assis, 57
Negreiros, Ignácio Xavier de, 117
Negreiros, João Xavier de, 141
Neves, Joaquim Teixeira, 57, 143
Neves, Mariana Candida das, 72–73
Nova América plantation, 181–83
Núcleos coloniais, 184–87, 189, 196
Nunes, Sebastião Machado, 103f

Occupations, town, 22
Oliveira, Antônio Galdino, 132–33
Oliveira, João Baptista de Mello, 191
Oliveira, Joaquina Nogueira de, 54
Oliveira, José Estanislau de, see Rio Claro, viscount of
Oliveira, Justiniano de Mello, 146
Oswald, Swiss resident in São Paulo, 102

Padrões, 31
Palmares plantation, 165, 167–68, 170
Palmeiras plantation, 26–27
Paranhos, Fernando da Rocha, 186–87
Parceria contract, see Indenture contracts
Parceiros, see Indentured plantation workers
Paternalism, 70, 72ff, 78, 113, 152–53, 181
Patrimônio, 21
Patronato Agrícola, 184, 224n44
Paulista, 41–42
Paulista West, xi, 51, 54, 116, 127, 158
Pecúlios, 132–34, 143–44, 149
Penteado and Dumont, brokers, 167
Pereira family, 11f
Piccoli, Luiz, 190
Pimentel, Salvador Pires, 74
Pinhal, count of, 42
Piracicaba, 4

Piracicaba, baron of, *see* Barros, Antônio Paes de (elder)
Piracicaba Falls, 3
Plantation: system, 18–19, 21, 24, 192, 194f; administration, 44, 53, 165–69, 179f; stores, 91, 97–98, 167, 175–76
Plantation labor, *see* Free plantation workers; Indentured plantation workers; Slave, plantation workers
Plantations, 25–27, 30, 39–40, 45, 55, 163–64, 166, 168, 170–71, 189–90f
Planter exploitation: of free labor, 20–21, 85, 96, 99, 102, 108, 118, 137, 140, 154, 156–57, 178, 180–81, 183f; of slaves, 52–53, 64–76 *passim*, 124–25, 130f, 139–46 *passim*; of indentured workers, 97–98, 102f, 110, 113–15
Planters: ideology, xiii, 64, 70, 81, 148–50f, 158, 172–73, 197, 213n41; social class, 10–12f, 15, 35–36, 43, 46, 48–49, 70, 85, 140, 191, 195ff; absenteeism, 15, 44, 191; and smallholders, 16–17, 19–20, 40, 89, 185; political control, 19, 21–22, 122; exercise of jurisdiction, 96, 169, 181; and abolition, 117, 123, 126, 129, 145–50 *passim*, 154, 156
Police repression, 66, 70, 83, 86–87, 98, 115, 139, 142, 146f, 152, 178, 182–83
Politics, 19, 21–22, 42, 44, 46, 48, 102, 122, 183, 186
Population, 2, 4, 6, 21, 160–61, 172, 192
*Por ajuste* contracts, 115–16, 119–20
Porto Feliz, baron of, 65, 75–76, 117
Portuguese indentured workers, 89–90, 93, 116–17
*Posse*, 15–16, 189
Pott, Matthias, 159
Prado, Lucas Ribeiro do, 150f
Prado, Martinho, 140, 164
Prates, Eduardo, 165
Pre-capitalist formations, 11, 13
Productivity, 106, 108–9, 161, 164–65, 173–74, 180, 196
Profitability, 52–53, 108–9, 197
Proletariat, town, 180
Provincial Assembly, 137–38, 157
Prussian government, 104

*Quadrados*, 45, 65

*Quilombos*, 83–84, 142, 144

Racial identity, free population, 6, 60
Racism, 88, 119, 153–54, 156, 173, 220n46
Railroads, 41–44, 162–63
Remittances, 122, 159, 192
Republican Party, xiii, 143
Ribeirão Claro, 4
Rio Claro, county of, 22
Rio Claro, viscount of, 41ff, 46–49, 122–23, 191
Rio Claro Railroad, 42, 42n, 43
Roads and trails, 3–4, 13, 40–41, 95
Romeiro, João, 137–38, 140
Rossi, Alfredo, Italian consul, 183–84
Rossi, Pedro, 190–91
Runaway slaves, *see* Escaped slaves

Saint-Hilaire, August de, 4, 27
Salles, Diogo, 181–83
Salles, Joaquim Augusto de, 146
Salles, Raul, 182–83
Santa Ana plantation, 45, 178, 181
Santa Caridade, Padre João de, 131
Santa Gertrudes plantation, 165–74 *passim*, 179, 181, 222n18
Santo Antônio plantation, 178
Santos, 35, 44, 142, 144
Santos, Gomes and Company, brokers, 167
São José do Corumbataí plantation, 164, 186
São José plantation, 117, 123, 139, 191
Schmid, J., administrator of Ibicaba "Colony," 100, 121
Schmidt, Cornélio, 153
Schmidt, Marcelo, 191
Schools, 162, 177, 187
Segregation, racial, 153
*Sesmarias*, 11–12, 24, 46ff, 202n11
Settlement, 3–4, 22–23, 55–56, 192, 195
Sexual exploitation, 62, 63n, 67–68, 74–75, 79, 224n39
Sharecropping, 172, 188–89
*Sitiantes, see* Smallholding
Skilled plantation workers, 37, 51–52, 170
Slave: plantation workers, 10, 27, 35, 50–53, 64, 71, 85, 93, 105, 108–9, 115, 122, 127; drivers, 36f, 71; living conditions, 45, 65; dealers, 48, 56; pop-

ulation, characteristics of, 51, 58, 60, 61–64, 76–77; craftsmen, 51–52; internal traffic, 51–58, 80, 136–38; women, 52, 58, 61–63, 67–68, 74–75, 77–79; prices, 54, 58, 129, 131, 136, 138–39; sales, 56f, 58, 79–80, 135, 138; children, 58, 74–75, 79–80; registration, 60, 63, 128–29, 141, 149; repression of, 64, 66, 68, 69–71, 79, 110, 125, 139, 143; festivities, 65–66; religious practices, 66, 80–82, 149–50; resistance, 68, 71, 84–86, 117, 124–25, 137–39, 144, 147; catchers, 69, 82, 143; self-help, 69–70, 75, 132–33; legal disabilities, 70; social organization, 71, 79, 82; marriages and families, 71–72, 74, 77–80, 128, 135–37; political consciousness, 86, 124–26, 128; moral qualities, 86–87. *See also* Escaped slaves
Slavery, xi, xiv, 20–21, 50–53, 60, 66, 71, 71n, 73, 115, 125, 128, 194f
Slaves, individual accounts by name: Tolentino, 68; Fausto, 69, 139; Marcelina, 69, 72–73; Amaro, 70; Catarina, 72; Manuel, 74; Antônia, 78; Antônio, 78; Francisca, 78; Francisco, 78; Joana, 79; Guilherme, 84; Romão, 84; Dita, 84–85; José, 132; Lourenço, 133; Mariano, 133; Liberato, 139–40
Smallholding, 10, 12–14, 16–19, 40, 80, 88–91, 120–22, 164, 172, 184–91, 196
Social mobility, 187–88, 191–92
Sociedade Promotora de Imigração, 157
Society of the Commonweal, 21
Soil conditions, 25, 31f, 180, 192
Souza, Brig. Luis Antônio de, 48
Souza, José Francisco de Paula, 146
Souza Queiroz family, 49
Spanish government, 184
Squatters, 15–18, 189
Strikes, 146f, 178ff
Subsidized immigration, *see* Immigration, subsidies
Sugar cultivation, 24–27, 33–34, 53
Sugar mills, 15, 25–26
Swidden farming, 7–8, 17

Swiss government, 100, 104, 111
Swiss indentured workers, *see* German-Swiss immigrant workers

Taunay, Afonso d'Escragnolle, 112
Telegraph, 44
Tenancy, 172, 188–89
*Terra roxa*, 31
Topography, 3–4
Torres, Joaquim José Rodrigues, 145
Torres, José Estevão, 67
Town center, 16, 19, 21, 43, 92, 162
Transport, *see* Mule trains; Railroads; Roads and trails
Três Rios, marquis (and count) of, 43, 138, 143, 165, 185
Tschudi, Johan Jacob von, 67, 103, 111
Tupi-Guarani aborigines, 2, 17–18
*Turmas*, 170

Underground railway, 142–43
"Uprising" of 1856–57, 101

Vagrancy, 17, 20, 129, 141f, 151
Valdetaro, Manuel de Jesus, 103, 108, 112
Vergueiro, José, 41, 69f, 85, 91, 103, 121, 156
Vergueiro, Luiz, 91, 99f, 103
Vergueiro, Nicolau Pereira de Campos, 15, 30, 44, 46–47, 71, 88–103 *passim*, 110f
Viana, Antônio José Simões, 56
Violence, 2, 17–18, 20–21. *See also* Planter exploitation; Slave, repression of; Slave, resistance
Viotti da Costa, Emília, 104, 129, 132
Vollet, João, 121, 159

Wage labor, *see* Free plantation workers
Wages, 20–21, 106–8, 116, 118–20, 132, 172, 175, 179, 180–81, 183, 195–96
Whitaker, Jorge, 167–68, 224n39
"Whitening" of population, 154

Zerrener-Bülow, 163, 178